DATABASE SECURITY

DATABASE SECURITY
Problems and Solutions

Christopher Diaz, Ph.D.

MERCURY LEARNING AND INFORMATION
Dulles, Virginia
Boston, Massachusetts
New Delhi

Publisher: David Pallai

MERCURY LEARNING AND INFORMATION
22841 Quicksilver Drive
Dulles, VA 20166
info@merclearning.com
www.merclearning.com
1-800-232-0223

C. Diaz. *Database Security.*
ISBN: 978-1-68392-663-4

Library of Congress Control Number: 2022940435
222324321 Printed on acid-free paper in the United States of America.

I thank my wife Sindy, who assisted with developing case studies, as well as my family for inspiration and support.

CONTENTS

PREFACE

After authoring my first textbook, *An Introduction to UNIX/Linux*, I later wanted to author another textbook. I considered a follow-up to that same topic, but realized a different topic had a larger void and greater need: Database Security. The idea of authoring a textbook in the field of database security arose with the rising trends of data science the past few years, the plethora of digital information that is created and used each day, and the ongoing needs for information security. While there are a few good database security textbooks that exist, many of those were written 10 to 20 years ago, so I believed it was time for a fresh look at this important topic.

Database security and information security may sound like similar concepts, but they are different in perspective and coverage. Database security does involve the information security principles of confidentiality, integrity, and availability. However, database security considers and implements those security measures or *controls* in more specific ways than are generally realized in the broader realm of information security. For example, to uphold the principle of confidentiality, we often turn to the information security control of encryption. But database security also involves other confidentiality approaches, such as techniques for account credential management, techniques to manage access to data, as well as techniques to manage the types of access. These are among the topics that we cover in Chapters 1, 3, 4, 5, 6, and 7.

To uphold the principle of integrity, we often consider the information security controls of hashing or digital signatures. With database security, in addition to those techniques we must also consider other, less realized, approaches such as database normalization, referential integrity, transactions, locks, and check constraints, all of which are some of the topics we cover in Chapters 1, 2, 7, 8, and 9.

Last but not least, to uphold the principle of availability we likewise discuss a variety of approaches in Chapters 1, 3, and 9.

The audiences for this textbook include professionals and self-learners, as well as classroom or workshop settings. The concepts presented in the text are demonstrated against databases that are provided, so that one can follow along in a hands-on approach and better learn these concepts. Each chapter also has a set of questions and follow up projects that one can use to reinforce their understanding of the material.

This textbook is not meant to be a complete reference of database security concepts and techniques, but rather focuses on the more typical ones. In addition, in this text we focus on DBMS considerations, and not database application considerations (such as SQL injection), which itself can involve enough content for its own textbook. With this background, the reader can expand on these concepts as necessary with various print and online resources.

1

INTRODUCTION TO INFORMATION SECURITY, DATA SECURITY, AND DATABASE SECURITY

Security is a vital need in many facets of everyday life. Whether we think of security for a room or security for digital information, the goal is similar: protect something important from unauthorized access or tampering! In terms of protecting a physical area such as a room, we consider *physical security* with doors, locks, and other mechanisms to prevent unauthorized physical access. In terms of protecting digital information, we can also employ physical security to prevent unauthorized physical access to devices that contain the information. However, for digital information we also must consider *other* forms of security, because physical security alone does not provide complete protection when digital information is accessible through an application, through a system, or over a network.

When it comes to forms of security involved with storing and managing digital information, we often think or hear of the terms *information security*, *data security*, and *database security*. These terms may seem equivalent and interchangeable when it comes to protecting digital information. However, while each term has security goals in mind, the actual goals of each vary in both scope as well as how to achieve those goals. In this first chapter, we introduce these terms and explain how they provide the basis for security concepts presented in subsequent chapters.

1.1 INFORMATION SECURITY

Information security refers to protecting data in general and in *any* form. Technically, the data may be digital or nondigital, although this text focuses on digital data. The data may be sitting in storage, in the act of being processed, and/or being communicated between parties. Information security is considered a *broad definition* of protection, encompassing every state or form in which the information exists. This broad definition also leads us to three goals, or *principles*, by which information security has been established: confidentiality, integrity, and availability. These principles are often referred to as the CIA (for confidentiality, integrity, and availability) Triad for Information Security.

Confidentiality

Confidentiality refers to the protection of information against unauthorized access. This principle keeps sensitive information confidential and therefore accessible only to an authorized *agent* (such as a person, application program, or system service). An example of confidentiality in practice is allowing only an authorized user to access certain information, such as their own account or an information that is delivered to them over a network. Such a restriction prevents access or disclosure of the information to any unauthorized party.

Integrity

The information security principle of *integrity* refers to the protection of information against unauthorized modification or deletion. A goal of integrity is to maintain information in a manner that is *expected* and *accurate*. As an example of this integrity goal, consider a financial document where a value in that document is accidentally—or intentionally—modified in an unauthorized manner. Such a modification could portray a higher or lower value than in reality, and that could lead to inaccurate, false, or invalid information being presented.

Another goal of integrity is to keep information *consistent* with other information, so that if one piece of information is changed (whether in an authorized or unauthorized manner), that change does not conflict—or become *inconsistent*—with other information. As an example of such inconsistency, again consider an unauthorized modification of a value in a financial document, and that value is also referenced to derive a second value, say a sum or average. But if that second value remains unchanged, the correlations between the modified value and the derived value become inconsistent with each other. In other words, to maintain integrity with consistency, both values must be updated so that the first modified value is reflected in the second value such as a sum or average. Even though these examples involve unauthorized modification of information, the same idea holds for unauthorized addition or removal of information, where that information derives other information such as a sum, average or even a count.

Availability

The third information security principle of *availability* provides timely accessibility of information to agents authorized to access that information. The types of information can be broad, such as information stored within a file or information provided by an application or service, such as a web server or database server. The goal of availability is to prevent situations where an authorized agent is unable to access information that should be accessible to them. As an example of availability in practice, consider a database server that stores financial information about bank accounts and is accessed by users that work at the bank or are customers of the bank to obtain such information. Such a user should be able to access the information of an account to which they are authorized and achieve this access in a timely manner. If the information is retrieved to the user within the expected time, the principle of availability is met. The problem lies when that information is not retrieved or made available within the specified time, presenting a delay (or maybe even no response at all) to the authorized user.

The factors that can affect availability are numerous and broad, but can be categorized into the following problems and solutions:

- *Hardware failure,* which usually involves a faulty storage device that prevents access to information stored on that device.
- *System outages,* caused by power failure, environmental damage, and even catastrophic events.
- *Software bugs or faulty software* that does not operate as intended.
- *User attacks* that overwhelm the system with busy or non-legitimate work, thereby preventing the system from being able to process legitimate work or the work that the system really should handle. Such an attack is commonly called a *Denial of Service (DOS) attack* when the attack is carried out by one source, and a *Distributed Denial of Service (DDOS) attack* when the attack is carried out by multiple sources.

1.2   SECURITY THREATS, CONTROLS, AND REQUIREMENTS

Now that we have a broad understanding of information security, before we move into more detailed approaches involving data security and database security, let's describe the concepts of security threats, security measures, and security requirements. These concepts are applicable to information security as well as data security and database security.

Security threats

A *security threat* is a malicious user, program, or service that attempts to compromise confidentiality, integrity, and/or availability. Typically, we view a security threat as occurring by an agent that is not associated with (or even not known by) the organizational environment. Such security threats are often referred to as *external* threats. As an example of an external threat, consider a person who is not affiliated with an organization and attempts to access sensitive information within the organization over a network. Certainly that user is not authorized to access that sensitive information. The sensitive information may be stored on one of the organization's servers, contained in one of the organization's transmitted emails, or other numerous possibilities. The principle of confidentiality helps prevent the unauthorized access of the sensitive information through one or more mechanisms (or *controls*, which we describe later), thereby keeping such information confidential against unauthorized parties.

In addition to external threats, we must also consider internal threats. An *internal threat* involves an agent that is affiliated with or recognized by the organization. Such threats can pose a greater security challenge, because the person has a familiarity with the environment, or the agent may already have authorized access to certain information or resources. As an example of an internal threat, consider a person that is part of the organizational environment and is allowed to access financial information but is not allowed to access human resource information. The person attempts to access human resource information about someone else. In this scenario, the principle of confidentiality aims to keep that human resource information confidential from that person. The concept of allowing or disallowing access to certain information not only applies to people or users, but to any agent within or outside of an organization, such as a running program or service, like a web server, file server, or application communicating on a network.

Security controls

Each security principle can be enforced by an implementation of one or more security mechanisms, or *controls*. The exact mechanism(s) or control(s) in a given situation can vary by many factors, such as the type of environment, operational needs, and organizational policies. As an example, a common control for confidentiality involves encryption, where an agent must have the required key (typically a password) to access the information. Without that key the information remains encrypted and thus confidential. However, in an environment where users are mobile and/or unable to practically provide a password, a control for confidentiality may instead involve a physical component that provides the required key—such as a card, fob, or wearable device.

A common control for integrity involves checksums or hashes on data to detect modifications to the data. As with confidentiality, other controls for integrity may be required depending on the situation.

Controls for availability can also vary depending on the situation. With regard to storage device failure, a variety of controls may be implemented. One approach may rely on regular data backups, so that data on a failed device can be restored onto a replacement device. For a faster and even automated approach, we may consider the use of redundant array of independent devices (RAID), where multiple storage devices are configured and used in ways to prevent the failure of a device to impact the accessibility to the stored data. Many RAID configurations exist, but the main idea is to use redundancy to store data one more than one device, so the failure of one of those devices still leaves the data accessible on a functional device. In terms of system outages, controls may range from uninterruptible power supplies (UPSs), backup power generators, antistatic measures, to even redundant or backup systems. Faulty programs may involve controls such as proper design, implementation, testing, and code reviews. Last but not least, threats by DOS and DDOS attacks may be mitigated by controls involving anti-malware programs, intrusion detection systems, or network devices such as firewalls.

Security requirements

Note that requirements as well as controls for confidentiality, integrity, and availability can vary greatly across types of applications or systems. We have listed some general security threats and solutions, and depending on the purpose or environment of the application or system, we may have to consider any of the threats and solutions we described, or other ones altogether.

Later we will discuss more such threats and solutions in the context of a database environment.

Requirements of confidentiality, integrity, and availability can also vary greatly across organizations. One organization (such as a financial institution) may have greater demands for confidentiality of information compared to another organization (such as an advertising agency that gathers mailing addresses). The greater demand may be in the form of requiring confidentiality for *larger amounts or percentages* of overall data. The greater demand may also be in a *stronger form* of confidentiality, such as requiring two factor authentication (for example, requiring a password and physical token or device card) rather than a password alone to access sensitive data. Integrity requirements can vary, depending on the amount of data to verify as well as how to verify the data. This can be further broken down into how the data is accessed, who accesses the data, how data is processed, as well as how data may relate with other data. Lastly, availability requirements can vary, depending on what data or resources are to be made accessible in a timely manner. We also must consider the window of time that defines a "timely manner." In more critical environments, that window may be within a minute or second of time. In less critical environments, that window may be an hour or even longer.

An organization's requirements for confidentiality, integrity, and availability will be identified within the organization's security and operational policies. It is important that the objectives of the organization's security and operational policies are met or exceeded with the security solution design, implementation, and configuration. The security solution should be tested to ensure those objectives are met not only once deployed, but also routinely afterwards to ensure that the security solution is effective as the data and environment changes or evolves.

1.3   DATA SECURITY

Data security has similar goals and objectives as information security—with the same fundamental principles of confidentiality, integrity, and availability. However, data security is often associated with only data that is at rest or saved in persistent storage, such as a magnetic disk, flash drive, or solid state device. Even though data security follows the same goals and objectives of information security, the goals are often much more focused on how to achieve and implement them. Such focus allows the goal to be more precisely defined and detailed in how the solution is achieved. As an example, to protect data against unauthorized modification (integrity), a data security approach may involve monitoring accesses to certain data to reveal who accesses the data as well as how the data is accessed. Such analysis can reveal anomalies to identify potential threats, such as when data is written unexpectedly (say, outside of normal work hours or outside of the expected processing pattern).

1.4   DATABASE SECURITY

"Database security refers to the range of tools, controls, and measures designed to establish and preserve database confidentiality, integrity, and availability."[1] We can view database security to have the same objectives and principles as data security and information security, but within the scope or level of a database environment. This further focuses the choice, design, implementation, and configuration of controls available at the database level.

Data confidentiality

To achieve confidentiality in database security, we can employ controls such as *privileges* (which we cover in Chapter 5, "Database Privileges") and *encryption* of stored data (which we cover in Chapter 7, "Other Database Security Controls"). Privileges are a database system control where the database system itself manages data access. As described earlier, encryption can provide confidentiality against agents that do not have the proper credentials and may be implemented by the database system, modules, or other programs.

To achieve database integrity, in addition to checksums or hashing, we can use a range of controls that appear as early as the database design phase. This includes proper database design with normalization, defining referential integrity constraints, and identifying when concurrent access may occur. We cover database design and normalization approaches to help maintain data integrity in Chapter 2, "Database Design," and other data integrity controls in Chapter 8, "Transactions for Data Integrity." We also cover mechanisms that help maintain integrity when multiple applications and/or users access the same data in Chapter 9, "Data Integrity with Concurrent Access."

---

[1]*https://www.ibm.com/cloud/learn/database-security*

Data integrity

We previously defined the term *integrity* to detect when data has been modified in an unauthorized manner. Within a database environment we also have four types of data integrity that we must also recognize, and describe now.

Entity integrity

The first type of data integrity to recognize within a database environment is entity integrity. The idea behind *entity integrity* is similar to the definition of a relation in the relational database model, which we describe in more detail shortly. In a database design model, an *entity* describes a set of data for a particular theme or context, such as for an employee. In the relational database model, we can consider an entity to be implemented as a table or relation. Each *instance* of an entity (or row in that table) represents one specific instance or case of that theme. For example, an instance of the employee entity (or each row in the employee table) represents one specific person and contains data to just that person.

Entity integrity requires that each entity instance (or each table row) to be uniquely identified by a *primary key* value. The primary key may consist of one or more attributes of the entity (or columns of the table). If the primary key is a single attribute, then all of the values in that one column must be unique. If the primary key contains multiple attributes (a *composite key*), the combined values of the columns must be unique. Primary key values for an entity should be not only unique, but non-null and contain no more attributes or columns than is necessary to provide uniqueness.

As examples, let's consider the following set of tables that hold data for an organization that manages employees, departments, and projects (Figure 1.1). Each theme is implemented as a table and contains data specific to that theme. For representation purposes, we will use one of the popular conventions of representing table names and column names with *PascalCase*, also known as *CapitalCase*, where the first letter of each word in the name is capitalized and all other letters are lower case. When reading a name, such capital letters indicate word separation without the use of other character separators such as an underscore symbol, hyphen, or space. Also, when using PascalCase, abbreviations within a name are commonly represented with all capital letters, such as ID for "identifier" or SSN for "social security number."

This textbook also follows the principles of the most common database model, the *relational database model*. The relational database model defines that each table (or relation) consists of a set of rows (or records), where each row contains a set of data to a specific entity of the table. Each column (or attribute) contains at most one piece of data in each row. In certain cases, no value (a null value) may be given to a column in a row. No two rows are identical; that is, no two rows have the same values for each corresponding column.

For the employee entity, a table named Employee holds data about the organization's employees, and each row in the table represents one employee. In order to uniquely identify an employee, we need to specify a *primary key* of one (or possibly more) attributes or columns, whose data values would refer to exactly one row in that table. The EmployeeId attribute serves this purpose, as every employee has a unique EmployeeId value in the organization. At times we may consider other attribute possibilities as unique identifiers, and that may be valid for certain tables and attributes. While this particular set of data for the Employee table does have unique last names, we may be tempted to specify LastName (or LastName and FirstName) as a primary key. However, in a practical scenario we could not assume that every employee does or will have a unique last name (or unique last name and first name). As such, relying on last name, or last name and first name, as a unique identifier would not provide entity integrity in general.

In a similar manner, data about departments is implemented with a Department table and each row contains data of a specific department. DepartmentID is chosen as a primary key value. We may have alternatively chosen DeptName as a primary key, presuming that no two departments have the same name. While that may be a valid assumption, we may also consider that DepartmentID may be an introduced key (or *surrogate key*) to help provide a more uniform and possibly easier way to specify a primary key value for a particular department (this idea may become clearer when we get to the ProjectAssignment table later).

Referential integrity

The next form of data integrity, *referential integrity*, may be the more familiar type of integrity to database users or administrators. Here, we look at requirements needed to support *relationships* of data across tables. In a database, data in one row can relate with data in another row (of another table or possibly the same table) to generate more complete information. For example, consider these tables in an organization where employees are assigned to at most one department.

Employee

EmployeeId	FirstName	LastName	Office	DeptID
1000	Sam	Smith	103	D2
1001	Scotty	Smalls	302	D3
1002	Alex	Hall	202	D1
1003	Bob	Brown	105	D2
1004	Susan	Shu	203	D1
1005	Marcia	Gold	201	D1
1006	Gary	Grant	101	D2
1007	Alice	Aziz	102	D2

Department

DepartmentID	DeptartmentName	Manager	AdminAsstEmpId
D1	Accounting	1003	1004
D2	Sales	1006	1005
D3	Marketing	1001	(null)

Project

ProjectID	ProjectName	Client
P1	Red	Ava's Volleyball Camp
P2	Blue	Katie's Krafts
P3	Yellow	Brittany's Boutique
P4	Green	Izzy's and Emily's Anime World
P5	Orange	Ron's Rock and Roll Collectables

ProjectAssignment

EmpId	ProjID
1000	P1
1000	P2
1001	P1
1001	P3
1001	P4
1002	P1
1002	P2
1002	P5
1003	P3
1003	P4
1006	P5

FIGURE 1.1. Example database tables for an organization.

The Employee table provides the first name, last name, and office of a particular employee. However, if we need more information about a given employee's department, such as department name or administrative assistant, we can derive that information by using the DeptID column value at that employee's row in `Employee` as a foreign key that relates to the primary key DepartmentID in Department. Take for example the Employee table row for Sam Smith with the DeptID attribute D2. We can then retrieve in the Department table the row identified by D2 to derive that employee Sam Smith is with the Sales department.

A *relationship* refers to the mapping of rows in one table to rows in another (or even the same) table to provide more information with combining data. A *relationship instance* refers to a specific example of a given relationship. For example, we just mentioned that the relationship between Employee and Department allows us to derive the department information of a given employee. A relationship instance refers to a specific example of a mapping from Employee to Department, for example, that the row for Sam Smith in Employee relates to the row for Sales in Department.

Referential integrity requires that for each relationship instance, a foreign key value *must* refer to an existing primary key value. Between the Employee and Department tables, referential integrity is maintained because each DeptID value in Employee refers to an existing DepartmentID in Department. As a specific example, or instance, of referential integrity being maintained between Employee and Department, consider another EmployeeId 1003, which has a `DeptID` of D1, associating Susan Shu with the Accounting department. Because D1 is an existing DepartmentID in Department, referential integrity is maintained. However, if an employee were to have a `DepartmentID` of, say D5, referential integrity is not maintained because DepartmentID D5 does not exist in Department.

The Employee and Department tables also have a second relationship, where a row in Department relates to a row in Employee to provide more information about a department's administrative assistant. For example, with DepartmentID D2, the AdminAsstEmpId value is 1005, referring to EmployeeId 1005 in Employee, which is Gary Grant. Because each foreign key value of AdminAsstEmpId in Department refers to an existing primary key value of EmployeeId in Employee, referential integrity is maintained for that particular relationship.

ProjectAssignment happens to be a table with two relationships, one with Employee and another with Project. In ProjectAssignment, EmpId is a foreign key to EmployeeId in the Employee table, and ProjID is a foreign key to ProjectID in Project. Referential integrity likewise requires that each row in ProjectAssignment has a foreign key value that corresponds to an existing primary key value in Employee as well as an existing primary key value in Project.

ProjectAssignment is also an example of an entity with a composite (multi-attribute) identifier, where EmpId and ProjID together form the primary key. Here, one must provide a value to both EmpId and ProjID to uniquely identify a row in ProjectAssignment. In the larger picture, ProjectAssignment is actually an *intersection table* that implements a many-to-many relationship between Employee and Project, where a given row in ProjectAssignment relates an employee with a project. As such, the composite primary key of ProjectAssignment not only uniquely identifies a row in ProjectAssignment, but also represents a relationship instance between a specific row in Employee and a specific row in Project.

While referential integrity requires a foreign key value to correspond to an existing primary key value, referential integrity *does not* require a foreign key value to always be defined or specified in every row of a table that has a relationship, as long as that foreign key is not part of a composite primary key to that table. When a foreign key is not part of the table's primary key, the idea here is that a foreign key value may not be known or not exist yet, in which case there may not be a foreign key value to specify (at least at that time). The assumption is that in the future this foreign key value will become known and added to the row, say after the value is determined, or after the corresponding primary key is added to the related table. As an example, in the Department table, Marketing currently does not have an administrative assistant. Perhaps there may not be a person to specify at this time because that person is not yet an employee and hence does not exist in the Employee table, or perhaps the person is a current employee and does exist in Employee but has not yet been appointed. In either case, a null value may be specified for AdminAsstEmpId in the Department row for Marketing, because AdminAsstEmpId is not part of Department's primary key. After the person is added to Employee or appointed, their EmployeeId value may be set as the AdminAsstEmpId value in Department for the Marketing row.

Entity integrity also plays a part in supporting this many-to-many relationship, requiring that every row of ProjectAssignment contain a value for

EmpId as well as ProjID. This means that in order to specify a project assignment, we must have both an employee and project—the absence of either is an invalid project assignment. Even though EmpId and ProjID are foreign keys in ProjectAssignment, because they also form the primary key in that table (and because of entity integrity), we will require that both EmpId and ProjID have non-null values in ProjectAssignment. In general, if a foreign key in a table also is part of the table's primary key, then entity integrity *does* require a non-null value of that foreign key in every row of that table.

Domain integrity

Domain integrity in a database environment refers to a data value that exists when expected and in the proper form. When a table is created, the definition and constraints defined for a column causes the database management system (DBMS) to play a huge role with enforcing domain integrity. For example, by defining the data type for a column when a table is created, we are defining the domain of values that are stored in that column. A column defined with an integer data type will store a value as a whole number, even if the value is provided as a decimal number. And if an inserted value cannot be converted to an integer, the DBMS will generate an error.

Domain integrity may even involve enforcing that a row's value for a column is present when required. Such a specification for a column can be defined by indicating its value must be NOT NULL. In contrast, a NULL specification indicates that the value may or may not be specified.

One can also employ the use of constraints to ensure that data values conform to an expected value or format. For example, consider a column that stores a value in U.S. dollars and cents. By specifying the data type of that column as a monetary type or number type with two decimal places, we ensure that a value stored has two digits for the cents value. An inserted number that has, say, one or three decimal digits that cannot be converted properly, will not be allowed by the DBMS. Other forms of constraints can ensure other types of criteria, such as ensuring a column value is within a range of values.

User-defined integrity

Even with the other three forms of data integrity that have been described, in a particular environment or situation we may still have requirements to define. *User-defined integrity* refers to the addition of those requirements, typically in the form of *business rules*. An example of a business rule involves a minimum number of items that can be placed in an order. Another example may be that a department must have at least two employees to exist. If data does not fulfill those requirements, then the data is considered to violate the data integrity of that organization. The concept of user-defined integrity may not be as formally defined as the others, but it may play a significant part in the data integrity of an organization.

Data availability

With database security, if availability is compromised such that data is lost or corrupted, as part of recovery we may have to use data backups, as described with information security. There are often various backup and restore approaches based on facilities provided by the operating system and/ or applications that carry out the backup and recovery tasks. Regarding databases, there are often built-in mechanisms within the DBMS itself that can be used to quickly and conveniently issue backup and restore operations. We cover some of those approaches in Chapter 3, "Database Management and Administration" and Chapter 9, "Data Integrity with Concurrent Access."

As with information security, in addition to hardware failure of storage devices, we may also have to consider other forms of hardware failure, such as with RAM, CPU, network connection, or network card. Controls to mitigate these threats also involve redundancy of hardware components, so that the operation of one failed component can be quickly replaced by operation of a similar functional component. If such a switchover is automatic, we can achieve *high availability*, where the system continues to operate in a manner that minimizes or eliminates the effect of the failure to users. High availability can involve RAID systems or other redundant hardware involving multiple RAM banks, CPUs, network connections, or network interface cards. High availability often requires special hardware, operating systems, and/or software that is particular to the system platform, operating system, and availability objectives. Depending on the security objectives of the database system, we may even involve multiple database servers to provide availability of the database information in the event that one of the databases fails, say by power outage or catastrophe.

Database security may also involve many of the availability controls mentioned earlier. This may include hardware and/or software controls such as UPSs, firewalls, and other network security mechanisms. When database applications are present, we may also have to consider attacks that could compromise availability (as well as confidentiality or integrity). Controls that include proper code design, reviews, and testing of database applications or mechanisms can reduce those threats.

1.5 SUMMARY

In this chapter, we introduced the concepts of information security as well how data security and database security involve more focused and specific usage of those concepts. Other security controls involving user account management can also play a role with database security. As with general user accounts, a security control may involve proper review of database user accounts to mitigate certain threats. Such threats include ensuring that an account of a former employee, or an account created for testing or backdoor purposes is properly disabled and inaccessible to a malicious agent. For accounts that are legitimately active, we must also ensure that proper data access or privileges are assigned to the account, so that an agent has access to the data in which they are allowed and does not have access to data that is disallowed. We describe the concepts of database user accounts and managing access to data in Chapter 4, "Database User Accounts," Chapter 5, "Database Privileges," and Chapter 6, "Roles."

CHAPTER 2

DATABASE DESIGN

While we may often consider database security in terms of managing the access to data, there are other areas we must also recognize that can threaten database security. The design of a database (that is, the structure of the tables and relationships between them) can also have a database security impact in terms of integrity. We typically refer to integrity in computer security as ensuring that data is not altered in an unauthorized manner. But with database security we must also consider cases where data is validly altered in an authorized manner, but the changes may not be seen as expected. Such phenomena can especially arise when data is duplicated in a database. As an example, suppose we have a data item that is replicated in a database (for example, the data item's value appears in multiple locations or tables). We issue an authorized change to one copy of a data value (at one location or table of the database). If we subsequently retrieve that same data value (at that same location), we will see the authorized change as expected. But suppose we instead retrieve the value of that same data item from another copy of the data (the data replicated at another location or table and was not changed) We would obtain the previous value. Because we can now retrieve more than one value for the same data item, we have a data inconsistency. Some retrievals of that data yield one value and other retrievals yield another value, so we are left with the undesirable question of which value (if any of them) is accurate or up-to date. This chapter explores these problems of data inconsistency with duplicated data and the solution to these problems with normalization. In Chapter 9, we will also see other forms of data inconsistencies that may result from concurrent database access and investigate other solutions to resolve that issue.

2.1 NORMALIZATION

Normalization is an important part of database design because that process can reduce or eliminate the potential for insert, update, or delete anomalies. Within a database environment, normalization also helps maintain integrity by preventing such anomalies, such as update anomalies and data inconsistencies that can result with duplicated data.

To provide examples of these anomalies and to see how we can resolve them, let's consider some data in a real estate agency scenario shown in Figure 2.1. We consider this data to be in *list form* because all of the data is contained within one list, and a particular row contains the data for a property, the realtor assigned to that property, and the realtor office. For brevity and to focus on the concepts, we only include some pertinent data items and not an exhaustive list of data that one would actually see in a more detailed listing scenario.

Listing

RealtorName	OfficeAdr	OfficeCity	Phone	PropAdr	PropCity	NBeds	Area	Price
Penny	137 Main	CityA	555-1111	17 Highland	CityA	3	2000	220000
Penny	137 Main	CityA	555-1111	1565 State Rd	CityB	4	2900	290000
Penny	137 Main	CityA	555-1111	997 George	CityA	4	2200	240000
Penny	137 Main	CityA	555-1111	123 Big Lane	CityA	8	5000	750000
Bob	455 Oak	CityB	555-2222	5 Lighthouse	CityB	4	2000	230000
Bob	455 Oak	CityB	555-2222	190 Brown	CityC	2	1700	140000
Bob	455 Oak	CityB	555-2222	123 Big Lane	CityA	8	5000	750000

FIGURE 2.1 Data in list form for a real estate agency.

Each row in this table (or relation, using the relational database model) represents the listing of a property for sale. For each row, we can obtain some basic information about the property itself (address, number of bedrooms, area or size of the interior, and price). Each row also yields information about the realtor (first name, office address and city location, and phone number for the realtor).

In the relational database model, the relation for this data set can be described with the structure or definition given in Figure 2.2.

Listing (RealtorName, OfficeAdr, OfficeCity, Phone, PropAdr, PropCity, NBeds, Area, Price)

FIGURE 2.2 Original relation structure or definition of Listing.

where Listing is the name of the relation, the relation attributes are comma-separated within parenthesis, and the attribute(s) that define the primary key are underlined. Here the primary key of Listing is the set of attributes (Phone, PropAdr, PropCity), so that, given a set of values for each of those attributes, we can derive a unique row or property listing and its listing realtor. For example, given the values ("555-1111," "997 George," "CityA"), we can uniquely derive the information in the third row of the Listing table.

While this relation can be used to store and retrieve data about a particular property and its realtor, this relation does present database integrity concerns. Because certain data is duplicated (such as RealtorName, OfficeAdr, PropAdr, and Price, to name a few), the potential for modification anomalies with updates and inconsistencies is introduced. As an example, suppose realtor Penny updates her office address from "137 Main" to "417 Main." Unless that address change is applied to every occurrence of the previous address, the previous address will coexist in the database along with the new address. This coexistence of different values for the same data is a data inconsistency, where a certain data retrieval operation may yield one address, but another data retrieval operation may yield a different address for the same realtor. To see how this may happen, suppose that OfficeAdr is changed to "417 Main" for only the first row of the relation (the row with a PropAdr value of "17 Highland"), as shown in Figure 2.3. A subsequent data retrieval with primary key values of ("555-1111," 17 Highland," "CityA") for (Phone, PropAdr, PropCity) yields the new OfficeAdr value of "417 Main." But a data retrieval with primary key values ("555-1111," "1565 State Rd," "CityB") yields the previous OfficeAdr value of "137 Main."

Realtor Name	Office Adr	Office City	Phone	PropAdr	Prop City	NBeds	Area	Price
Penny	137 Main	CityA	555-1111	17 Highland	CityA	3	2000	220000
Penny	417 Main	CityA	555-1111	1565 State Rd	CityB	4	2900	290000
Penny	137 Main	CityA	555-1111	997 George	CityA	4	2200	240000
Penny	137 Main	CityA	555-1111	123 Big Lane	CityA	8	5000	750000
Bob	455 Oak	CityB	555-2222	5 Lighthouse	CityB	4	2000	230000
Bob	455 Oak	CityB	555-2222	190 Brown	CityC	2	1700	140000
Bob	455 Oak	CityB	555-2222	123 Big Lane	CityA	8	5000	719000

FIGURE 2.3 Real estate data with two data inconsistencies.

Another example of a data inconsistency exists with the "123 Big Lane" property. Suppose Bob reduces the price of that property to $719,000, also as shown in Figure 2.3. Because that property is listed with multiple realtors, a change to that property's data (such as a price change) must be applied to each realtor's listing, otherwise the old price and new price will coexist in the databases, resulting in another data inconsistency. The only way we can resolve such database integrity issues with inconsistencies is to either ensure that all duplicate occurrences of a data value are updated (which may be tricky to accomplish) or better, normalize the relations that hold the data.

To help eliminate duplication and the possibility of data inconsistencies, we can apply database normalization techniques that split tables as necessary to create new tables and new relationships between those tables. The normalization technique we demonstrate is based on the use of functional dependencies to achieve Boyce-Codd Normal Form (BCNF), which can eliminate most forms of duplication.

The concept of a functional dependency is a way to represent which attributes can derive a unique set of other attributes. Given a set of values for the attributes on the left side of a functional dependency, we can derive a unique set of values for the attributes on the right side of that functional dependency. Because the primary key of (RealtorPhone, PropAdr, PropCity) together can derive a unique row in Listing, the functional dependency for Listing with that understanding is given in Figure 2.4.

(Phone, PropAdr, PropCity) -> (RealtorName, OfficeAdr, OfficeCity, NBeds, Area, Price)

FIGURE 2.4 Functional dependency for original Listing table based on the primary key.

Here, given a set of values for (Phone, PropAdr, PropCity), we can derive a unique set of values for (RealtorName, OfficeAdr, OfficeCity, NBeds, Area, Price), which in this case derives a unique row in the Listing relation.

The process of normalization (for our purposes to BCNF) is based on functional dependencies and candidate keys. Like a primary key, a *candidate key* consists of one or more attributes that can derive a unique row in a table. A table can have only one primary key but can actually have multiple candidate keys. If a table has only one candidate key, that key becomes the table's primary key. On the other hand, if a table has multiple candidate keys, one is chosen to be the table's primary key, and the others exist as alternate retrieval keys that can still derive a unique row.

To achieve BFNF normalization, for each functional dependency, the attributes that compose the left side of that functional dependency must be a primary or candidate key to some table. If that is not the case then we split a table into two tables to fulfill that goal. The specific table to split and how we split that table is based on the left and right sides of that functional dependency.

To illustrate the concept of BCNF normalization and see how it can reduce data duplication and resolve the potential of data inconsistencies, let's consider the relational form of the Listing table and the functional dependencies of those attributes. We already established the table definition for Listing in Figure 2.2 and the functional dependency based on its primary key in Figure 2.4.

Suppose we also note the following functional dependencies also exist, given in Figure 2.5. Combined with the functional dependency given in Figure 2.4, we are now considering three functional dependencies total.

Phone -> (RealtorName, OfficeAdr, OfficeCity)
(PropAdr, PropCity) -> (NBeds, Area, Price)

FIGURE 2.5 Other functional dependencies for original Listing table.

Note that we do not need to consider the actual table data for this normalization task, although the data may be considered in deriving the functional dependencies themselves. However, we will consider the table data by removing duplicate rows that may appear after splitting tables, as we will soon see.

The process of normalization to BCNF is shown in Figure 2.6. The main idea is to examine every functional dependency and determine whether to split a table. If a table is to be split, steps 1, 2, and 3 define how to split the table based on the functional dependency. The last step (3b) establishes a relationship between the table that was split and the new table.

```
For each functional dependency F:
   If the left side of F itself is not a candidate key to some table
   then
      Step 1: Create a new table T that consists only of the attributes
              in both sides of F.
      Step 2: Set the primary key of T as the attributes in F's left
              side.
      Step 3: In the existing table E that already had the attributes
              of F:
              a Remove the attributes of F's right side that are not
                part of E's primary key.
              b Set the attributes in F's left side to be a foreign key
                into T.
```

FIGURE 2.6 Normalization process to BCNF.

Looking at the first functional dependency, shown in Figure 2.4 we confirm whether the left side (Phone, PropAdr, PropCity) is itself a primary or candidate key to some table. Because that is the primary key of Listing, we do not need to go any further with that first functional dependency and proceed with the second.

Looking at the second functional dependency, the first in Figure 2.5 we confirm whether the left side, Phone, is itself a candidate key to some table. Note that while Phone is part of the primary key in Listing, Phone by itself is not a primary key or candidate key, so we proceed with the three steps to split Listing. In step 1, we first create a new table that consists only of the attributes Phone, RealtorName, OfficeAdr, and OfficeCity. Let's call this new table Realtor. In step 2, we then set Phone to be the primary key of Realtor. Finally, for step 3, in the Listing table we remove RealtorName, OfficeAdr, and OfficeCity. We leave Phone in Listing but set Phone as a foreign key in Listing that relates to the primary key Phone in Realtor. After being split because of the second functional dependency, the result is the two tables defined in Figure 2.7.

```
Listing (Phone, PropAdr, PropCity, NBeds, Area, Price)
Realtor (RealtorName, OfficeAdr, OfficeCity, Phone)
```

FIGURE 2.7 Original Listing table split into two tables.

Note that in the Listing table, Phone is both underlined and italicized. This means that Phone is part of the primary key, and is itself a foreign key into Realtor. Figure 2.8 shows how the split tables appear with their data at this time.

Because, by definition in the relational database model, a table does not have duplicate rows (that is, rows with the same value in each corresponding column), we remove any duplicate rows that may exist after splitting a table. In this example, after the normalization process we have 5 duplicate rows in Realtor, and after removing them the Realtor table is now reduced to that shown in Figure 2.9.

Now on to the last functional dependency. We confirm whether the left side (PropAdr, PropCity) is itself a primary or candidate key to some table. It is not, so we likewise proceed with the three steps to split the Listing table. In step 1, we first create a new table that consists only of the attributes PropAdr, PropCity, NBeds, Area and Price. Let's call this new table Property. In step 2, we then set (PropAdr, PropCity) to be the primary key of Property. Finally, for step 3, in the Listing table we remove NBeds, Area, and Price. We leave (PropAdr, PropCity) in Listing but set it as a foreign key in Listing that relates to Property. The result is now the following three tables, whose definitions are given in Figure 2.10.

Listing

Phone	PropAdr	PropCity	NBeds	Area	Price
555-1111	17 Highland	CityA	3	2000	220000
555-1111	1565 State Rd	CityB	4	2900	290000
555-1111	997 George	CityA	4	2200	240000
555-1111	123 Big Lane	CityA	8	5000	750000
555-2222	5 Lighthouse	CityB	4	2000	230000
555-2222	190 Brown	CityC	2	1700	140000
555-2222	123 Big Lane	CityA	8	5000	750000

Realtor

RealtorName	OfficeAdr	OfficeCity	Phone
Penny	137 Main	CityA	555-1111
Penny	137 Main	CityA	555-1111
Penny	137 Main	CityA	555-1111
Penny	137 Main	CityA	555-1111
Bob	455 Oak	CityB	555-2222
Bob	455 Oak	CityB	555-2222
Bob	455 Oak	CityB	555-2222

FIGURE 2.8 Split tables with their data.

Realtor

RealtorName	OfficeAdr	OfficeCity	Phone
Penny	137 Main	CityA	555-1111
Bob	455 Oak	CityB	555-2222

FIGURE 2.9 Realtor table with duplicate rows eliminated.

Listing (*Phone, PropAdr, PropCity*)
Realtor (RealtorName,OfficeAdr,OfficeCity,Phone)
Property (PropAdr,PropCity,NBeds,Area,Price)

FIGURE 2.10 Resulting table definitions after normalization of real estate data.

The tables with their data are shown in Figure 2.11.

Because we have analyzed all the stated functional dependencies and the left side of each is now a candidate key to some table, we have established these tables to be in BCNF. Hence, duplicated data has been reduced, and

Listing

Phone	PropAdr	PropCity
555-1111	17 Highland	CityA
555-1111	1565 State Rd	CityB
555-1111	997 George	CityA
555-1111	123 Big Lane	CityA
555-2222	5 Lighthouse	CityB
555-2222	190 Brown	CityC
555-2222	123 Big Lane	CityA

Realtor

RealtorName	OfficeAdr	OfficeCity	Phone
Penny	137 Main	CityA	555-1111
Bob	455 Oak	CityB	555-2222

Property

PropAdr	PropCity	NBeds	Area	Price
17 Highland	CityA	3	2000	220000
1565 State Rd	CityB	4	2900	290000
997 George	CityA	4	2200	240000
123 Big Lane	CityA	8	5000	750000
5 Lighthouse	CityB	4	2000	230000
190 Brown	CityC	2	1700	140000

FIGURE 2.11 Resulting real estate tables with data normalized to BCNF.

the corresponding data inconsistencies have been resolved. For example, if Penny now updates her office address from "137 Main" to "417 Main," that involves changing the data in exactly one location (in the Realtor table). The office address is not duplicated anywhere else, so there is now no possibility of a data inconsistency involving the new address and previous address. In a similar manner, if we were to now change the price of the "123 Big Lane" property, that change is applied to exactly one location (in the Property table) and there is now no possible data inconsistency involving the new price and previous price.

2.2 SURROGATE KEYS AND DATA INTEGRITY

The normalization we applied to achieve BCNF did reduce data duplication and potential for data inconsistencies. However, the potential of a data inconsistency—and database integrity concern—still remains if a change is made to one of our primary key values. The reason is because in our scenario, we still have a natural key chosen as a primary key for the Realtor table. A *natural key* is one whose values have meaning associated with the scenario. In Realtor, we chose Phone as the primary key, and Phone has a meaning associated with the scenario (that is, Phone contains the actual phone number of a realtor).

To see how the potential of a data inconsistency still remains, consider that Bob changes his phone number to "555-3333." That data value exists not only in the Realtor table, but potentially in multiple database locations as a foreign key, in our case with the Listing table. There are some ways in which we can eliminate this type of data duplication and its data inconsistency potential. One way is to define and enforce referential integrity constraints with cascading updates, where if a primary key value changes, the database system will automatically apply that change to every foreign key reference of that primary key. With a cascading update defined between Realtor and Listing in our real estate listing scenario, if Bob changes his phone number and we apply that change to the Phone column in the Realtor table, the database system will automatically apply that same change to the Phone column in Listing to rows that have the previous value in Phone. While cascading updates are effective, this approach does lead to a performance overhead consideration, in that if a primary key value appears as a foreign key value a large number of times, the cascade of the update may take a significant amount of time to update to all occurrences of that foreign key value.

A second way to resolve such data duplication and data inconsistencies and avoid cascading overhead is to introduce a surrogate key. A *surrogate key* is an added primary key that is not part of the original data or and does not contain values meaningful to the scenario, but is rather introduced to generate a unique value in each row. We will introduce a surrogate key named RealtorID in the Realtor table, so the Realtor relation has the structure and data given in Figure 2.12. The data of the surrogate key has unique values in the RealtorID column such as those shown.

Note that RealtorID is now the primary key, rather than Phone. However, Phone can still exist as a candidate key as an alternative means to retrieve a unique row in Realtor.

We also have similar database integrity concerns with the use of PropAdr and PropCity as a natural primary key for Property and duplication of its values as foreign keys (although changes to PropAdr and PropCity may be less

```
Realtor(RealtorID, RealtorName, OfficeAdr, OfficeCity, Phone)
```

Realtor

RealtorID	RealtorName	OfficeAdr	OfficeCity	Phone
R001	Penny	137 Main	CityA	555-1111
R002	Bob	455 Oak	CityB	555-2222

FIGURE 2.12 Realtor table structure and data with surrogate key.

likely unless a misspelling or inaccurate value was initially provided and needs correcting). As with Realtor, we can introduce a surrogate key for Property to avoid such integrity concerns. But we will also see another advantage of surrogate keys: a surrogate key also provides the benefit of simplifying a composite primary key and reducing the primary key to just one column. With a surrogate key named PropID introduced in the Property table, we will have the following Property table structure and data given in Figure 2.13.

```
Property (PropID, PropAdr, PropCity, NBeds, Area, Price)
```

Property

PropID	PropAdr	PropCity	NBeds	Area	Price
P001	17 Highland	CityA	3	2000	220000
P002	1565 State Rd	CityB	4	2900	290000
P003	997 George	CityA	4	2200	240000
P004	123 Big Lane	CityA	8	5000	750000
P005	5 Lighthouse	CityB	4	2000	230000
P006	190 Brown	CityC	2	1700	140000

FIGURE 2.13 Property table with surrogate key.

In addition to reducing database integrity concerns with data duplication, reducing data inconsistencies that may arise when the primary key value changes, and reducing the size of a primary key, a surrogate key can also enforce referential integrity when a foreign key value is specified for an added or changed row. As an example, if one were to add a new row to Listing but mistype the phone number "555-1111" as "555-1112," we have a referential integrity constraint violation because "555-1112" is not a primary key in the current Realtor table. Likewise, because we now have a surrogate key in Property, we no longer have to specify a composite foreign key in Listing, which may otherwise result with mistyped values and referential integrity constraint violations. Because we now use surrogate keys for Realtor and

Property, such mistyping of foreign key values may become less likely. The new Listing table structure and its data are as shown in Figure 2.14.

Listing (*RealtorID*, *PropID*)

Listing

RealtorID	PropID
R001	P001
R001	P002
R001	P003
R001	P004
R002	P005
R002	P006
R002	P004

FIGURE 2.14 Referencing surrogate keys.

Now data duplication of values to Phone no longer exists, which helps enforce integrity. A change to a Phone value requires only one change, and that is in the Realtor table.

2.3 NORMALIZATION, ACCESS RESTRICTIONS, AND BEYOND

In addition to reducing data duplication and enforcing database integrity, normalization can also provide other database security benefits. By splitting tables according to themes and functional dependencies, we may more easily manage access to the data by allowing or disallowing access based on tables. As an example in this real estate scenario, suppose we wanted to allow a person to see data about properties, but not about realtors or listings. With the normalized set of tables in the real estate scenario, we could allow the person access to see the Property table but disallow that person to have access to Realtor or Listing. Based on this concept, the original Listing table that held all of the data could not support such discernment of access, because we could then either allow access to all of the data or disallow access to all of the data.

However, even after normalization the data may be broken down (or *fine-grained*) enough to support all or future security requirements in terms of tables. Now suppose a new regulation or business requirement requires a potential buyer to be signed with a realtor in order to see a property's street address and area size. In other words, the general public cannot see a property's address or area. Based on the normalized Property table structure, we can only either allow the public to see all Property data or disallow the public to see any Property data. To enforce the restriction to the public of street address and area based on table-level security, we can further break down Property into two tables. One table (let's name PropertyPublic) will contain the columns in which we allow public access, and another table (let's name PropertyPrivate) will contain the remaining columns that the public cannot access. Both tables would contain the same primary key values to properly identify each row, as shown with the table structures and data in Figure 2.15.

```
PropertyPublic(PropID,PropCity,NBeds,Price)
PropertyPrivate(PropID,PropAdr,Area)
```

PropertyPublic

PropID	PropCity	NBeds	Price
P001	CityA	3	220000
P002	CityB	4	290000
P003	CityA	4	240000
P004	CityA	8	750000
P005	CityB	4	230000
P006	CityC	2	140000

PropertyPrivate

PropID	PropAdr	Area
P001	17 Highland	2000
P002	1565 State Rd	2900
P003	997 George	2200
P004	123 Big Lane	5000
P005	5 Lighthouse	2000
P006	190 Brown	1700

FIGURE 2.15 Splitting tables further to isolate sensitive data.

We could then allow the public to access the first table but not the second. Persons who have signed with a realtor are authorized to access both tables, so can be given access to both.

2.4 SUMMARY

In this chapter, we described database design techniques that can remove certain data integrity risks from the start. While database design is an often overlooked or underestimated phase of database implementation, it plays a vital role in the security management of the database. We looked at design approaches to manage access to certain data through tables. We explore this idea of using tables to manage data access further in Chapter 5, "Database Privileges."

CHAPTER 3

DATABASE MANAGEMENT AND ADMINISTRATION

In this chapter, we explore and demonstrate a variety of tasks and controls that a database administrator can carry out to maintain the information security objectives of confidentiality, integrity, and availability of the data in a database.

For representation purposes, in this text we will represent SQL keywords with all capital letters. For names of databases, tables, columns, and other components we will use PascalCase (uppercase for the first letter of each word with no underscores). There are other conventions to represent SQL keywords and names of database components, and we opted for those conventions to distinguish SQL keywords from component names and possibly help with grasping the syntax and structure of the SQL statements that we will introduce. SQL keywords are case insensitive, so if you wish to use another convention, such as lower-case or camelCase for SQL keywords, you may do so. Many DBMSs also use case insensitive names for databases, tables, columns, and other components. However, some DBMSs do employ (or can be configured to employ) case sensitive names for components, so the best practice is to choose a convention and consistently use that.

We will also use certain fonts to distinguish an item's context or purpose. We represent in bold font the names of system commands as well as their options and arguments. We also represent names of environment variables in bold font. SQL keywords are represented in italics font. Names of files, users and similar items are represented in normal (non-bold, non-italic) font.

3.1   BACKUP AND RECOVERY

The first database management and administration task that we discuss is an important one that helps support the information security objective of availability. One risk to the availability of the data in a database is the loss or inaccessibility of that data due to a variety of threats that include corruption by hardware failure, user alteration, or user deletion. For those last two threats we have to include both cases where the user action was authorized or unauthorized. A common solution to such availability problems is to recover or *restore* that data to an earlier point in time with a previously obtained *backup*, or copy of that data. By doing so, we recover the ability to access and use that data as we could beforehand.

In addition to an availability solution, we also present these backup and recovery techniques as a way to create a *checkpoint* of a database as we walk through demonstrations in this text. In this manner, you can use the backup and recovery techniques to restore the data to a previous checkpoint so that you may repeat certain demonstrations that occur after that checkpoint. You can also use these techniques to go back to a previous valid set of data in the event that a demonstration was not carried out properly and altered the data with a different result than expected.

Notice that to recover the data to a database, we must have previously obtained a backup of that data. An important administrative task is to backup the data so that we have one or more known *restore points* for that data. This can furthermore include deciding what data to backup, as well as when or how frequently to issue the backup. In the event of data loss, it is these restore points that we can refer to when considering which data set to restore. One consideration is to restore the most recent data, that is, the most recently backed up data set. Another consideration may be to restore a data set that we know contains valid data, which may not necessarily be the most recent backup if we notice or suspect a data corruption occurred before the most recent backup.

Database backups can exist in a variety of formats. A common format is a set of files that contain the necessary SQL statements that can insert the data into the database tables. We can also generate a set of SQL statements that contain the necessary data definition language (DDL) statements to create the necessary structures and functionality, such as databases, tables, views, constraints, procedures, and functions. With these files, we can rerun the SQL statements to rebuild the backed up database(s) if necessary, as well as to replace the data in the backed up databases. An advantage of this backup format is the ability to use those files on compatible DBMSs. Another advantage is that we can easily view and edit the database components or data if needed, before we rebuild the database or restore the data. While other backup formats exist as well, including comma-separated value (CSV) files or XML files, and although we can manage those formats similarly, we will focus on the SQL statement format.

In MySQL, Oracle, and MariaDB, we can use the **mysqldump** command to backup various parts of a DBMS. For now we will assume a single-session DBMS environment where at most one user or application is connected to the DBMS at a given time. The following describes how we can issue backups to maintain data availability in single-session DBMS environments. If multiple user or application sessions to the DBMS may exist at the same time, we can also use these same approaches, but should also take an additional measure to ensure data integrity of the generated backup. We describe and demonstrate that additional measure in Chapter 9, "Data Integrity with Concurrent Access."

Backup and restore of a specific database

With the simplest form of **mysqldump**, we can backup one specific database as shown in Figure 3.1. The generated backup will contain all that database's tables, views, constraints, and data (do not be concerned if some of those terms seem unfamiliar now, as we will explain and demonstrate their purposes in later chapters).

As an example, Figure 3.1 shows how we can obtain a backup of the Financial database, which includes its tables and data, into the file financial_backup.sql. That database and others mentioned in upcoming examples will be used further when we demonstrate concepts in the following chapters. The empty box that appears in the last line of Figure 3.1, and also appears in other figures in the text that portray command line screenshots, represents the cursor location at which typed input appears, as well as where the typed input stops (more on that later).

```
$ mysqldump -u root -p --databases Financial > financial_backup.sql
Enter password:
$ []
```

FIGURE 3.1 Using mysqldump to create a backup of a specific database.

In Figure 3.1, we specify the **-u** option followed by the username root for a DBMS administrator user and the **-p** option to indicate that we will provide the corresponding password on a separate prompt. You can replace the username specification as appropriate for your DBMS administrator. We can optionally provide the password immediately (that is, with no space) after the **-p** option to avoid the password prompt and provide the password as an option, but that is considered less secure and a risk to confidentiality, because an attacker who lists process information while the backup is in progress may see the password as part of the command. To reinforce safe practices, we will omit the password in the command for these examples and require the password to be provided on a separate prompt.

In this example, we also use the **--databases** option, (note there are two hyphens) followed by the name of the database. Even though the **--databases** option is not absolutely necessary for a single database backup, and we can just specify the name of the database, that option does simplify the restore operation, as we will explain later.

The greater-than (**>**) symbol in Figure 3.1 represents *output redirection* to the file that follows, which is financial_backup.sql in this example. With output redirection, the generated SQL statements for the backup are written to the specified output or backup file. If the output file is to be generated in a directory other than the current working directory, we can prefix the output filename with the path to output file's location. Without output redirection, the generated SQL statements for the backup are sent to the screen by default.

The file mydb_backup.sql generated in Figure 3.1 contains all of the necessary SQL statements to create and populate that database's tables, views, and data. With this single backup file, we can easily and quickly restore that database. Using a command-line interface to the DBMS, we have two approaches to issue such a restore operation with such a backup file. The first approach, shown in Figure 3.2, involves issuing a **mysql** command to initiate a client connection to the DBMS, in the same way we would normally do so to establish a user connection or *session*. As with establishing a user session, we must provide a DBMS administrator username and password prompt specification, which you can change according to your environment, to carry out the restore operation.

```
$ mysql -u root -p Financial < financial_backup.sql
Enter password:
$ □
```

FIGURE 3.2 Restoring a backup created with the **--databases** option of a single database, without an existing user session.

Additionally, we also include at the end of that **mysql** command in Figure 3.2 a form of *input redirection* that indicates we want that session to read its input from a particular file, in this case the restore information saved in a previous backup, rather than from the keyboard. We specify input redirection with the less-than (**<**) symbol followed by the restore file name. If the restore file is not in the current working directory, we can prefix the restore filename with the path to its location. That **mysql** restore command then reads the SQL statements one after the other and applies them to the DBMS, thus recreating the DBMS components and data defined in the backup file.

Notice that this form of restore requires that the backup was generated with the **--databases** option. If that is not the case, then we have to issue additional steps to restore the backup, namely choose the database in which to restore and even possibly create that database first, as we do in Section 3.1.3, "Backup and Restore of Specific Tables."

Notice that the **mysql** command given in Figure 3.2 does not require a DBMS session to already exist for the restore operation. The **mysql** command given in Figure 3.2 also does not leave the session open for subsequent use, but rather closes the session immediately after restoring from the input file.

The second approach to restore from a backup file uses an existing DBMS administrator session. Figure 3.3 illustrates this approach by first establishing a session for a DBMS administrator. As before, you can replace the username and password as appropriate for your DBMS administrator. Once the session is established, we can issue the restore operation with the SQL *SOURCE* command followed by the name of the backup file to restore. If the file to restore resides in a directory other than the current working directory, we can also prefix the backup file with its path. The *SOURCE* command will then read the backup file and issue the file's SQL statements one after the other within that session to recreate the backup up content. For brevity, Figure 3.3 does not show the Enter key pressed and the results of all the SQL statements in the backup file after they are carried out by the restore operation.

This second approach to restore can be helpful if we had already established a session, say, to carry out some DBMS administrative work before and/or after the restore operation, such as creating and choosing the database in which to restore if the backup was not created with the **--databases** option.

```
$ mysql -u root -p
Enter password:
Welcome to the MySQL monitor.  Commands end with ; or \g.
Your MySQL connection id is 9
Server version: 8.0.29 MySQL Community Server - GPL

Copyright (c) 2000, 2022, Oracle and/or its affiliates.

Oracle is a registered trademark of Oracle Corporation and/or its
affiliates. Other names may be trademarks of their respective
owners.

Type 'help;' or '\h' for help. Type '\c' to clear the current input statement.

mysql> SOURCE financial_backup.sql []
```

FIGURE 3.3 Restoring a backup created with the **--databases** option of a single database, with an existing user session.

Backup and restore of multiple specific databases

To create a backup of multiple, specific, databases, we must use the **--databases** option, followed by a list of space-separated database names. Figure 3.4 shows how we may create a backup of the Financial and MedicalCaseStudy databases into the file financial_medical_backup.sql.

```
$ mysqldump -u root -p --databases Financial MedicalCaseStudy > financial_medical_backup.sql
Enter password:
$ []
```

FIGURE 3.4 Using **mysqldump** to create a backup of multiple specific databases.

To restore the content in a backup that consists of multiple databases, we use the same techniques as we did to restore a backup of a single database created with the **--databases** option shown in Figure 3.2 or Figure 3.3.

Backup and restore of specific tables

To create a backup of only a specific table within a database, we simply add to the **mysqldump** command the database name followed by the name of the table. Figure 3.5 shows how we can generate a backup of only the Employee table from the BusinessTLS database into the backup file BTLS_employee.sql.

```
$ mysqldump -u root -p BusinessTLS Employee > BTLS_employee.sql
Enter password:
$ ▯
```

FIGURE 3.5 Using **mysqldump** to create a backup of a specific table.

If we wish to backup multiple tables within a database, we simply add to the previous example. After the database name we specify the table names as a comma-separated list. Figure 3.6 shows how we can generate a backup of the Employee and HR tables from the BusinessTLSSplitHR database into the backup file BTLSSHR_employee_hr.sql.

```
$ mysqldump -u root -p BusinessTLSSplitHR Employee HR > BTLSSHR_employee_hr.sql
Enter password:
$ ▯
```

FIGURE 3.6 Using **mysqldump** to create a backup of specific tables.

Unlike restoring a backup that consists of one or more entire databases, to restore a backup that consists of only tables, we must specify the database in which to restore those tables. If the database already exists, then we can restore the backup with or without a previously established DBMS session. To restore without an established session, we can use the **mysql** command as we did before to restore a database backup. Figure 3.7 shows how we can take that approach to restore into the existing database BusinessTLSSplitHR the two tables obtained in the previous backup. Notice that although we specified to restore into the same database name as was specified for the backup, we can also specify the name of another existing database in which to restore, say if we wanted to transfer all or part of one database into another database.

```
$ mysql -u root -p BusinessTLSSplitHR < BTLSSHR_employee_hr.sql
Enter password:
$ ▯
```

FIGURE 3.7 Restoring tables into an existing database without a previously established DBMS session.

If the database in which to restore does not already exist, we must first create the database. A common approach is to first establish a DBMS session, create the database, choose that database to use, then issue the restore operation. This is an example of carrying out administrative tasks before and/or after the restore operation as we described for Figure 3.3. As an example, let's again restore the Employee and HR tables from the previous backup into the database BusinessTLSSplitHR, but this time suppose the database in which to restore does not already exist. This may be the case, for example, if we deleted that database after creating the backup, are restoring the backup into a fresh DBMS, or are restoring into another new database. Let's suppose we want to restore the backed up Employee and HR tables into a new database named EmployeeData.

In Figure 3.8, we first establish a DBMS session like we did before. We then create the database with the *CREATE DATABASE* statement. Next, with the *USE* statement we choose that database to be the one in which subsequent operations will occur. We then issue the *SOURCE* command and the backup filename with optional path. Like before, we do not show Enter pressed at the end of the *SOURCE* command for brevity. Note that we could also use this approach to restore into an existing database by just omitting the *CREATE DATABASE* statement.

```
mysql> CREATE DATABASE EmployeeData;
Query OK, 1 row affected (0.11 sec)

mysql> USE EmployeeData;
Database changed
mysql> SOURCE BTLSSHR_employee_hr.sql []
```

FIGURE 3.8 Restoring tables into a database that does not already exist.

Backup of users, privileges, and other components

In addition to user-created databases, a DBMS may contain other components that are necessary for an organization or environment. One such set of components involve database user accounts and associated privileges. These components are maintained and stored by the DBMS within *internal* databases and tables that are not by default included with the backup approaches described thus far. While we could specifically name those internal databases in a list similar to the **mysqldump** command given in Figure 3.4, we must be careful to specify all of the necessary internal databases to include all of their tables and data that are required. To compound this matter, DBMSs typically have varying names for internal databases and tables, so for example, MySQL, MariaDB, and Oracle each manage user accounts with internal databases and tables that have different names.

Fortunately, we can easily include user account and privilege information, as well as other DBMS internals, in a backup with the **--all-databases** option to **mysqldump**. Figure 3.9 shows how we can issue a backup of all user and

DBMS internal databases to the backup alldbs_backup.sql, where "alldbs" refers to "all databases."

```
$ mysqldump -u root -p --all-databases > alldbs_backup.sql
Enter password:
$ []
```

FIGURE 3.9 Using **mysqldump** to create a backup of all user and DBMS databases and tables, including user account information.

A database may also contain stored procedures or functions, also known as *routines*. In later chapters we use stored procedures and functions as solutions to certain data confidentiality and integrity problems. These routines are normally not included in a backup that we create, but we can specify that we want to include them with the **--routines** option in a **mysqldump** command. Figure 3.10 shows how we can create an even more comprehensive backup of all databases, with their tables, views, data, stored procedures and stored functions, into the file dbms_backup.sql.

```
$ mysqldump -u root -p --all-databases --routines > dbms_backup.sql
Enter password:
$ []
```

FIGURE 3.10 Using **mysqldump** to create a backup of all databases, user account information, and stored routines.

Deciding what to backup

While a backup of the entire DBMS or of only select components is useful as an availability solution, we do have considerations among which approach to employ in a given situation. A backup of the entire DBMS is an easy and safe way to ensure we have all DBMS content, so that we can restore the entire DBMS as it existed at the point of that backup. Such a complete backup is especially helpful, because while we may often consider which organizational or user database(s) or table(s) to backup, we may not as easily consider other vital components such as database users, privileges, or stored routines. As such, the organization's data may be only part of the necessary operational components. If we inadvertently omit other vital components such as users or privileges in a backup, after a restore operation we may have security risks with availability (by a user not being able to access the data to which they should have the ability because their account is not available), or with confidentiality (by quickly allowing "open" access for any user, whether authorized or unauthorized), until we accurately recreate those users and privileges as they existed previously. Add to this consideration that certain components, such as user and privileges information, is stored in certain internal databases and tables that vary among DBMSs, so unless we are certain which of those internal databases and tables are necessary for functionality, we may wish to consider a full DBMS backup of all databases and routines.

While a full DBMS backup can be a reliable solution for availability, for DBMSs with a lot of content, the file size of a full DBMS backup may be large. If file size is a consideration, we may wish to create a smaller backup of only a specific database, a small set of databases, or only certain tables. We may also wish to use this approach if we will share a backup file with another party that should only have access to specific databases or tables. That way we can include only those databases or tables in the backup and not risk confidentiality by sharing a complete DBMS backup that happens to include content the other party is unauthorized to access. We could even employ a backup solution that uses the best of both approaches, such as a complete DBMS backup, say, every day, and of specific databases or tables more frequently, such as every hour. This may be particularly attractive if certain components, such as users and privileges, change infrequently, but user data in other databases or tables change more frequently.

3.2 USER ACCOUNT SECURITY CONFIGURATIONS

To better secure database user accounts, a DBMS administrator can employ a variety of security controls that manage user accounts.

Password expiration

One common control is password *expiration*, or the length of time that a user's password will remain in effect before the user is required to change that password. This control helps protect a user's account against unauthorized access in scenarios such as unauthorized use of an old password that has been compromised without the user's knowledge. By requiring the user to eventually change that password, an attacker will no longer be able to use that password to gain unauthorized access. Password expiration can also prevent potential future unauthorized use of a password that is in the process of being compromised, such as when an attacker issues a brute force password attack. For example, if an attacker needs on average one year to brute force compromise a user's password, and the user's password expires in 120 days, after that password expires and the user puts a second password into effect, should the attacker compromise the first password, it is no longer used and therefore of no value to the attacker. Essentially, password expiration reduces or closes the window of opportunity by which an attack can compromise and use the password for unauthorized access.

Password expiration values exist for each user as well as a system default. Each user can have a unique expiration value, and that value is initially the system default in effect when the user account is created. After a user account is created, we can change the expiration value for that specific user without affecting the expiration values of other users.

To see the number of days for which a specific user account can use a password without changing the password, we can issue the *SELECT* statement whose general syntax is given in Figure 3.11 for MySQL or MariaDB DBMSs. Here we would replace username with the user name of the account, and hostname for an optional host specification for that account. We also specify single straight quotes (or alternatively left-quotes) around the username and hostname for reasons that we explain in Chapter 4. Note that smart quotes are not recognized as quotes in many DBMSs and may generate a syntax error if used.

SELECT password_lifetime *FROM* mysql.user
WHERE user='**username**' *AND* host='**hostname**';

FIGURE 3.11 General syntax to show the password expiration for a specific user in MySQL or MariaDB.

This chapter contains some examples with general syntax and not with specific user accounts. Rather, these concepts for user password and account management are meant as a reference for now, and when we later create user accounts, you can refer back to these concepts and apply them to those accounts (or other accounts that you create) if you wish.

To change the password expiration interval for a specific user, we can issue the statement whose general syntax is given in Figure 3.12. We would replace ndays with the number of days in the expiration interval, and again replace username with the user name of the account, and hostname for an optional host specification for that account.

UPDATE mysql.user *SET* password_lifetime=**ndays**

WHERE user='**username**' *AND* host='**hostname**';

FIGURE 3.12 General syntax to change the password expiration for a specific user in MySQL or MariaDB.

The default password expiration can vary across DBMSs. MySQL and MariaDB typically have a default of 0 days, which means no password expiration. To confirm the default expiration interval in days for those DBMSs, we can examine the **default_password_lifetime** global variable value, as demonstrated in Figure 3.13.

```
mysql> SHOW GLOBAL VARIABLES LIKE 'default_password_lifetime';
+---------------------------+-------+
| Variable_name             | Value |
+---------------------------+-------+
| default_password_lifetime | 0     |
+---------------------------+-------+
1 row in set (0.01 sec)

mysql> []
```

FIGURE 3.13 Showing the default password expiration interval in MySQL or MariaDB.

We can change the default password expiration in a MySQL or MariaDB DBMS either by changing the DBMS server's configuration file or by setting the **default_password_lifetime** global variable within the DBMS. In Figure 3.14, we show how a MySQL or MariaDB DBMS administrator can redefine that global variable to set the default password expiration at 120 days, with the *SET* statement. We then show the new default password expiration with the *SHOW* statement.

```
mysql> SET GLOBAL default_password_lifetime=120;
Query OK, 0 rows affected (0.00 sec)

mysql> []
```

FIGURE 3.14 Setting the default password expiration interval to 120 days in MySQL or MariaDB.

Oracle often installs with a password expiration default of 180 days. To confirm the default password expiration for an Oracle DBMS, we can issue a *SELECT* statement on one of the DBMS internal tables as shown in Figure 3.15.

```
SQL> SELECT * FROM dba_profiles WHERE resource_name = 'PASSWORD_LIFE_TIME';

PROFILE                RESOURCE_NAME                   RESOURCE LIMIT
---------------        --------------------------      -----------------------
DEFAULT                PASSWORD_LIFE_TIME              PASSWORD 180

SQL> []
```

FIGURE 3.15 Showing the default password expiration interval in Oracle.

If we wish to change the default password expiration in an Oracle DBMS, we can issue an *ALTER* statement to change the DBMS internal tables. Figure 3.16 shows how we can specify no password expiration in Oracle.

```
SQL> ALTER PROFILE default LIMIT PASSWORD_LIFE_TIME unlimited;
Profile altered.

SQL> █
```

FIGURE 3.16 Setting no password expiration in Oracle.

Notice that no password expiration introduces a security risk with confidentiality. Figure 3.17 shows how we can change the default password expiration in Oracle to 120 days.

```
SQL> ALTER PROFILE default LIMIT PASSWORD_LIFE_TIME 120;
Profile altered.

SQL> []
```

FIGURE 3.17 Setting the default password expiration interval to 120 days in Oracle.

Notice that a default password expiration value applies only to user accounts created after that value is put into effect and does not affect user accounts that already exist. Each user account contains information that includes the time interval in which their current password will expire. To modify the password expiration for an existing account, we have to change that account's password expiration as we discuss next.

A DBMS administrator can set the number of days in which a given user's password will continue to be valid before expiring. To set the number of days before expiration in MySQL or MariaDB, a DBMS administrator can issue a form of the *ALTER USER* statement, whose general syntax in given in Figure 3.18. Here we would replace username with the username of the account, along with optional hostname restriction, and ndays with the number of days until password expiration.

ALTER USER '**username**' *PASSWORD EXPIRE INTERVAL* **ndays** *DAY*;

FIGURE 3.18 General syntax to set the password expiration interval to a given number of days for a given user in MySQL and MariaDB.

A DBMS administrator can also immediately expire a password for a given user account. This action may be a decision if the user's password has a low suspicion to be compromised, and as a precautionary measure we will simply allow the user to continue using their account but with a new password. To immediately expire an account's password in MySQL, MariaDB, as well as Oracle, a DBMS administrator can issue the *ALTER USER* statement whose general syntax is shown in Figure 3.19. Here we would replace username with the username of the account, along with optional hostname restriction,

ALTER USER '**username**' *PASSWORD EXPIRE*;

FIGURE 3.19 General syntax to immediately expire a user's password in MySQL, MariaDB, and Oracle.

If a user's password expires—either by reaching the number of days since setting the current password or by an immediate expire by a DBMS administrator—the user password must be *reset* before the user can regain their normal access with that account. Either the user or a DBMS administrator can reset the password for an expired account with the *ALTER USER* statement, as described in Chapter 4, "Database User Accounts." By default, the user can still log into their database account with an expired password, but has extremely limited access. In that situation, the user still has the ability to log change their password so they can relogin in and regain normal control of their account.

If we wish to have no password expiration, a DBMS administrator can issue the *ALTER USER* statement, whose general syntax is shown in Figure 3.20. Remember that while no password expiration may be a user convenience, it introduces security risks with user account confidentiality.

ALTER USER '**username**' *PASSWORD EXPIRE NEVER;*

FIGURE 3.20 General syntax to never expire a user's password in MySQL, MariaDB and Oracle.

Disabling/enabling user accounts

We may have situations in which a user account should be disabled such that no one can log into that account but it is not necessarily removed. This may be a temporary action, say, for when a user account is suspected to be compromised and for security purposes is not allowed to be used until the matter is assessed. Should the compromise turn out to be true, we can keep the account disabled until the breach is assessed, or however else is specified in the organization's security policy. In other situations, the disabling of an account may be a longer term solution, say because the user associated with the account is no longer with the organization, but for various functional or availability needs we still need the presence of that account so that, say, certain data or resources are still accessible. In both cases, we do not want anyone logging into that account for the time being.

To disable (or lock) a user's account in MySQL, MariaDB, and Oracle so that logins to that account are denied, we can issue an *ALTER USER* statement whose general syntax is shown in Figure 3.21. Here we replace **username** with the user and any applicable hostname.

ALTER USER '**username**' *ACCOUNT LOCK;*

FIGURE 3.21 General syntax to disable or lock a user account in MySQL, MariaDB, and Oracle.

When applicable, we can reenable a disabled user account, so that logins by that user are now permitted. In one of the previous scenarios. where we disabled a user account that was suspected of compromise, suppose the assessment yielded a false alarm. In that case, we can reenable the user's account so the user can access the DBMS as before. To reenable (or unlock) a user's account, we can also issue an *ALTER USER* statement, whose general syntax is given in Figure 3.22.

ALTER USER '**username**' *ACCOUNT UNLOCK;*

FIGURE 3.22 General syntax to reenable or unlock a user account in MySQL, MariaDB and Oracle.

A DBMS may have other security controls for passwords and user accounts, and while these can vary among DBMSs, we introduced some common ones in this chapter. We continue in Chapter 4, "Database User Accounts," with other security controls for user accounts, such as with host-restricted access, which limits the system(s) by which a user account can access the DBMS.

3.3   SUMMARY

In this chapter, we introduced some tasks by which a database administrator can provide or maintain some of the security objectives with availability and confidentiality. While not an exhaustive discussion of administrative concepts, we described some of the important ones with backups, restores, password expiration, and account disabling. The concept of backups and restore can be especially useful as we follow along with the hands-on demonstrations of security concepts in upcoming chapters and wish to repeat them.

4

DATABASE USER ACCOUNTS

In this chapter, we describe the concept of database users and show how to manage them using SQL. While many DBMSs also provide a graphical user interface (GUI), the SQL approach is beneficial for many reasons. First, when issuing a task through a GUI, we often have limited features compared to issuing the task through SQL. Secondly, SQL is very uniform across DBMS, while GUIs vary in appearance and design not only across DBMS, but also across versions of a given DBMS. So understanding the SQL approach is not only more powerful, but it allows us to carry out an operation in a more uniform manner across types and versions of DBMSs.

We consider a *database user* to be a person or agent (such as an application or system service) that is authorized to interact with a database. A database user can be specified by a *database username*, and is part of the credential a database user provides to log into or gain access to a database. The database username can be defined in many ways, such as based on the user's actual name and/or a number to help make the username unique. The other part of the credential is an optional password that the user provides for authentication. A database user can also be specified with a *database user ID*, which is a unique identifier assigned to a user when the database user account is created. The database username or user ID is how we will specify which user is allowed or disallowed a type of data access.

The manner in which a particular database user can interact with the database's data is defined by the user's needs or responsibilities. As an example, we may have one user that requires the capability to add, retrieve, and change certain data. We may also have another user that does not require any of that capability, in which case that user should be denied any access to that data.

4.1. CREATING AND REMOVING DATABASE USER ACCOUNTS

Before we can go further with discussing how to allow or disallow certain access to data, we need some database users. So, let's first explain how to create database user accounts. To cover a broad range of use, we will describe how to carry out this task as well as other database security tasks with SQL directly in the MySQL, MariaDB, and Oracle DBMSs. While the figures indicate use of MySQL DBMS, the exact same SQL statements will apply to MariaDB and Oracle unless otherwise noted.

In this scenario, we will create database user accounts for the employees within a business organization. We will choose the database username of an employee to be that employee's last name in lowercase, which in this scenario happens to be unique. In general, if employee last names were not unique, we would have to define the database username on something that is unique, such as combining the last name with first name and/or a number.

When creating a database user account, we can optionally specify an authentication password. To reinforce this form of security, we will specify a password, although for ease of demonstration we will use passwords that are easy to remember for each user. Keep in mind that in practice, we would want to use stronger passwords. Figure 4.1 gives the usernames and passwords for the database accounts in our business scenario.

username	password
roberts	passroberts
garrett	passgarrett
chu@localhost	passchu
donnelly@localhost donnelly@192.168.2.8	passdonnelly passdon28
gardner@192.168.2.10	passgardner
sanford@localhost sanford@192.168.2.%	passsanford passsan2all
smith@localhost	passsmith

FIGURE 4.1 Database usernames and the corresponding authentication password for our business scenario.

The SQL *CREATE USER* statement can be used to create database accounts. The basic syntax for the *CREATE USER* statement with the MySQL, MariaDB, and Oracle DBMSs is given in Figure 4.2.

CREATE USER '**username**'[@'**hostname**'] [*IDENTIFIED BY* '**password**'];

FIGURE 4.2. Basic SQL syntax to create a database user account.

To understand this command representation, the italic characters are SQL symbols or keywords that are specified exactly as is. The bold content represents where we fill in the specifications for our specific needs, such as username, hostname and password for this statement. The content within square brackets is optional and can be omitted or specified depending on whether we wish to leverage that particular feature.

The easiest SQL statement to create a user account for user roberts is one that specifies only the username, as shown in Figure 4.3, where we create a database account for user roberts with no password. This command consists of the SQL keywords *CREATE USER* followed by the username for the new account. The username does not require enclosing quotes if the username consists of only alphanumeric or underscore characters. If the username does contain hyphens (-), periods (.), or other special symbols, the entire username must be enclosed within quotes.

```
mysql> CREATE USER 'roberts';
Query OK, 0 rows affected (0.17 sec)

mysql> █
```

FIGURE 4.3 Creating a user account with no password.

Tip: The *CREATE USER* statement must be issued by the database root account or some other database administrative account that has been given the capability to issue those statements.

In Figure 4.3, we did enclose the username with straight single quotes ('), although technically quotes were not required in this specific example. Even though enclosing quotes may not always be required for a username (and as we see later, for a hostname), it is common practice to always use enclosing quotes for a predictable and uniform appearance, as well as to avoid surprise errors in situations when quotes are required. As such, the examples in this text will always enclose the username (and hostname). Most DBMSs and users prefer the use of straight single quotes when quotes are necessary, and that is the convention we follow. However, many DBMSs also allow use of straight double (") or back (') quotes in situations where quotes are required. No matter which form of quote you use, the form must be the same for each pair of matching quotes.

Tip: Be careful to use straight single or double quotes with SQL. Smart quotes are not recognized as single or double quotes in many DBMSs and may generate a syntax error if used.

That database user can then log into the database by specifying only the username with the SQL command shown in Figure 4.4.[1] Here the **mysql** command includes the **-u** option, followed by one or more spaces and the username. The **-u** option specifies that the username is to follow next.

```
$ mysql -u roberts []
```

FIGURE 4.4 Logging into a database user account with no password.

While a simple way to create a database account, note that this approach does not involve any security measures—such as use of a password—with that account. Because we are reinforcing database security concepts, we should involve such security measures. Let's now incorporate a password for that account.

To add (as well as change) a password to an existing database user account, we can use the SQL *ALTER USER* statement, followed by the username of the account. This statement also contains the *IDENTIFIED BY* keywords which allow us to specify a security control for the account. All DBMSs provide a password-based control, and some DBMSs may also provide other security controls. For a password-based control, we follow those keywords with the password, enclosed in single quotes, as shown in Figure 4.5.

```
mysql> ALTER USER 'roberts' IDENTIFIED BY 'passroberts';
Query OK, 0 rows affected (0.16 sec)

mysql> []
```

FIGURE 4.5 Setting (or changing) a password for a database user account.

---

[1]In an Oracle DBMS, after creating the account for 'username', we must then issue "GRANT CREATE SESSION TO 'username'" to allow that account to log into the DBMS. MySQL and MariaDB do not require this extra step.

Now if a login attempt is made to the account roberts without a password, the login is denied, as shown in Figure 4.6.

```
$ mysql -u roberts
ERROR 1045 (28000): Access denied for user 'roberts'@'localhost' (using password: NO)
$ []
```

FIGURE 4.6 Failed login attempt without a password.

In order to log into the account now, we have to specify a password in one of two ways. One way involves specifying the password as part of the login command. We can do so with the mysql command we previously attempted, but also with the **-p** option immediately followed by the password (that is, no spaces between the option and password), as shown in Figure 4.7.

```
$ mysql -u roberts -ppassroberts
mysql: [Warning] Using a password on the command line interface can be insecure.
Welcome to the MySQL monitor.  Commands end with ; or \g.
Your MySQL connection id is 9
Server version: 8.0.29 MySQL Community Server - GPL

Copyright (c) 2000, 2022, Oracle and/or its affiliates.

Oracle is a registered trademark of Oracle Corporation and/or its
affiliates. Other names may be trademarks of their respective
owners.

Type 'help;' or '\h' for help. Type '\c' to clear the current input statement.

mysql> []
```

FIGURE 4.7 Logging into a database user account with a password.

While the database account for roberts is now password-protected, this login approach does raise a new security concern. This concern stems from the inclusion of the password as part of the login command. On some systems, a user may be able to issue the operating system to generate a full process or command listing that would show the mysql command and its options while the mysql session is running. If the operating system does show all of the program or command options in plaintext, then the user account password may be compromised. More recently however, some operating systems will mask out passwords (such as with x's or other synbols) that are part of a command or process listing, so that particular password vulnerability would not exist in that case.

The second way in which we can specify a password when logging in is similar to the first method, but does not include the password itself as part of the command. Here we issue the same command but omit the password itself after the **-p** option, as shown in Figure 4.8. If nothing immediately follows the **-p** option, the DBMS will prompt the user for the password. This slight change to the login command yields two security benefits. First, as with most password prompts, the password itself will not be reflected on the screen as it is typed in, for security purposes pertaining to shoulder-surfing. Secondly, because the password is not included within the command itself, the password will not be revealed by a command or process listing, whether or not the operating system masks the password in the listing.

```
$ mysql -u roberts -p
Enter password: []
```

FIGURE 4.8 Logging in a database user account with a prompted password.

We have other mysql options that we may provide when logging in, such as **-D** followed by a space and name of a database. The effect is that upon logging in, we do not have to specify the database name to access its components, as if we had chosen the database with the SQL *USE* statement. We will demonstrate this option later with our next scenario.

For the next database user account, let's see how we can create the account and set the password in one command. This approach combines the two commands we issued to separately create the account and set the password. We specify the *CREATE USER* statement followed by the username for the new account. We then add the *IDENTIFIED BY* keywords followed by the password enclosed with single quotes, as shown in Figure 4.9. As before, the username does not require surrounding quotes if the username consists of only alphanumeric or underscore characters. The password must be enclosed within quotes regardless.

```
mysql> CREATE USER 'garrett' IDENTIFIED BY 'passgarrett';
Query OK, 0 rows affected (0.13 sec)

mysql> []
```

FIGURE 4.9 Creating a database user account with a password.

There may be times when we want to remove a database user account. For example, if we did not create the account properly, we may find it easier to remove the account and start over. Figure 4.10 gives the syntax to remove a particular database user's account.

DROP **'user'**[@'**hostname'**];

FIGURE 4.10 General SQL syntax to remove a database user account.

The [@'**hostname**'] portion of the statement is optional (we did not use it up to this point), but we incorporate that later in this chapter.

4.2. LISTING USER ACCOUNTS

Before we create more database users, let's now explain how to list the database accounts that we currently have. Doing so involves our familiar SQL *SELECT* to retrieve certain data from a table that holds user account related details. These tables are typically DBMS-specific, so the exact statement may vary across DBMSs. In the MySQL DBMS, to show a simple listing of users and the hosts from where they can log in, we can issue the *SELECT* statement shown in Figure 4.11. In addition to listing the users that we create, we also see some other entries for the default DBMS root and administrative accounts. You will notice a percent sign (%) in the host column for users garrett and roberts because we created those accounts with no host restriction. This means that one can log into those database user accounts from any system or host.

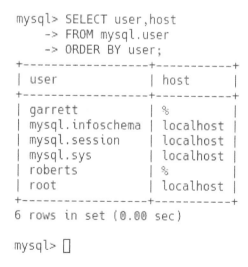

```
mysql> SELECT user,host
    -> FROM mysql.user
    -> ORDER BY user;
+------------------+-----------+
| user             | host      |
+------------------+-----------+
| garrett          | %         |
| mysql.infoschema | localhost |
| mysql.session    | localhost |
| mysql.sys        | localhost |
| roberts          | %         |
| root             | localhost |
+------------------+-----------+
6 rows in set (0.00 sec)

mysql> []
```

FIGURE 4.11 Listing database users and their hosts in MYSQL.</fc>

In the Oracle DBMS, we can similarly obtain a list of database user account names and the hosts from which they login by using the SQL statement shown in Figure 4.12. Figure 4.12 shows only the accounts we created and not any Oracle system accounts.

```
SQL> SELECT USERNAME FROM all_users ORDER BY USERNAME;

USERNAME
-----------------
garrett
roberts

SQL> []
```

FIGURE 4.12 Listing database users and their hosts in Oracle.

Chapter 5 and Chapter 6 follow up with more advanced listings of MySQL, MariaDB, and Oracle database user accounts combined with security controls.

4.3 HOST-RESTRICTED ACCOUNTS

For enhanced security, we can create database user accounts with additional specifications and settings. As an example, we can restrict which system(s) or host(s) a user must be on in order to log into the database system. The first two account creations had no such restriction, so a user on any system may log into the database with username roberts or garrett.

If we wish to restrict which systems can be used to log into a particular account, we can combine the username with a hostname from which the login attempt must occur in order to be successful. Any login attempt to that account from another system is automatically denied. We combine the username and hostname with an at (@) symbol in between them and no added spaces, similar to that of an email address format. In Figure 4.13, we show how to create the account for chu and restrict logins to that account from only the localhost, or system running the DBMS.

```
mysql> CREATE USER 'chu'@'localhost' IDENTIFIED BY 'passchu';
Query OK, 0 rows affected (0.10 sec)

mysql> []
```

FIGURE 4.13 Creating a database user account with a password and host restriction.

As with usernames, if the hostname contains special symbols such as a hyphen (-) or percent sign (%), the entire hostname must be enclosed within a set of quotes. Note that while periods in a username were considered a special symbol, periods in a hostname are not considered a special symbol.

So, if we specify a hostname with one or more periods, we are not required to enclose the hostname within quotes. Furthermore, we can also specify a system with its network or IP address rather than hostname. In a similar manner, we do not have to enclose an IPv4 address within quotes because of the periods involved. However, we do have to enclose an IPv6 address within quotes because a semicolon (:) is considered a special character.

Even though quotes were not required for the hostname in Figure 4.13, we provided quotes anyway because as with usernames, it is good practice to always enclose hostnames within a set of quotes for a predictable and uniform appearance, as well as to avoid the omission of quotes in situations where required.

As an important note, we do not enclose both the username and hostname within one set of quotes. Even though an error may not be generated, doing so has the effect of specifying the username as everything within that pair of quotes, including the at symbol (@) and hostname. The hostname portion will be assumed nonexistent.

In cases where we want to allow a user to log into the DBMS from multiple hostnames or IP addresses, we can specify multiple user accounts, one for each hostname or IP address. For example, if we want to allow user donnelly to log in from the DBMS system itself as well as the IPv4 address 192.168.2.8, we create two user@hostname accounts or instances for donnelly, as shown in Figure 4.14.

```
mysql> CREATE USER 'donnelly'@'localhost' IDENTIFIED BY 'passdonnelly';
Query OK, 0 rows affected (0.61 sec)

mysql> CREATE USER 'donnelly'@'192.168.2.8' IDENTIFIED BY 'passdonnelly';
Query OK, 0 rows affected (0.09 sec)

mysql> []
```

FIGURE 4.14 Creating a database user account with access from multiple systems.

Note that because each user@hostname account or instance is associated with its own password, we can either assign the same password to all instances or accounts for a particular user, or assign different passwords for each of those instances or accounts. Figure 4.1 shows different passwords for each of the multiple accounts that users donnelly and sanford have.

While using the same password for multiple user accounts may be easier to remember from a user perspective, that can introduce a security vulnerability. If that password becomes compromised, an attacker can use that password among all of those user accounts and thus access the database system from all of the hosts by which that user is authorized. Specifying different passwords for a user's set of accounts may be more demanding from a user perspective to remember all of those passwords, but can add a greater degree of security. Namely, if one of those passwords becomes compromised, only the account associated with that password is vulnerable. An attacker can then use that password to gain access only when logging in from the host(s) associated with that particular account. Because the other accounts for that user have a different password, they are still safe. As a result, the *attack surface* can be minimized in the event a password becomes compromised. For example, if the password for donnelly@localhost becomes compromised, an attacker can only use that password to gain access when logging in from the DBMS system. If attempting to log in from 192.168.2.8, that account is secured by another password and so remains safe.

To help reduce the number of user accounts or instances involved when allowing a user to log in from multiple specific systems, the SQL wildcard characters can play a role with specifying multiple hostnames or IP addresses. This is particularly helpful if the set of allowable hostnames or addresses fall within a certain range or network. To restrict an account to log in from a range of hostnames or network addresses, we can specify the range by using a SQL single character underscore (_) wildcard symbol to represent which single character can vary. For example, to represent the IPv4 address range 192.168.2.100 to 192.168.2.109, we can use an underscore (_) in place of the last digit, as shown in Figure 4.15.

```
mysql> CREATE USER 'gardner'@'192.168.2.10_' IDENTIFIED BY 'passgardner';
Query OK, 0 rows affected (0.21 sec)

mysql> []
```

FIGURE 4.15 Creating a database user account with access from a range of IPv4 addresses.

Note that because we created only this account for gardner, we have effectively restricted that user to log into the DBMS from only systems that have an IP address within the range 192.168.2.100 to 192.168.2.109, and not from the DBMS system itself (unless for some reason the DBMS maps the name localhost to an address within that range).

To specify a larger hostname or IP address range, we can use multiple consecutive single character wildcards. But we have to consider that because each wildcard symbol represents one character that can vary, a given number of single character wildcards matches against that many characters. For example, a specification of two consecutive single wildcard characters will match against exactly two characters.

To represent a multiple character wildcard match against any number of characters, we can use the SQL multiple character wildcard percent sign (%) symbol. As an example, suppose we want to allow user sanford to have access from the DBMS system itself as well as from any system within the 192.168.2 network (that is, any system in the IPv4 address range 192.168.2.0 to 192.168.2.255). We can specify % to match any value for the fourth number in the IP address, as shown in Figure 4.16.

```
mysql> CREATE USER 'sanford'@'localhost' IDENTIFIED BY 'passsanford';
Query OK, 0 rows affected (0.43 sec)

mysql> CREATE USER 'sanford'@'192.168.2.%' IDENTIFIED BY 'passsan2all';
Query OK, 0 rows affected (0.09 sec)
mysql> []
```

FIGURE 4.16 Creating a database user account with access from a host and network.

A multiple character wildcard is also common with a hostname specification that involves an entire network domain or subdomain. For example, if we wanted to allow access from any system in the subdomain x.y.z, we could specify 'x.y.z.%' for the hostname.

As an important note, when creating a user account, specifying a wildcard for the hostname such as 'username'@'%' has the same effect as specifying 'username' alone. In both cases, there is no restriction on the host or system in which the login attempt occurs.

Now that all user accounts for the business scenario have been created, the listing of those usernames and their hosts should appear like that in Figure 4.17 for MySQL and MariaDB, and in Figure 4.18 for Oracle.

```
mysql> SELECT user,host
    -> FROM  mysql.user
    -> ORDER BY user;
+-------------------+----------------+
| user              | host           |
+-------------------+----------------+
| chu               | localhost      |
| donnelly          | 192.168.2.8    |
| donnelly          | localhost      |
| gardner           | 192.168.2.10_  |
| garrett           | %              |
| mysql.infoschema  | localhost      |
| mysql.session     | localhost      |
| mysql.sys         | localhost      |
| roberts           | %              |
| root              | localhost      |
| sanford           | 192.168.2.%    |
| sanford           | localhost      |
+-------------------+----------------+
12 rows in set (0.02 sec)

mysql> []
```

FIGURE 4.17 Showing the complete list of database users and their hosts in MYSQL.

```
SQL> SELECT USERNAME FROM all_users ORDER BY USERNAME;

USERNAME
----------------
chu
donnelly
gardner
garrett
roberts
sanford

SQL> []
```

FIGURE 4.18 Showing the complete list of database users and their hosts in Oracle.

4.4 SUMMARY

The user accounts that we created allows one to log into the overall DBMS, which itself can contain one or more databases, and each database can have one or more tables. The next chapter describes how we can manage a user's access to these databases and their table contents once the user logs into the DBMS.

CHAPTER 5

DATABASE PRIVILEGES

We touched on the topic of privileges in Chapter 4, where we created a database user in Oracle and had to assign the the *CREATE SESSION* privilege so that user had the ability to login into the DBMS. In this chapter we explore other privileges that can manage what data a user can access as well as what type(s) of access a user can issue on data.

A comprehensive use of security in an organizational environment must consider the various contexts of data, who or what will access the data, and how they are allowed to access the data. The concept of *privileges* is a way to define and manage what data may be accessed by a user, as well as what types of accesses that user is allowed to issue on that data. Such practices can implement higher security compared to approaches that give all users the same level of access to data.

For example, if we were to say that certain data is readable in general, say to all employees, then we are permitting any employee to read the data. Now consider if that data should be readable to only certain employees (such as an employee's personal information, which may only be readable to that employee and a human resource representative). Then we want a certain type of access to that data for some employees (such as "read-write" access) and other types of access for other employees (such as "no access"). The use of privileges allows us to employ detailed specifications that involve *which* agents may access a given piece of data, as well as *how* a given agent may access the data. The latter allows us to define the type of access an agent is allowed to issue, such as whether the agent can only retrieve or see the given data, whether the agent can view and modify that data, or whether that agent has no access to the data whatsoever.

Let's demonstrate this idea with the following business scenario that has data for employees as well as company budgets. Figure 5.1 shows the normalized tables structures and data. We have these tables provided in a database named BusinessTLS, where TLS is an abbreviation for *table-level security*, representing the level or means by which we are going to manage data access for this scenario at first.

Employee (EmpID,FName,LName,Title,Office,Address,SSN,DOB,Salary)

Budget (BudgetID,Year,Quarter,Sales,Expenses)

Employee

EmpID	FName	LName	Title	Office	
E01	Tom	Roberts	CEO	A110	
E02	Alison	Garrett	CFO	A118	
E03	Betty	Chu	HR Director	A203	...
E04	Cindy	Donnelly	Sales Director	B116	
E05	Alex	Gardner	Sales Assoc	B118	
E06	Miguel	Sanford	CIO	A202	

Employee (cont)

	Address	SSN	DOB	Salary
	212 Orchid Ave	000-404-1234	03/01/1957	175000
	1234 Brown St	000-145-0909	05/25/1966	140000
...	67 Tulip Lane	000-223-7888	10/13/1973	80000
	101 Harrison Ave	000-132-5673	02/17/1970	60000
	73 East Liberty	000-454-9654	10/16/1982	48000
	43 Falcon Dr	000-065-7788	02/15/1967	16000

Budget

BudgetID	Year	Quarter	Sales	Expenses
B01	2021	1	1600000	1450000
B02	2021	2	1700000	1460000
B03	2021	3	1550000	1380000
B04	2021	4	1760000	1430000
B05	2022	1	1710000	1395000
B06	2022	2	1775000	1435000
B07	2022	3	1920000	1520000
B08	2022	4	1830000	1480000

FIGURE 5.1 Table definitions and table data for our business scenario.

Now that we have a database with data and user accounts created in Chapter 4, we can manage how these users can access this data. Because data is organized in a relational DBMS with databases, tables, and columns and rows, we can manage access at those levels with various strategies. At the highest level, the database-level, we can manage as a single unit how a user may access all of the data within that database. At the next lower level, the table-level, we can manage in a single unit how a user may access all of the data within a given table of a database. The table-level represents the largest granularity or unit by which we can manage a user's type(s) of access. The smallest levels of granularity are the column-level and row-level, where we can manage user access to specific columns or rows, respectively. We will start with an overview of privileges with database-level granularity.

5.1 OVERVIEW OF PRIVILEGES AND DATABASE-LEVEL PRIVILEGES

Even though a database user has an account and can log into the DBMS, that does not mean that user suddenly has access to the databases – and their data - contained within that DBMS. Unless otherwise specified when a database user account is created, a user's access to database tables is by default *disallowed* (or default secure) in most DBMSs. The concept of *default secure* is where an asset (such as that table) has strong security and very limited or no access by default or when created, and then we assign the required access to the asset.

Figure 5.2 illustrates the failed attempt that user roberts would experience at this time if, after logging into the DBMS, roberts attempts to choose the BusinessTLS database itself with the SQL *USE* statement or attempts to directly access a component of the database such as the BusinessTLS. Employee table with the SQL *SELECT* statement.

```
mysql> USE BusinessTLS;
ERROR 1044 (42000): Access denied for user 'roberts'@'%' to database 'BusinessTLS'
mysql> SELECT * FROM BusinessTLS.Employee;
ERROR 1142 (42000): SELECT command denied to user 'roberts'@'localhost' for table 'Employee'
mysql> []
```

FIGURE 5.2 A default secure database that is inaccessible after login.

Should roberts alternatively attempt to choose the database as part of the login process, such as with the MySQL **-D** option, a failed attempt will similarly result, as shown in Figure 5.3.

```
$ mysql -u roberts -D BusinessTLS -p
Enter password:
ERROR 1044 (42000): Access denied for user 'roberts'@'%' to data 'BusinessTLS'
$ []
```

FIGURE 5.3 A default secure database that is inaccessible during login.

Access to a database must first be assigned or *granted* before a user can access that database. To allow a database user to access our BusinessTLS database or its data, we can assign one or more privileges with the SQL *GRANT* statement. The *GRANT* statement covers a broad range of privileges that can simply or comprehensively manage a user's access to a database, its tables, its columns, and so on. The privileges that we commonly manage and assign are shown in Table 5.1, with the SQL keyword(s) that represents the privilege given along with a description of the privilege.

SQL Privilege/ Keyword	Description of Privilege
ALL	allows a user to have all of the following privileges
SELECT	allows a user to retrieve data from the given table(s) with the SQL *SELECT* statement
UPDATE	allows a user to modify existing data in the given table(s) with the SQL *UPDATE* statement
INSERT	allows a user to add rows to the given table(s) with the SQL *INSERT* statement
DELETE	allows a user to remove rows from the given table(s) with the SQL *DELETE* statement
CREATE	allows a user to create new tables and databases with the SQL *CREATE* statement
DROP	allows a user to remove entire tables and databases with the SQL *DROP* statement

TABLE 5.1 Common SQL privileges.

To obtain an overall understanding of the SQL *GRANT* statement, let's first examine its general form, and we will expand into more intricate use. Figure 5.4 shows the general syntax of the SQL *GRANT* statement in the MySQL, MariaDB, and Oracle DBMSs with use on databases and tables. As before, the SQL keywords are capitalized and bold, and are specified exactly as is. Italicized content represents where we fill in our specifications, and content within square brackets is optional.

```
GRANT privilege(s)

ON [database(s).]table(s)

TO 'username'[@'hostname'];
```

FIGURE 5.4 General syntax of SQL *GRANT* statement to assign privileges to database users.

Taking a look at the clauses of the *GRANT* statement in Figure 5.4, following the SQL keyword *GRANT*, we specify the privilege(s) we want to manage by their SQL keyword. We can specify one privilege, or multiple privileges, by comma-separating them. In the next clause, after the keyword *ON* we specify the database and table(s) that we want the statement to manage. A database name is optional if we already have chosen the necessary database with the SQL *USE* statement or when logging in with the **-D** option. We can specify a single database by its name or all databases with the * wildcard. Likewise, we can specify a single table by its name or all tables within the database(s) with an * wildcard. To specify multiple databases or tables by name, we can issue separate *GRANT* statements with each database or table. Finally, in the third clause after the SQL keyword TO we specify the database username (with applicable hostname if necessary) that we have previously created.

As with the *CREATE USER* statement, a *GRANT* statement must be issued by the database root account or some other database administrative account. A database administrative account is one that has the privileges to issue those statements. Later we will cover as well as demonstrate that such administrative access as a type of privilege itself!

Focusing first at the database-level, Figure 5.5 shows how we can grant user roberts all access to the database BusinessTLS.[1] The keyword *PRIVILEGES* is optional in most recent versions of MySQL, MariaDB and Oracle but is included here for completeness, to highlight the context of the command, as well as to maintain uniformity with other documentation resources. We also split the clauses onto their own lines to help emphasize the parts of the statement, although we could have certainly issued the statement with a single line.

Tip: the keyword *PRIVILEGES* is optional in most recent versions of MySQL, MariaDB, and Oracle.

---

[1]While the use of a .* wildcard in this manner can be viewed as table-level management that happens to involve all tables, we will consider it database-level management because it affects all tables in a database at once.

```
mysql> GRANT ALL PRIVILEGES
    -> ON BusinessTLS.*
    -> TO 'roberts';
Query OK, 0 rows affected (0.10 sec)

mysql> []
```

FIGURE 5.5 Granting database access.

Now user roberts can successfully access the database and its components. This example demonstrates the simplest form of granting database privileges, where we allow the user all types of access (noted by the keyword *ALL*) to all components within the database (noted by the .*). This means we granted roberts the capability to retrieve, as well as to add, update, or delete components within the database, which includes the data as well as entire tables themselves. Though easy to grant access in this manner, such open database access, especially to casual or end users can pose a huge security vulnerability in an operational environment, and we look at that very shortly.

Now that we have begun to work with privileges, let's take a moment to mention that traditionally after the granting (or as we will later discuss, removing with the SQL *REVOKE* keyword) of a privilege, tvhe SQL *FLUSH PRIVILEGES* statement was subsequently required to ensure the previously issued privilege changes were recognized by the DBMS and took effect. However, in recent versions of MySQL, MariaDB, and Oracle DBMSs, *FLUSH PRIVILEGES* has become optional when following *GRANT* or *REVOKE* statements, as those statements automatically flush their changes so as to be immediately recognized by the DBMS. So, issuing a separate command to flush privileges in that case is no longer required. But many tutorials and documentation sources may still issue a *FLUSH PRIVILEGES* just to be sure the changes take effect. There is no adverse effect of flushing privileges if they have already been flushed automatically or by the user, so if you wish to issue a flushing of privileges after granting or revoking a privilege, you can safely do so. Figure 5.6 shows how we could have issued the previous grant example (this time alternatively expressed in a single line) with a subsequent flushing of privileges. From here onward, we will not issue a flushing of privileges in conjunction with the *GRANT* or *REVOKE* statements for brevity; however, you may issue that yourself if you wish.

```
mysql> GRANT ALL PRIVILEGES ON BusinessTLS.* TO 'roberts';
Query OK, 0 rows affected (0.08 sec)

mysql> FLUSH PRIVILEGES;
Query OK, 0 rows affected (0.04 sec)

mysql> []
```

FIGURE 5.6 Granting database access and flushing privileges.

Even though flushing of privileges is typically optional with *GRANT* or *REVOKE* statements, flushing or privileges is usually required with changes made *directly* to the internal DBMS tables that store privilege and other user data with other SQL statements, such as *UPDATE, INSERT, DELETE,* or *ALTER.* Such direct internal table changes are typically not automatically flushed, and must be followed with a *FLUSH PRIVILEGES* statement in order for the DBMS to recognize those changes.

In addition to simply allowing or disallowing database access to a user, we can achieve greater database security when access is allowed by limiting the type(s) of database access allowed. As an example, if we would like to allow user garrett to have read-only (or retrieve-only) access to the BusinessTLS database, we can issue the *GRANT* statement like that in Figure 5.7. Here, as well as onward, we will issue *GRANT* statements in a single line for brevity, but you may alternatively use multiple lines, as we previously issued for roberts, if you wish. This particular *GRANT* statement replaces the keyword *ALL* with *SELECT* to limit the privilege(s) given to garrett. That user will only be able to issue *SELECT* statements on tables in the database, effectively permitting only data retrieval or read-only access.

```
mysql> GRANT SELECT ON BusinessTLS.* TO 'garrett';
Query OK, 0 rows affected (0.06 sec)

mysql> []
```

FIGURE 5.7 Granting database read-only access.

While garrett can now successfully retrieve data by issuing a *SELECT* on the BusinessTLS database, other operations to add, make any changes to, or delete data or tables will not be allowed. As an example, if garrett attempts to delete some data in that database, that particular access will be denied.

Figure 5.8 illustrates user garrett issuing a successful data retrieval followed by an unsuccessful attempt to delete data.

```
mysql> SELECT * FROM BusinessTLS.Employee;
+-------+--------+----------+----------------+--------+-----------------+--------------+------------+--------+
| EmpID | FName  | LName    | Title          | Office | Address         | SSN          | DOB        | Salary |
+-------+--------+----------+----------------+--------+-----------------+--------------+------------+--------+
| E01   | Tom    | Roberts  | CEO            | A118   | 212 Orchid Ave  | 000-404-1234 | 1957-03-01 | 175000 |
| E02   | Alison | Garrett  | CFO            | A118   | 1234 Brown St   | 000-145-0909 | 1966-05-25 | 140000 |
| E03   | Betty  | Chu      | HR Director    | A203   | 67 Tulip Lane   | 000-223-7888 | 1973-10-13 |  80000 |
| E04   | Cindy  | Donnelly | Sales Director | B116   | 101 Harrison Ave| 000-143-5673 | 1970-02-17 |  60000 |
| E05   | Alex   | Gardner  | Sales Assoc    | B118   | 73 East Liberty | 000-454-9654 | 1982-10-16 |  48000 |
| E06   | Miguel | Sanford  | CIO            | A202   | 43 Falcon Drive | 000-065-7788 | 1967-02-15 | 160000 |
+-------+--------+----------+----------------+--------+-----------------+--------------+------------+--------+
6 rows in set (0.01 sec)

mysql> DELETE FROM BusinessTLS.Employee WHERE EmpID='E01';
ERROR 1142 (42000): DELETE command denied to user 'garrett'@'localhost' for table 'Employee'
mysql> []
```

FIGURE 5.8 Successful read-only access to data.

5.2 CAPABILITY TO MANAGE PRIVILEGES

As previously mentioned, the database root account by default has the capability to assign (and as we will soon see, to remove) user privileges. We can also assign those abilities to another user account, say to an administrative account that is to have those responsibilities. To assign this capability to another account, the root account (or other previously assigned administrative account) must issue two *GRANT* statements. Figure 5.9 shows the root account assigning the capability to manage privileges to the user sanford, who will later be the organization's Chief Information Officer and the one most suited for such responsibilities in this organization.

```
mysql> GRANT ALL PRIVILEGES ON *.* TO 'sanford'@'localhost';
Query OK, 0 rows affected (0.09 sec)

mysql> GRANT ALL PRIVILEGES ON BusinessTLS.* TO 'sanford'@'localhost' WITH GRANT OPTION;
Query OK, 0 rows affected (0.05 sec)

mysql> []
```

FIGURE 5.9 Assigning the capability to manage privileges.

The first *GRANT* statement gives sanford all access to databases in the DBMS; this is necessary to allow sanford the necessary access to issue administrator operations.[2] The second *GRANT* statement contains the *WITH GRANT OPTION* clause that gives the capability to manage user privileges.

---

[2]Note that, for greater security, if we typically do not want the administrative user to have access to certain nonsystem databases, we can selectively remove those databases from the administrative user privileges using techniques described in the "Removing Privileges" section.

sanford may have to log out of the current DBMS session and log back in for that recently applied effect to be recognized. Similar to the root account, sanford can now manage privileges for other users, and we will demonstrate that shortly.

Tip: The *WITH GRANT OPTION* privilege allows a user to manage the privileges of other users.

In addition to allowing a user to manage privileges, this example also shows how we can implement security measures that define or limit the types of access for a particular user based on from what system the user is logging into the DBMS. Because we assigned the administrative capability to manage privileges to only the 'sanford'@'localhost' account and not to the other sanford account, we are requiring sanford to log in from the DBMS system itself. This security measure disallows sanford the capability to manage privileges when logged into the DBMS from another system, and organizations often limit what administrative access may occur remotely or over a network. By creating multiple database accounts for a user, with each account associated with a different host or group of hosts, and assigning certain privileges to those accounts, we can define a user's access based on from what system the user logs into the DBMS.

You may have also noticed that 'sanford'@'192.168.2.%' still has no database privileges, other than to log into the DBMS. Depending on what access we want to allow that user when logged in over that network, we can define nonadministrative access, such as we did for roberts or garrett, or administrative as we did for 'sanford'@'localhost'. For our demonstration, let's give 'sanford'@'192.168.2.%' all access to BusinessTLS but nonadministrative, as shown in Figure 5.10.

```
mysql> GRANT ALL ON BusinessTLS.* TO 'sanford'@'192.168.2.%';
Query OK, 0 rows affected (0.11 sec)

mysql> []
```

FIGURE 5.10 Granting nonadministrative database access.

5.3   LISTING PRIVILEGES

Let's now explain the ways in which we can see the privileges of a database user. To list their own set of assigned privileges, a database user can issue the SQL *SHOW GRANTS* statement, whose general syntax is given in Figure 5.11.

```
SHOW GRANTS [ FOR 'user'[@'hostname'] ];
```

FIGURE 5.11 General SQL syntax to show a user's privileges.

The simplest form of the *SHOW GRANTS* statement is when issued by a user to show their own privileges, and involves just those two keywords. Figure 5.12 shows user garrett listing their privileges.

```
mysql> SHOW GRANTS;
+----------------------------------------------------------+
| Grants for garrett@%                                     |
+----------------------------------------------------------+
| GRANT USAGE ON *.* TO `garrett`@`%`                      |
| GRANT SELECT ON `BusinessTLS`.* TO `garrett`@`%`         |
+----------------------------------------------------------+
2 rows in set (0.00 sec)

mysql> []
```

FIGURE 5.12 A database user listing their own privileges.

Examining this listing, we notice two sets of privileges. The first privilege is assigned when the database user account is created; this privilege only allows access into the DBMS and not to any of its databases. The second privilege represents the read-only access to the BusinessTLS database that we assigned. Both privileges indicate the username, and note that because we did not specify a hostname when we created the database account for garrett, a wildcard is represented for any hostname of that user. You will notice a similar listing of privileges for roberts except that the second indicates that all privileges have been given to the database.

While a nonadministrative database user can only see their own privileges by default, the DBMS root account or other administrative account can see privileges for themselves as well as for other users. Figure 5.13 shows the database root account listing their own privileges. You will notice quite a number of privileges listed for the root user, including the more common *SELECT, INSERT, UPDATE, DELETE, CREATE, DROP*, along with and many others. Because of the longer lines resulting from the longer list of privileges, the output of a privilege listing may be a little difficult to read without increasing the width of the terminal window. Figure 5.13 has the right side border edited out and some lines shortened to help make it more readable.

```
mysql> SHOW GRANTS;
+--------------------------------------------------------------------------------------+
| Grants for root@localhost                                                            |
+--------------------------------------------------------------------------------------+
| GRANT SELECT, INSERT, UPDATE, DELETE, CREATE, DROP, RELOAD, SHUTDOWN, PROCESS, FILE, REFERENCES, INDEX, ALTER, SHOW D
ATABASES, SUPER, CREATE TEMPORARY TABLES, LOCK TABLES, EXECUTE, REPLICATION SLAVE, REPLICATION CLIENT, CREATE VIEW, SHO
W VIEW, CREATE ROUTINE, ALTER ROUTINE, CREATE USER, EVENT, TRIGGER, CREATE TABLESPACE, CREATE ROLE, DROP ROLE ON *.* TO
 `root`@`localhost` WITH GRANT OPTION
| GRANT APPLICATION_PASSWORD_ADMIN,AUDIT_ADMIN,BACKUP_ADMIN,BINLOG_ADMIN,BINLOG_ENCRYPTION_ADMIN,CLONE_ADMIN,CONNECTION
_ADMIN,ENCRYPTION_KEY_ADMIN,FLUSH_OPTIMIZER_COSTS,FLUSH_STATUS,FLUSH_TABLES,FLUSH_USER_RESOURCES,GROUP_REPLICATION_ADMI
N,INNODB_REDO_LOG_ARCHIVE,INNODB_REDO_LOG_ENABLE,PERSIST_RO_VARIABLES_ADMIN,REPLICATION_APPLIER,REPLICATION_SLAVE_ADMIN
,RESOURCE_GROUP_ADMIN,RESOURCE_GROUP_USER,ROLE_ADMIN,SERVICE_CONNECTION_ADMIN,SESSION_VARIABLES_ADMIN,SET_USER_ID,SHOW_
ROUTINE,SYSTEM_USER,SYSTEM_VARIABLES_ADMIN,TABLE_ENCRYPTION_ADMIN,XA_RECOVER_ADMIN ON *.* TO `root`@`localhost` WITH GR
ANT OPTION
| GRANT PROXY ON ''@'' TO 'root'@'localhost' WITH GRANT OPTION
+--------------------------------------------------------------------------------------+
3 rows in set (0.00 sec)

mysql> []
```

FIGURE 5.13 Showing the privileges of the database root account, edited for brevity.

To see the privileges of another database user, the root or an administrative account can issue the *SHOW GRANTS* statement and specify the desired user, in this case roberts, as shown in Figure 5.14. Note that this time, both the root account and administrative account 'sanford'@'localhost' are capable of listing another user's privileges.

```
mysql> SHOW GRANTS FOR 'roberts';
+----------------------------------------------------------+
| Grants for roberts@%                                     |
+----------------------------------------------------------+
| GRANT USAGE ON *.* TO `roberts`@`%`                      |
| GRANT ALL PRIVILEGES ON `BusinessTLS`.* TO `roberts`@`%` |
+----------------------------------------------------------+
2 rows in set (0.00 sec)

mysql> []
```

FIGURE 5.14 Showing privileges of another database user.

Note that in order to list the privileges of a database user account associated with a hostname, we must include the full username@hostname specification. For example, if we were to use the root or an administrative account to list the privileges for 'chu' rather than 'chu'@'localhost', the response would be that there is no user by that username with no host restriction, as illustrated in Figure 5.15. In a similar manner, you will notice different privileges for 'sanford'@'localhost' and 'sanford'@'192.168.2.%'.

```
mysql> SHOW GRANTS FOR 'chu';
ERROR 1141 (42000): There is no such grant defined for user 'chu' on host '%'
mysql> SHOW GRANTS FOR 'chu'@'localhost';
+-----------------------------------------+
| Grants for chu@localhost                |
+-----------------------------------------+
| GRANT USAGE ON *.* TO `chu`@`localhost` |
+-----------------------------------------+
1 row in set (0.00 sec)

mysql> []
```

FIGURE 5.15 Showing privileges for a database user's two accounts.

If we want to see a list of the privileges to *all* users, there is not a built-in or native way to do so with MySQL, MariaDB, or Oracle DBMSs. However, there are various approaches that may accomplish this goal. Figure 5.16 shows one approach for MySQL that executes in a Linux command line prompt (this will prompt you for the database root password twice). Only part of the result is shown for brevity.

```
$ mysql -u root -p -sNe" `mysql -u root -p -se"SELECT CONCAT('SHOW GRANTS FOR \'',user,'\'@\'',host,'\';') FROM mys
ql.user; "`"
Enter password:
Enter password:
GRANT USAGE ON *.* TO `garrett`@`%`
GRANT SELECT ON `BusinessTLS`.* TO `garrett`@`%`
GRANT USAGE ON *.* TO `roberts`@`%`
GRANT ALL PRIVILEGES ON `BusinessTLS`.* TO `roberts`@`%`
```

FIGURE 5.16 Showing the privileges of all users.

5.4 REMOVING PRIVILEGES

In addition to adding privileges with *GRANT*, we can also remove privileges with the SQL *REVOKE* statement. Either the database root account or an administrative account can remove a user's privileges. Figure 5.17 shows the general syntax for *REVOKE* in MySQL, MariaDB, and Oracle.

```
REVOKE privilege(s)

ON [database.]table

FROM 'username'[@'hostname'];
```

FIGURE 5.17 General syntax of SQL REVOKE statement to remove privileges.

Similar to *GRANT*, the privilege(s) that we can revoke are among those listed in Table 5.1. To demonstrate the removal of privileges, let's consider the *principle of least privilege*, which defines that a user should be given only the access or privileges needed to carry out their task or role, and nothing more. Suppose we determine that the previous decision to give roberts all privileges to BusinessTLS raises a security vulnerability and is insecure, and that read-only access is appropriate. We can lower that user's privileges by first removing all of the privileges and then adding only the privilege to read or retrieve data. As shown in Figure 5.18, we first issue the *REVOKE* statement that takes away all of the privileges that roberts has, and then with *GRANT* add only the privilege to *SELECT* on the database. If we list the privileges of roberts now, we will see that only *SELECT* privilege remains.

```
mysql> REVOKE ALL PRIVILEGES ON BusinessTLS.* FROM 'roberts';
Query OK, 0 rows affected (0.08 sec)

mysql> GRANT SELECT ON BusinessTLS.* TO 'roberts';
Query OK, 0 rows affected (0.05 sec)

mysql> []
```

FIGURE 5.18 Reducing a user's privileges.

We can also revoke specific privileges rather than all privileges, and in certain situations we may be able to remove certain privileges without the need to add back others and achieve our security objective. For example, if a user currently has only *SELECT* and *UPDATE* privileges, and we determine that only *SELECT* is necessary, we only need to revoke the *UPDATE* privilege and not have to subsequently grant any privileges back.

However, we must also be careful when removing privileges from a user that currently has all privileges assigned. Assigning privileges with the SQL keyword *ALL* can refer to a large set of privileges (and that set can vary among DBMSs). So unless we can be sure that we revoke a complete set of extra privileges, we risk leaving more privileges than is necessary and compromising the principle of least privilege.

As an example of this situation, suppose we gave 'chu'@'localhost' all privileges, then decide that we only want that user to have *SELECT* privilege. However, we attempt to implement this downgrade of privileges with only a revoke statement for the SQL operations that we think of offhand. Figure 5.19 illustrates this chain of events.

```
mysql> GRANT ALL ON BusinessTLS.* TO 'chu'@'localhost';
Query OK, 0 rows affected (0.08 sec)

mysql> REVOKE INSERT,DELETE,UPDATE ON BusinessTLS.* FROM 'chu'@'localhost';
Query OK, 0 rows affected (0.09 sec)

mysql> []
```

FIGURE 5.19 Adding all, then removing only some user privileges.

Without considering all possible privileges that were initially granted, after revoking we can see in Figure 5.20 the user has not only the *SELECT* privilege we intended, but many other privileges that we overlooked.

```
mysql> SHOW GRANTS FOR 'chu'@'localhost';
+---------------------------------------------------------------------------------------------+
| Grants for chu@localhost                                                                    |
+---------------------------------------------------------------------------------------------+
| GRANT USAGE ON *.* TO `chu`@`localhost`                                                     |
| GRANT SELECT, CREATE, DROP, REFERENCES, INDEX, ALTER, CREATE TEMPORARY TABLES, LOCK TABLES, EXECUTE, CREATE VIEW, SHO
W VIEW, CREATE ROUTINE, ALTER ROUTINE, EVENT, TRIGGER ON `BusinessTLS`.* TO `chu`@`localhost` |
+---------------------------------------------------------------------------------------------+
2 rows in set (0.00 sec)

mysql> []
```

FIGURE 5.20 Listing user privileges that were overlooked.

Note that if a user currently has a set of database privileges, and we attempt to revoke one or more privileges that are not in that set of privileges, there is no error. Likewise, if a user has a set of privileges that is fewer than all privileges, we can still revoke the remaining privileges with the *ALL* keyword.

To "clean up" from the last example of leaving overlooked privileges if it was carried out (and that would be necessary to set up our next examples), we can revoke the privileges that remain for 'chu'@'localhost' as shown in Figure 5.21 and list the user's privileges to confirm no privileges remain for that user.

```
mysql> REVOKE ALL ON BusinessTLS.* FROM 'chu'@'localhost';
Query OK, 0 rows affected (0.07 sec)

mysql> SHOW GRANTS FOR 'chu'@'localhost';
+----------------------------------------+
| Grants for chu@localhost               |
+----------------------------------------+
| GRANT USAGE ON *.* TO `chu`@`localhost` |
+----------------------------------------+
1 row in set (0.00 sec)

mysql> []
```

FIGURE 5.21 Removing any remaining privileges.

As a side note, to revoke a certain privilege we must specify the database(s) in the same manner as they were specified when the privilege was granted. In particular, if a user was assigned privileges to one or more databases specified by the database name(s) and not a *.* wildcard, we must revoke the privileges in a similar manner. In other words, we cannot revoke privileges from those databases with a *.* database wildcard. We must list the databases by name just as they were assigned and as they also appear in a privilege listing. As an example, given that 'sanford'@'192.168.2.%' was previously granted privileges to the database BusinessTLS, to revoke any of those privileges we have to specify BusinessTLS by name rather by *.*.

In general, if we want to restrict the database privileges of a user who currently has all privileges, it is safer from a security standpoint to revoke all privileges and then grant the desired privilege(s). However, if a user has a limited set of privileges, then we may be able to safely revoke certain privileges and leave only those that maintain the principle of least privilege.

5.5   WORKING WITH TLS AND TABLE-LEVEL PRIVILEGES

In our business scenario, let's suppose that the principle of least privilege has led to increased security restrictions, such that the tables in the BusinessTLS database will be accessed by each user according to the type of access listed in Table 5.2. Note that we have listed each user's type of allowed access in high-level terms, which can be helpful when planning and identifying the types of accesses with nontechnical personnel.

User Account	Employee	Budget
roberts	read	read,write
garret	read	read,write,add, remove
chu@localhost	read-write,add,remove	read
gardner@192.168.2.10_	read	read
donnelly@localhost	read	read
donnelly@192.168.2.8	read	read
sanford@localhost	read,grant	read,grant
sandord@192.168.2.%	read	read

TABLE 5.2 Defining user data access requirements for tables in the BusinessTLS database.

In general, we want to allow all employees the capability to read the Employee table data, but only allow human resources personnel to read and write that data. To implement this security objective, we will employ two sets of privileges for the Employee table: one that allows all employees (except for human personnel) to read the Employee table and one that allows human resources personnel to read and write that table. Managing this type of access will involve the SQL *GRANT* statement similar to how we managed database-level access, but in this case with individual tables.

Table 5.2 illustrates a situation where a particular user (donnelly) will have the capability to log in from multiple systems, but will have the same type of access regardless of which system they log in from. That user is able to log into the DBMS directly (from) localhost or from the system with the IP address 192.168.2.8, and in both cases will have read-only access to both tables.

But a situation may alternatively call for a user to have one set of privileges when logging in from a certain system and another of privileges when logging in from another system or network. Table 5.2 also illustrates that situation with user sanford, who will have read and grant privileges when logging into the DBMS directly, and has only read privilege when logging in from any system in the 192.168.2 network.

Before we begin assigning privileges to meet our security objective with table access, let's consider that we previously assigned database-level privileges for at least some users, and we now want to manage access by table-level. As we saw with database-level privileges, we may find it more effective from a security point-of-view to remove all privileges first and start new with assigning privileges, especially if we are unsure about the extent to which privileges have been previously given. Following this idea, we will revoke any existing privileges to BusinessTLS for all users first. Recall that because we had previously granted 'roberts', 'garrett', 'sanford'@'localhost' and 'sanford'@'192.168.2.%' access to BusinessTLS.*, we must revoke their privileges from that specific database rather than with the *.* database wildcard. Figure 5.22 shows the commands by which we can revoke their privileges. If you have privileges remaining for the other users, similarly revoke theirs as well.

```
mysql> REVOKE ALL ON BusinessTLS.* FROM 'roberts';
Query OK, 0 rows affected (0.08 sec)

mysql> REVOKE ALL ON BusinessTLS.* FROM 'garrett';
Query OK, 0 rows affected (0.10 sec)

mysql> REVOKE ALL ON BusinessTLS.* FROM 'sanford'@'localhost';
Query OK, 0 rows affected (0.07 sec)

mysql> REVOKE ALL ON BusinessTLS.* FROM 'sanford'@'192.168.2.%';
Query OK, 0 rows affected (0.09 sec)

mysql> []
```

FIGURE 5.22 Removing all privileges to start with a new assignment.

Recall that we had also granted 'sanford'@'localhost' the capability to manage user privileges, so we will also have to remove that privilege with the *REVOKE* statement shown in Figure 5.23. Note that if we happen to revoke the *GRANT OPTION* privilege while other privileges coexist for that same database or table, those other privileges will remain.

```
mysql> REVOKE GRANT OPTION ON BusinessTLS.* FROM 'sanford'@'localhost';
Query OK, 0 rows affected (0.08 sec)

mysql> []
```

FIGURE 5.23 Removing the capability to manage user privileges.

We want every user to have a list of privileges like that shown for roberts in Figure 5.24.

```
mysql> SHOW GRANTS FOR 'roberts';
+------------------------------------+
| Grants for roberts@%               |
+------------------------------------+
| GRANT USAGE ON *.* TO `roberts`@`%` |
+------------------------------------+
1 row in set (0.00 sec)

mysql> []
```

FIGURE 5.24 User with no assigned privileges.

Now that we have a "clean slate" of user privileges, we can begin implementing our security objective for table access. Looking at the types of accesses specified in Table 5.2, we will have to define the type of accesses in terms of SQL privileges, using some mapping of high-level access to SQL privilege level specification such as that in Table 5.3. Note that we have distinguished read-write access to involve only an *UPDATE* privilege and not itself include the *INSERT* or *DELETE* privileges. Such a distinction allows us to permit one to modify existing data, but not to add or remove data. Such a restriction may be required by a compliance standard, where an employee may be able to modify data but cannot fabricate new data or destroy its existence. However, if a situation calls for a user to have the capability to read, write, add, and remove data, we can combine high-level accesses and their corresponding SQL privileges.

High-level access	SQL Privilege(s)
read or read-only	*SELECT*
read,write or read-write	*SELECT* and *UPDATE*
add	*INSERT*
remove	*DELETE*
grant	*GRANT OPTION*

TABLE 5.3 Mapping of high-level access to SQL table privilege.

Starting with the Employee table, we can specify that username 'roberts' has read-only access to the Employee table, as shown in Figure 5.25. The same read-only privilege should also be granted to 'garrett', 'gardner'@'192.168.2.10_', 'donnelly'@'localhost', 'donnelly'@'192.168.2.8', and 'sanford'@'192.168.2.%'.

```
mysql> GRANT SELECT ON BusinessTLS.Employee TO 'roberts';
Query OK, 0 rows affected (0.06 sec)

mysql> []
```

FIGURE 5.25 Assigning read-only access to the Employee table.

You may have noticed that we did not list 'sanford'@'localhost' in that last set of users. That is because we have to also assign that user the capability to manage user privileges. As a result, we will have to assign both read-only and grant privileges as shown in Figure 5.26.

```
mysql> GRANT SELECT ON BusinessTLS.Employee to 'sanford'@'localhost' WITH GRANT OPTION;
Query OK, 0 rows affected (0.09 sec)

mysql> []
```

FIGURE 5.26 Assigning read-only access and user privilege management to the Employee table.

As a side note, if we had included 'sanford'@'localhost' in that read-only privilege assignment with the other users in Figure 5.25, we can add just the *GRANT OPTION* privilege to that user, as shown in Figure 5.27. That privilege will add the capability to manage user privileges.

```
mysql> GRANT GRANT OPTION ON BusinessTLS.Employee to 'sanford'@'localhost';
Query OK, 0 rows affected (0.06 sec)

mysql> ▯
```

FIGURE 5.27 Assigning user privilege management to the Employee table.

Because of their job requirements, we now must allow only human resources personnel (that is, Betty Chu) the capability to read as well as write Employee table data. In terms of database table access, this will include the capability to read and write, as well as add and delete data. We can assign those privileges to the human resource personnel with the grant statements shown in Figure 5.28.

```
mysql> GRANT SELECT,UPDATE,INSERT,DELETE ON BusinessTLS.Employee TO 'chu'@'localhost';
Query OK, 0 rows affected (0.07 sec)

mysql> ▯
```

FIGURE 5.28 Assigning read-write, add, and remove access to the Employee table.

To review the privileges that were assigned to the Employee table, let's show the privileges for roberts and demonstrate both the capability to retrieve data as well as incapability to change data in the Employee table. Figure 5.29 shows user roberts listing their privileges, attempting to retrieve data and attempting to change data, such as their address. Because only the *SELECT* privilege appears for BusinessTLS.Employee, the retrieve operation is successful, but attempts to change, add, or remove data are denied.

```
mysql> SHOW GRANTS;
+---------------------------------------------------------+
| Grants for roberts@%                                    |
+---------------------------------------------------------+
| GRANT USAGE ON *.* TO `roberts`@`%`                     |
| GRANT SELECT ON `BusinessTLS`.`Employee` TO `roberts`@`%` |
+---------------------------------------------------------+
2 rows in set (0.00 sec)

mysql> SELECT * FROM BusinessTLS.Employee WHERE EmpID='E01';
+-------+-------+---------+-------+--------+----------------+--------------+------------+--------+
| EmpID | FName | LName   | Title | Office | Address        | SSN          | DOB        | Salary |
+-------+-------+---------+-------+--------+----------------+--------------+------------+--------+
| E01   | Tom   | Roberts | CEO   | A110   | 212 Orchid Ave | 000-404-1234 | 1957-03-01 | 175000 |
+-------+-------+---------+-------+--------+----------------+--------------+------------+--------+
1 row in set (0.02 sec)

mysql> UPDATE BusinessTLS.Employee SET Address='54 Oak St' WHERE EmpID='E01';
ERROR 1142 (42000): UPDATE command denied to user 'roberts'@'localhost' for table 'Employee'
mysql> ▯
```

FIGURE 5.29 Demonstrating read-only access to the Employee table.

All of the other users (except for chu) should have similar listed privileges to that of roberts, specifically the capability to retrieve data, but incapability to access the Employee table in any other way. For the human resource personnel, let's show the privileges for chu and demonstrate both the capability to retrieve and change data (such as for the address of roberts) in the Employee table. Both operations are allowed because of the presence of *SELECT* and *UPDATE* privileges for BusinessTLS.Employee, as shown in Figure 5.30. Also note that operations by chu to add or remove data are also allowed, as indicated by the presence of *INSERT* and *DELETE* privileges.

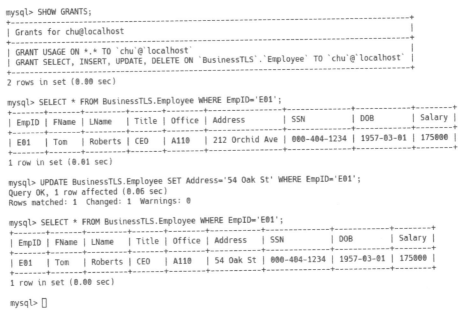

FIGURE 5.30 Demonstrating read-write access to the Employee table.

Even though the operations may appear as expected for a given user, for a more thorough security assessment, we may need to test further. As examples, we may have to repeat such tests for each database user account, even if a user has the same privileges as another user that we previously tested successfully. We may also have to consider issuing operations that should not be allowed and confirming those accesses are denied, such as attempting to *DROP* (delete) the entire Employee table or create another table.

Moving onto the Budget table, suppose we similarly want any employee to read Budget data, but only allow the CEO and CFO to read and write that data. Additionally, we want to allow only the CFO to also add or remove Budget table data. Similar to the Employee table, we can assign read-only privilege to all employees except for the CEO and CFO, of whom we would assign read-write privileges. Starting with the employees from first to last, we have read-write access given to 'roberts' as shown in Figure 5.31.

```
mysql> GRANT SELECT ON BusinessTLS.Employee TO 'roberts';
Query OK, 0 rows affected (0.06 sec)

mysql> GRANT SELECT,UPDATE ON BusinessTLS.Budget TO 'roberts';
Query OK, 0 rows affected (0.08 sec)

mysql> []
```

FIGURE 5.31 Assigning read-write access to the Budget table.

We additionally issue to garrett the capability to create and delete Budget table data, as shown in Figure 5.32.

```
mysql> GRANT SELECT,UPDATE,INSERT,DELETE ON BusinessTLS.Budget TO 'garrett';
Query OK, 0 rows affected (0.07 sec)

mysql> []
```

FIGURE 5.32 Assigning read-write access to the Budget table.

For all other employee accounts, we will assign read-only access, as we do for chu in Figure 5.33. Repeat that *GRANT* statement for the remaining database user accounts, namely 'garrett', 'gardner'@'192.168.2.10_', 'donnelly'@'localhost', 'donnelly'@'192.168.2.8', and 'sanford'@'192.168.2.%'.

```
mysql> GRANT SELECT ON BusinessTLS.Budget TO 'chu'@'localhost';
Query OK, 0 rows affected (0.06 sec)

mysql> []
```

FIGURE 5.33 Assigning read-only access to the Budget table.

As with the Employee table, we will also include the user privilege management *GRANT OPTION* privilege for 'sanford'@'localhost', as shown in Figure 5.34. Also, as with the Employee table, if we had already given 'sanford'@'localhost' read-only access to Budget, we could assign just the *GRANT OPTION* privilege.

```
mysql> GRANT SELECT ON BusinessTLS.Budget TO 'sanford'@'localhost' WITH GRANT OPTION;
Query OK, 0 rows affected (0.05 sec)

mysql> []
```

FIGURE 5.34 Assigning read-only access and user privilege management to the Budget table.

At this point there may be some questions or observations. You might have noticed that we have given 'sanford'@'localhost' only *SELECT* privilege combined with the *GRANT OPTION*. At first thought we might consider that if a user has the capability to manage privileges of a database or table, that same user should also have *all* privileges to that database or table. However, we should also consider the principle of least privilege, and that even though a user requires the capability to manage privileges of a database or table, that user may likely *not* require the capability to issue all types of data access, such as make changes to the data of that database or table, or in some cases, even retrieve the data. Consequently, because sanford is the CIO and is on the technology side, we did want 'sanford'@'localhost' to have the capability to manage user access to the Employee and Budget tables but not have the capability to change, add, or remove their data.

Also, you may have noticed that when a database user has the same access to both Employee and Budget, we granted those privileges one table at a time rather than together. For example, given a user with read-only access to both tables, we granted that user *SELECT* privilege to each table in separate statements, one table at a time. Alternatively, we could have granted that user *SELECT* privilege to both tables in one statement by specifying a BusinessTLS.* database-level privilege. While such a shortcut of reducing the number of SQL statements may seem tempting, we do have to consider the security vulnerability introduced with doing so. In particular, when we assign a database-level privilege, we assign that privilege to *all* tables in the database, both *current* tables as well as any tables added in the *future*. And while a database-level privilege may fulfill the principle of least privilege at present (as is the case with Employee and Budget), if a table is later added to the database, that new table will automatically inherit the database-level privilege. And we may not want the user to have that privilege with the new table. Consequently, if a table is later added and the privileges to that table are not the same as those of the other tables, we would have to take the steps to identify and revoke all extra privileges in order to uphold the principle of least privilege. Otherwise we introduce a security vulnerability by allowing a user to have more privileges to the new table than the user should have. Consequently, it is safer practice to avoid table wildcards at the onset and specify all tables by name. That way, if a table is added in the future, the new table is automatically secure from any access, and then we can assign the necessary privileges for that table. This is an example of being default secure.

To ensure that the privileges have been properly assigned, we should now list each user's privileges and confirm they appear as expected. In addition, we should also test a user's access to confirm the outcome is as expected. Figure 5.35 shows a series of operations, when logged in as user roberts and after choosing the BusinessTLS database, to confirm successful read-write access, as well as unsuccessful add and remove access, to the Budget table. Specifically, the presence of normal output by the *SELECT* operation and "Query OK" result by the *UPDATE* indicates these accesses were successful, and that the allowed privileges appear to be assigned properly. Furthermore, the presence of "command denied" errors for both the *INSERT* and *DELETE* attempts indicates that no additional privileges were inadvertently assigned.

```
mysql> USE BusinessTLS;
Reading table information for completion of table and column names
You can turn off this feature to get a quicker startup with -A

Database changed
mysql> SHOW GRANTS;
+----------------------------------------------------------------+
| Grants for roberts@%                                           |
+----------------------------------------------------------------+
| GRANT USAGE ON *.* TO `roberts`@`%`                            |
| GRANT SELECT, UPDATE ON `BusinessTLS`.`Budget` TO `roberts`@`%`|
| GRANT SELECT ON `BusinessTLS`.`Employee` TO `roberts`@`%`      |
+----------------------------------------------------------------+
3 rows in set (0.00 sec)

mysql> SELECT * FROM Budget WHERE Year=2022 AND Quarter=1;
+----------+------+---------+------------+------------+
| BudgetID | Year | Quarter | Sales      | Expenses   |
+----------+------+---------+------------+------------+
| B05      | 2022 |       1 | 1710000.00 | 1395000.00 |
+----------+------+---------+------------+------------+
1 row in set (0.00 sec)

mysql> UPDATE Budget Set Sales=1910000.00 WHERE Year=2022 AND Quarter=1;
Query OK, 1 row affected (0.07 sec)
Rows matched: 1  Changed: 1  Warnings: 0

mysql> INSERT INTO Budget VALUES('B09',2023,1,2000000.00,1720000.00);
ERROR 1142 (42000): INSERT command denied to user 'roberts'@'localhost' for table 'Budget'
mysql> DELETE FROM Budget WHERE Year=2022 AND Quarter=1;
ERROR 1142 (42000): DELETE command denied to user 'roberts'@'localhost' for table 'Budget'
mysql> []
```

FIGURE 5.35 Confirming that user roberts has read-write access.

To confirm the privileges for garrett, Figure 5.36 shows another series of operations, this time logged in as user garrett and after choosing the BusinessTLS database, to list the privileges as well as confirm successful read-write, add, and remove access to the Budget table. Similar to before when testing for roberts, the presence of normal output with the *SELECT* operation and "Query OK" result by the other operations indicates these accesses were successful and that the allowed privileges appear to be assigned properly.

```
mysql> USE BusinessTLS;
Reading table information for completion of table and column names
You can turn off this feature to get a quicker startup with -A

Database changed
mysql> SHOW GRANTS;
+----------------------------------------------------------------------------+
| Grants for garrett@%                                                       |
+----------------------------------------------------------------------------+
| GRANT USAGE ON *.* TO `garrett`@`%`                                        |
| GRANT SELECT, INSERT, UPDATE, DELETE ON `BusinessTLS`.`Budget` TO `garrett`@`%` |
| GRANT SELECT ON `BusinessTLS`.`Employee` TO `garrett`@`%`                  |
+----------------------------------------------------------------------------+
3 rows in set (0.00 sec)

mysql> SELECT * FROM Budget WHERE Year=2022 AND Quarter=1;
+----------+------+---------+------------+------------+
| BudgetID | Year | Quarter | Sales      | Expenses   |
+----------+------+---------+------------+------------+
| B05      | 2022 |       1 | 1910000.00 | 1395000.00 |
+----------+------+---------+------------+------------+
1 row in set (0.00 sec)

mysql> UPDATE Budget Set Sales=1710000.00 WHERE Year=2022 AND Quarter=1;
Query OK, 1 row affected (0.06 sec)
Rows matched: 1  Changed: 1  Warnings: 0

mysql> INSERT INTO Budget VALUES('B09',2023,1,2000000.00,1720000.00);
Query OK, 1 row affected (0.06 sec)

mysql> DELETE FROM Budget WHERE Year=2023 AND Quarter=1;
Query OK, 1 row affected (0.06 sec)

mysql> []
```

FIGURE 5.36 Confirming that user garrett has expected access.

As with the Employee table, for a more thorough security assessment, we may consider testing all users, as well as issuing all types of operations that should be allowed as well as those that should not, and confirm the results are as expected.

5.6 TLS AND NORMALIZATION REVISITED

The concept of normalization presented in Chapter 2, "Database Design," can lead to better security management of the granting of privileges at the table-level in an effective and efficient manner, as we described by grouping related data together and separating data that may not be related. However, we also mentioned that even with normalization, not all security requirements may be supported with security defined on a table basis, or *table-level security*. In these cases, if we still wish to manage security on a table-level we can break the table down further, so that columns with less restricted access are placed in one table that itself has less restricted access, and the columns that require greater restriction are placed in another table that itself is given the greater restricted access. We saw this in Chapter 2, where we split the Property table into two tables, one that contained all publicly accessible columns and another table that contained all publicly restricted columns.

As another example of managing data privileges at the table-level, let's reconsider the Employee table, and say we want to allow employees to retrieve certain data of other employees (for example, to obtain another employee's office or title). However, note that the Employee table contains not only information that we can safely share among employees, but also both personal information (PI) such as Address, DOB, and Salary, as well as personally identifiable information (PII) such as SSN. Because we should keep one's PI and PII confidential, we want an employee's PI and PII to be accessible only to authorized individuals, namely that particular employee and human resources personnel. In other words, non-human resources personnel should not be able to access the PI or PII of another employee. To implement this security requirement with table-level privileges, we will have to separate the PI and PII data into one table and the non-PI and non-PII data into another table. As illustrated in Figure 5.37, we kept the non-PI and non-PII data in the Employee table, but split the PI and PII data into a new table named HR. These tables and their data are available in the BusinessTLSSplitHR database.

```
Employee (EmpID, FName, LName, Title, Office)

HR (EmpID, Address, SSN, DOB, Salary)
```

Employee

EmpID	FName	LName	Title	Office
E01	Tom	Roberts	CEO	A110
E02	Alison	Garrett	CFO	A118
E03	Betty	Chu	HR Director	A203
E04	Cindy	Donnelly	Sales Director	B116
E05	Alex	Gardner	Sales Assoc	B118
E06	Miguel	Sanford	CIO	A202

HR

EmpID	Address	SSN	DOB	Salary
E01	212 Orchid Ave	000-404-1234	03/01/1957	175000
E02	1234 Brown St	000-145-0909	05/25/1966	140000
E03	67 Tulip Lane	000-223-7888	10/13/1973	80000
E04	101 Harrison Ave	000-132-5673	02/17/1970	60000
E05	73 East Liberty	000-454-9654	10/16/1982	48000
E06	43 Falcon Dr	000-065-7788	02/15/1967	160000

FIGURE 5.37 Employee data with PI and PII in separate tables.

Now we can increase security on the PI and PII with table-level privileges by specifying different access requirements to the non-PI and non-PII data in the Employee table compared to the PI and PII data in the HR table. Specifically, we want to allow only human resources to have read-write—as well as add and remove—access to both tables. We also want to allow all other employees to have just read-only access to Employee, and no access at all to the HR table. Table 5.4 lists the user access specifications for the new database.

User Account	Employee	HR	Budget
roberts	read	none	read, write
garret	read	none	read, write, add, delete
chu@localhost	read, write, add, delete	read, write, add, delete	read
gardner@192.168.2.10_	read	none	read
donnelly@localhost	read	none	read
donnelly@192.168.2.8	read	none	read
sanford@localhost	read, grant	none, grant	read, grant
sandord@192.168.2.%	read	none	read

TABLE 5.4 Defining user data access requirements for tables in the BusinessTLSSplitHR database.

Note the privileges we previously applied to BusinessTLS have no effect on BusinessTLSSplitHR, so we have a clean slate upon which to work; as previously mentioned, it is generally good practice to start default secure in order to prevent inadvertently leaving a user with too many privileges. Because the access requirements for BusinessTLSSplitHR.Employee are the same as with BusinessTLS.Employee, we can apply the same privileges to that table, as shown in Figure 5.38. In this example, we first choose to use the BusinessTLSSplitHR database so we do not have to specify the database name in each grant statement. We also issue the first privileges to 'sanford'@'localhost', because as an administrator account, that user could then issue the remaining privilege grants. We then assign read-only privileges to all of the non-human resource personnel as a precaution. By specifying a series of lower privileges before assigning the higher privilege, we can help avoid accidently assigning human resource privileges to a non-human resource employee, especially if we are recalling and editing previous statements.

```
mysql> USE BusinessTLSSplitHR;
Reading table information for completion of table and column names
You can turn off this feature to get a quicker startup with -A

Database changed
mysql> GRANT SELECT ON Employee to 'sanford'@'localhost' WITH GRANT OPTION;
Query OK, 0 rows affected (0.09 sec)

mysql> GRANT SELECT ON Employee to 'roberts';
Query OK, 0 rows affected (0.05 sec)

mysql> GRANT SELECT ON Employee to 'garrett';
Query OK, 0 rows affected (0.06 sec)

mysql> GRANT SELECT ON Employee to 'donnelly'@'localhost';
Query OK, 0 rows affected (0.08 sec)

mysql> GRANT SELECT ON Employee to 'donnelly'@'192.168.2.8';
Query OK, 0 rows affected (0.06 sec)

mysql> GRANT SELECT ON Employee to 'gardner'@'192.168.2.10_';
Query OK, 0 rows affected (0.05 sec)

mysql> GRANT SELECT ON Employee to 'sanford'@'192.168.2.%';
Query OK, 0 rows affected (0.05 sec)

mysql> GRANT SELECT,UPDATE,INSERT,DELETE ON Employee to 'chu'@'localhost';
Query OK, 0 rows affected (0.08 sec)

mysql> []
```

FIGURE 5.38 Assigning privileges to the nonconfidential employee data.

Also note that rather than create a new BusinessTLSSplitHR database with the split tables, we could have instead edited BusinessTLS and moved the PI and PII columns out of the Employee table into a new HR table. In this manner, the grants that were previously issued to the Employee table would still exist, and in this case can be used as is because the access to that nonconfidential data did not change in this particular scenario. However, in practice we should carefully assess whether it is best from a principle of least privilege goal to start with a default secure new database and add the necessary privileges for user data access requirements, or modify the current database and manage its privileges accordingly, which may involve adding as well as removing privileges. Depending on the situation, either approach may be best in terms of or require fewer steps to implement.

To the newly split HR table, we now must assign human resources personnel read, write, add, and remove access, as shown in Figure 5.39.

```
mysql> GRANT USAGE ON HR TO 'sanford'@'localhost' WITH GRANT OPTION;
Query OK, 0 rows affected (0.05 sec)

mysql> GRANT SELECT,UPDATE,INSERT,DELETE ON HR TO 'chu'@'localhost';
Query OK, 0 rows affected (0.05 sec)

mysql> []
```

FIGURE 5.39 Assigning privileges to the confidential employee data.

Note that in Figure 5.39 we designate that 'sanford'@'localhost' has the capability to manage privileges even though that user has no access to the table's data. Such a designation allows us to implement the situation that 'sanford'@'localhost' (or any other such database administrator) has the capability to add or remove user privileges to the HR table as necessary, while keeping the PI and PII confidential or inaccessible to themselves. To assign such a privilege, we can assign no data access to the table by specifying only the *USAGE* privilege along with the *WITH GRANT OPTION* clause.

Another way we can assign the capability to manage user privileges to a table but have no other data access is by specifying *GRANT OPTION* as the privilege, as shown in Figure 5.40.

```
mysql> GRANT GRANT OPTION ON HR TO 'sanford'@'localhost';
Query OK, 0 rows affected (0.04 sec)

mysql> []
```

FIGURE 5.40 Alternative approach to assign no data access but capability to manage privileges.

Regardless of how we specify a no-access privilege, we can then list the privileges of 'sanford'@'localhost' and see the capability to grant privileges but no read or other access to the data. Figure 5.41 shows the user's privileges, and in particular the privilege listing for the BusinessTLSSplitHR.HR table shows *USAGE* privilege and the capability to manage user privileges.

```
mysql> SHOW GRANTS FOR 'sanford'@'localhost';
+------------------------------------------------------------------------------------+
| Grants for sanford@localhost                                                       |
+------------------------------------------------------------------------------------+
| GRANT USAGE ON *.* TO `sanford`@`localhost`                                        |
| GRANT SELECT ON `BusinessTLSSplitHR`.`Employee` TO `sanford`@`localhost` WITH GRANT OPTION |
| GRANT USAGE ON `BusinessTLSSplitHR`.`HR` TO `sanford`@`localhost` WITH GRANT OPTION |
| GRANT SELECT ON `BusinessTLS`.`Budget` TO `sanford`@`localhost` WITH GRANT OPTION   |
| GRANT SELECT ON `BusinessTLS`.`Employee` TO `sanford`@`localhost` WITH GRANT OPTION |
+------------------------------------------------------------------------------------+
5 rows in set (0.00 sec)

mysql> []
```

FIGURE 5.41 Showing no data access but capability to manage privileges.

We can complete the necessary privileges for our new database by assigning them for the Budget table. The privileges for the Budget table and its user access specifications are identical to that in the BusinessTLS database, so we can assign the privileges in a similar manner, as shown in Figure 5.42.

```
mysql> GRANT SELECT ON Budget TO 'sanford'@'localhost' WITH GRANT OPTION;
Query OK, 0 rows affected (0.05 sec)

mysql> GRANT SELECT ON Budget TO 'chu'@'localhost';
Query OK, 0 rows affected (0.05 sec)

mysql> GRANT SELECT ON Budget TO 'donnelly'@'localhost';
Query OK, 0 rows affected (0.04 sec)

mysql> GRANT SELECT ON Budget TO 'donnelly'@'192.168.2.8';
Query OK, 0 rows affected (0.09 sec)

mysql> GRANT SELECT ON Budget TO 'gardner'@'192.168.2.10_';
Query OK, 0 rows affected (0.05 sec)

mysql> GRANT SELECT ON Budget TO 'sanford'@'192.168.2.%';
Query OK, 0 rows affected (0.08 sec)

mysql> GRANT SELECT,UPDATE ON Budget TO 'roberts';
Query OK, 0 rows affected (0.08 sec)

mysql> GRANT SELECT,UPDATE,INSERT,DELETE ON Budget TO 'garrett';
Query OK, 0 rows affected (0.08 sec)

mysql> []
```

FIGURE 5.42 Assigning privileges to the confidential employee data.

We can now keep PI and PII confidential to non-human resource personnel. We should test all user access to ensure the defined access requirements are met as expected. As examples, Figure 5.43 shows that roberts has no capability to access the HR table (that should be the case for all non-human resources personnel).

```
mysql> SELECT * FROM BusinessTLSSplitHR.HR;
ERROR 1142 (42000): SELECT command denied to user 'roberts'@'localhost' for table 'HR'
mysql> []
```

FIGURE 5.43 Demonstrating that user roberts has no access to the HR data.

Figure 5.44 issues a data retrieval to confirm that 'chu'@'localhost' has read access to the HR table. We could also test further to show that particular user also has the capability to change, add, and remove data to that table.

```
mysql> SELECT * FROM BusinessTLSSplitHR.HR;
+-------+-----------------+--------------+------------+--------+
| EmpID | Address         | SSN          | DOB        | Salary |
+-------+-----------------+--------------+------------+--------+
| E01   | 212 Orchid Ave  | 000-404-1234 | 1957-03-01 | 175000 |
| E02   | 1234 Brown St   | 000-145-0909 | 1966-05-25 | 140000 |
| E03   | 67 Tulip Lane   | 000-223-7888 | 1973-10-13 |  80000 |
| E04   | 101 Harrison Ave| 000-143-5673 | 1970-02-17 |  60000 |
| E05   | 73 East Liberty | 000-454-9654 | 1982-10-16 |  48000 |
| E06   | 43 Falcon Drive | 000-065-7788 | 1967-02-15 | 160000 |
+-------+-----------------+--------------+------------+--------+
6 rows in set (0.00 sec)

mysql> []
```

FIGURE 5.44 Demonstrating that user chu has access to the HR data.

TLS can often provide a great deal of data security in a flexible manner. However, there may be cases when TLS may not fully meet our data needs. Consider that in our goal to keep PI and PII confidential, a non-human resource employee does not have the capability to see their own data or manage their data directly. For such requirements, we have to turn to other levels of data security, such as column-level or row-level security, or employ other data access mechanisms. We will describe all of those, starting with column-level security next.

5.7   COLUMN LEVEL SECURITY (CLS)

We saw with the BusinessTLS database that data access requirements may vary among tables, as well as among columns within a table. In both cases, we can implement these data security requirements by splitting a table into multiple tables and employing TLS with table-level privileges. However, we can also implement such data security requirements with approaches based on *column-level security* (CLS). With CLS we can manage the security requirements for each column individually, and this can be especially beneficial in situations where the security requirements vary among the columns of a table. One CLS approach involves granting and revoking privileges on a column basis, also known as *column-level privileges*, which we will now explore.

Referring to the business scenario and original Employee table before we split that into two tables, let's consider how we may implement CLS with privileges to keep the PI and PII confidential. In other words, we will use CLS privileges to achieve the data security for the PI and PII that we had with the split Employee table, but with the original nonsplit Employee table.

Recall that for the nonconfidential (the non-PI and non-PII) data, we want human resources personnel to have read, write, add, and remove access. All other employees have read-only access. To demonstrate CLS in our business scenario, we will use the database *BusinessCLS*, which contains two tables: the original *Employee* table and a revised Budget table that contains an additional column that will introduce another security requirement in this scenario. Both tables have no assigned privileges, so we have a clean slate on which to implement our CLS.

When implementing CLS with column-level privileges, it is helpful to define the required and allowed user accesses, not only for each table, but also for each column. For the table as a whole, we define the TLS requirements that will be implemented with table-level privileges. These should be considered "blanket requirements," in that they will apply to the entire table, not only as the table exists now, but also as the table exists in the future. As we previously described, if we later add a column to that table, the new column automatically inherits the table-level privilege and has the same type of access as the other table columns. Consequently, we must be aware and careful to avoid inadvertently permitting such access to a column that is added in the future. We will soon see an actual example of this type of problem with the Budget table.

We also define the CLS requirements that will be implemented with column-level privileges. We should consider the TLS requirements as *minimal requirements* that are supplemented with the CLS requirements. In other words, the TLS and CLS requirements should work together, and not where one corrects or bypasses the security of the other. Table 5.5 illustrates how we may define TLS requirements that are supplemented with CLS for our business scenario.

User Account	Employee	Budget
roberts	read	read,write
garret	read	read,write,add,remove
chu@localhost	read-write,add,remove	read
gardner@192.168.2.10_	read	read
donnelly@localhost	read	read
donnelly@192.168.2.8	read	read
sanford@localhost	read,grant	read,grant
sandord@192.168.2.%	read	read

TABLE 5.5 Defining user access for tables in the BusinessTLS database.

The first detail you may notice in Table 5.5 is that read or write access is *not* specified for either table. We specify that type of access at the column-level. Instead, we define the higher, TLS requirements, namely whether a user has the capability to generally access the table (with the *USAGE* privilege), manage privileges (with the *GRANT OPTION* privilege), add a new row of data (with the *INSERT* privilege), and delete a row of data (with the *DELETE* privilege). Notice that we specify the capability to add or remove a row of data at the table-level and not at the column-level.

> **Tip:** The privilege to add or remove a row of data is specified at the table-level and not at the column-level.

Table 5.6 illustrates the read and/or write data access specifications of each database user to the Employee table data at the column-level. Here we can specify in detail the type of access (or lack thereof) each user has to each column in the table.

user	EmpID	FName	LName	Title	
roberts	read	read	read	read	
garrett	read	read	read	read	
chu@localhost	read,write	read,write	read,write	read,write	. . .
gardner@192.168.2.10_	read	read	read	read	
donnelly@localhost	read	read	read	read	
donnelly@192.168.2.8	read	read	read	read	
sanford@localhost	read	read	read	read	
sandord@192.168.2.%	read	read	read	read	

	Office	Address	SSN	DOB	Salary
	read	none	none	none	none
	read	none	none	none	none
. . .	read,write	read,write	read,write	read,write	read,write
	read	none	none	none	none
	read	none	none	none	none
	read	none	none	none	none
	read	none	none	none	none
	read	none	none	none	none

TABLE 5.6 User data access requirements for the Employee table columns.

We previously granted each user the *USAGE* privilege on all database tables with *.*, so each user already has *USAGE* privilege with the BusinessCLS database Employee and Budget tables. No other privileges have been set. Because user garrett is the CFO and needs the capability to add or remove a row of data in the Budget table, and because 'chu'@'localhost' requires the capability to add or remove a row of data in the Employee table, we can assign those privileges, as shown in Figure 5.45. Also shown in that figure, we also assign to 'sanford'@'localhost' the capability to manage user privileges on both tables. We specified the BusinessCLS database and these tables just to emphasize that we are now using that particular database for these examples. You may alternatively choose the database with the SQL *USE* keyword and then issue these statements without the database specification.

```
mysql> GRANT INSERT,DELETE ON BusinessCLS.Budget TO 'garrett';
Query OK, 0 rows affected (0.05 sec)

mysql> GRANT INSERT,DELETE ON BusinessCLS.Employee TO 'chu'@'localhost';
Query OK, 0 rows affected (0.05 sec)

mysql> GRANT GRANT OPTION ON BusinessCLS.Employee TO 'sanford'@'localhost';
Query OK, 0 rows affected (0.06 sec)

mysql> GRANT GRANT OPTION ON BusinessCLS.Budget TO 'sanford'@'localhost';
Query OK, 0 rows affected (0.07 sec)

mysql> []
```

FIGURE 5.45 Assigning necessary table-level privileges to the Employee table for CLS.

At this point, we can specify the finer-grain security requirements at the column-level. Figure 5.46 shows how we assign column-level privileges of the Employee table to roberts according to the user data access requirements given in Table 5.6. We would assign the same column-level privileges to all other non-human resources personnel.

```
mysql> GRANT SELECT (EmpID,FName,LName,Title,Office) ON BusinessCLS.Employee TO 'roberts';
Query OK, 0 rows affected (0.08 sec)

mysql> []
```

FIGURE 5.46 Assigning column-level privileges to the Employee table for non-human resource personnel.

You may notice the structure of a column-level *GRANT* statement is very similar to that of a table-level one. The difference is that we must specify the affected column(s) of a privilege in a set of parentheses immediately after the privilege. If a privilege applies to multiple columns, as in Figure 5.46, the column names are given in a comma-separated list. We can also specify multiple comma-separated privileges in the one statement; however, in that case we must also specify the column(s) that are affected by each privilege.

Let's briefly demonstrate the security provided by the CLS that we just implemented. As a simple test of the privileges for roberts, let's confirm the user can retrieve the nonconfidential employee data. Figure 5.47 shows a successful retrieval by roberts of the non-PI and non-PII data in the Employee table. While this example did retrieve all columns of which *SELECT* privilege was assigned, we could also retrieve only one or a subset of those columns as needed. Other non-human resource personnel assigned those privileges should have a similar successful retrieval with one or more of those columns.

```
mysql> SELECT EmpID,FName,LName,Title,Office FROM BusinessCLS.Employee;
+-------+--------+----------+----------------+--------+
| EmpID | FName  | LName    | Title          | Office |
+-------+--------+----------+----------------+--------+
| E01   | Tom    | Roberts  | CEO            | A110   |
| E02   | Alison | Garrett  | CFO            | A118   |
| E03   | Betty  | Chu      | HR Director    | A203   |
| E04   | Cindy  | Donnelly | Sales Director | B116   |
| E05   | Alex   | Gardner  | Sales Assoc    | B118   |
| E06   | Miguel | Sanford  | CIO            | A202   |
+-------+--------+----------+----------------+--------+
6 rows in set (0.00 sec)

mysql> □
```

FIGURE 5.47 Successful retrieval of non-PI and non-PII Employee data.

As part of testing that data security requirements are met, we should also attempt to access data for which a user is not authorized. As an example, let's consider an attempt to retrieve some of the PI and/or PII data by roberts, as shown in Figure 5.48. You will notice a similar denial by the DBMS if roberts or other non-human resource personnel attempt to retrieve any subset of the PI or PII data. This is an example of how we can provide confidentiality with column-level privileges.

```
mysql> SELECT SSN,Salary FROM BusinessCLS.Employee;
ERROR 1143 (42000): SELECT command denied to user 'roberts'@'localhost' for column 'SSN' in table 'Employee'
mysql> □
```

FIGURE 5.48 Unsuccessful retrieval of PI and PII Employee data.

In a similar manner, a retrieval of any or all Employee columns is unsuccessful if the user does not have *SELECT* privilege to one or more of the given columns. Figure 5.49 shows an attempt by roberts to retrieve columns that contain both nonconfidential and confidential data. Even though roberts is authorized to retrieve the nonconfidential columns, the retrieval fails because the retrieval includes confidential columns. Likewise, an attempt to retrieve all columns in the Employee table is unsuccessful because roberts is not given *SELECT* access to all Employee columns.

```
mysql> SELECT EmpID,FName,LName,Title,Office,Salary FROM BusinessCLS.Employee;
ERROR 1143 (42000): SELECT command denied to user 'roberts'@'localhost' for column 'Salary' in table 'Employee'
mysql> SELECT * FROM BusinessCLS.Employee;
ERROR 1142 (42000): SELECT command denied to user 'roberts'@'localhost' for table 'Employee'
mysql> □
```

FIGURE 5.49 Unsuccessful retrieval of nonconfidential and confidential data.

Moving to the human resource personnel, we can assign read and write access for 'chu'@'localhost' with the *GRANT* statement shown in Figure 5.50. Even though the user data access requirements in Table 5.6 specify that 'chu'@'localhost' has read-write access to all columns, we still list the columns in the *GRANT* statement to provide that CLS. Notice that in Figure 5.50 we show how to assign multiple privileges at the column-level in one statement, although we could have issued one statement for the *SELECT* privilege and a second statement for the *UPDATE* privilege.

```
mysql> GRANT SELECT (EmpID,FName,LName,Title,Office,Address,SSN,DOB,Salary),
    ->        UPDATE (EmpID,FName,LName,Title,Office,Address,SSN,DOB,Salary)
    -> ON BusinessCLS.Employee TO 'chu'@'localhost';
Query OK, 0 rows affected (0.09 sec)

mysql> □
```

FIGURE 5.50 Assigning column-level privileges to Employee for human resources personnel.

We may be tempted to issue 'chu'@'localhost' a table-level read-write privilege for brevity, like that in Figure 5.51, because the user is defined to have read-write access to all Employee columns. Notice that we are not actually executing this statement, but rather showing it for discussion.

```
mysql> GRANT SELECT,UPDATE ON BusinessCLS.Employee TO 'chu'@'localhost';□
```

FIGURE 5.51 Alternatively assigning table-level privileges to Employee for human resources personnel (note this can be less secure than assigning column-level privileges).

However, in such a case, assigning that privilege at the table-level introduces a security vulnerability. That vulnerability is like the one we described with assigning a database-level privilege with a .* wildcard when that privilege applies to all tables in the database. Specifically, just because a user has a certain privilege to all table columns at the present time, a column with a different security requirement may be added to that table in the future. And by assigning a table-level privilege now, we open the door for any future columns to automatically inherit the table-level privilege. For example, say a new column is later added to Employee, and that column is to be inaccessible to human resources personnel, or at least have a different set of access requirements than the other columns. The assignment of a read-write table-level privilege to Employee now will allow human resource personnel to have read-write access to that new column when it is later added. Consequently, when assigning privileges for CLS, it is safer practice to specify all columns by name, because if a new column is added in the future, 'chu'@'localhost' will not have access to the new column unless we assign a privilege for that column. This is also an example of being default secure.

Tip: Assigning a privilege with a wildcard for columns can introduce a security vulnerability!

Moving on to the Budget table, Table 5.7 illustrates the defined user specifications for that data at the column-level.

User	BudgetID	Year	Quarter	Sales	Expenses
roberts	read, write	read, write	read, write	read, write	read, write
garrett	read, write	read, write	read, write	read, write	read, write
chu@localhost	read	read	read	read	read
gardner@192.168.2.10_	read	read	read	read	read
donnelly@localhost	read	read	read	read	read
donnelly@192.168.2.8	read	read	read	read	read
sanford@localhost	read	read	read	read	read
sandord@192.168.2.%	read	read	read	read	read

TABLE 5.7 User data access requirements the Budget table columns.

All employees are to have read-only access to all of the columns except for the CEO and CFO, who both have read-write access to all columns. Even though we consider all Budget table columns to have the same access for a given user, for best security practices we will assign column-level privileges and specify all columns by name. Figure 5.52 shows the read-only privilege we will assign to human resources personnel; we are to assign similar privileges to the other non-CEO and non-CFO employees.

```
mysql> GRANT SELECT (BudgetID, Year, Quarter, Sales, Expenses) ON BusinessCLS.Budget TO 'chu'@'localhost';
Query OK, 0 rows affected (0.07 sec)

mysql> []
```

FIGURE 5.52 Assigning column-level privileges to Budget for read-only access.

For the CEO and CFO, we now assign read-write access to the Budget table. Figure 5.53 shows the assigning of read-write privilege for roberts. We want to repeat that same statement for garrett.

```
mysql> GRANT SELECT (BudgetID, Year, Quarter, Sales, Expenses),
    ->        UPDATE (BudgetID, Year, Quarter, Sales, Expenses)
    -> ON BusinessCLS.Budget TO 'roberts';
Query OK, 0 rows affected (0.05 sec)

mysql> []
```

FIGURE 5.53 Assigning column-level privileges to Budget for read-write access.

On to testing the assigned read-write privilege for human resources. In Figure 5.54, logged in as chu directly into the DBMS, we issue a retrieval of employee PI and PII, as well as change an employee's address, confirm both are successful, and then change the address back to its original value. Note that human resources can retrieve any or all columns in Employee because read-write access has been granted to that user for all columns.

```
mysql> SELECT Address, SSN, DOB, Salary FROM BusinessCLS.Employee;
+------------------+--------------+------------+--------+
| Address          | SSN          | DOB        | Salary |
+------------------+--------------+------------+--------+
| 212 Orchid Ave   | 000-404-1234 | 1957-03-01 | 175000 |
| 1234 Brown St    | 000-145-0909 | 1966-05-25 | 140000 |
| 67 Tulip Lane    | 000-223-7888 | 1973-10-13 |  80000 |
| 101 Harrison Ave | 000-143-5673 | 1970-02-17 |  60000 |
| 73 East Liberty  | 000-454-9654 | 1982-10-16 |  48000 |
| 43 Falcon Drive  | 000-065-7788 | 1967-02-15 | 160000 |
+------------------+--------------+------------+--------+
6 rows in set (0.00 sec)

mysql> UPDATE BusinessCLS.Employee SET Address='Test 123' WHERE EmpID='E01';
Query OK, 1 row affected (0.05 sec)
Rows matched: 1  Changed: 1  Warnings: 0

mysql> SELECT * FROM BusinessCLS.Employee WHERE EmpID='E01';
+-------+-------+---------+-------+--------+----------+--------------+------------+--------+
| EmpID | FName | LName   | Title | Office | Address  | SSN          | DOB        | Salary |
+-------+-------+---------+-------+--------+----------+--------------+------------+--------+
| E01   | Tom   | Roberts | CEO   | A110   | Test 123 | 000-404-1234 | 1957-03-01 | 175000 |
+-------+-------+---------+-------+--------+----------+--------------+------------+--------+
1 row in set (0.00 sec)

mysql> UPDATE BusinessCLS.Employee SET Address='212 Orchid Ave' WHERE EmpID='E01';
Query OK, 1 row affected (0.06 sec)
Rows matched: 1  Changed: 1  Warnings: 0

mysql> []
```

FIGURE 5.54 Testing that human resources has read and write access to Employee data.

Notice that we already assigned 'chu'@'localhost' the capability to add or remove rows in Employee with a table-level privilege. We should test that user's capability to add and remove a fictitious employee, as illustrated in Figure 5.55.

```
mysql> INSERT INTO BusinessCLS.Employee VALUES ('E07', 'John', 'Doe', 'Test', 'A00', '123 Main', '000-000-0000', '1970-
01-01', 10000);
Query OK, 1 row affected (0.06 sec)

mysql> SELECT * FROM BusinessCLS.Employee WHERE EmpID='E07';
+-------+-------+-------+-------+--------+----------+--------------+------------+--------+
| EmpID | FName | LName | Title | Office | Address  | SSN          | DOB        | Salary |
+-------+-------+-------+-------+--------+----------+--------------+------------+--------+
| E07   | John  | Doe   | Test  | A00    | 123 Main | 000-000-0000 | 1970-01-01 | 10000  |
+-------+-------+-------+-------+--------+----------+--------------+------------+--------+
1 row in set (0.00 sec)

mysql> DELETE FROM BusinessCLS.Employee WHERE EmpID='E07';
Query OK, 1 row affected (0.09 sec)

mysql> []
```

FIGURE 5.55 Testing that human resources can add and remove Employee data.

We can list the privileges for column-level privileges in the same way we did so for table-level privileges. Figure 5.56 illustrates how we can list the privileges assigned to roberts, which will include the user's table-level and/or column-level privileges. In that listing, notice that for the BusinessCLS. Employee table, *SELECT* privilege is associated with the set of columns (EmpID, FName, LName, Title, Office) rather than tables, indicating the *SELECT* privilege was assigned to only those columns for that user. Because we assigned the privileges to those columns specifically, those privileges are not associated with the table itself and as such, if any columns are later added to BusinessCLS.Employee, they will be default secure. The other non-human resources personnel should have a similar privilege listing for the BusinessCLS.Employee table.

```
mysql> SHOW GRANTS FOR 'roberts';
+-----------------------------------------------------------------------------------------------+
| Grants for roberts@%                                                                          |
+-----------------------------------------------------------------------------------------------+
| GRANT USAGE ON *.* TO `roberts`@`%`                                                           |
| GRANT ALL PRIVILEGES ON `BusinessTLS`.* TO `roberts`@`%`                                      |
| GRANT SELECT (`BudgetID`, `Expenses`, `Quarter`, `Sales`, `Year`), UPDATE (`BudgetID`, `Expenses`, `Quarter`, `Sales`
, `Year`) ON `BusinessCLS`.`Budget` TO `roberts`@`%`                                            |
| GRANT SELECT (`EmpID`, `FName`, `LName`, `Office`, `Title`) ON `BusinessCLS`.`Employee` TO `roberts`@`%` |
| GRANT SELECT, UPDATE ON `BusinessTLSSplitHR`.`Budget` TO `roberts`@`%`                         |
| GRANT SELECT ON `BusinessTLSSplitHR`.`Employee` TO `roberts`@`%`                               |
| GRANT SELECT, UPDATE ON `BusinessTLS`.`Budget` TO `roberts`@`%`                                |
| GRANT SELECT ON `BusinessTLS`.`Employee` TO `roberts`@`%`                                      |
+-----------------------------------------------------------------------------------------------+
8 rows in set (0.00 sec)

mysql> []
```

FIGURE 5.56 Showing table and column-level privileges for the CEO, edited for brevity.

Additionally, notice that for the BusinessCLS.Budget table, user roberts has *SELECT* and *UPDATE* privileges for all columns of that table. The columns are also listed individually, indicating that the column names were explicitly stated for the assigning of those privileges. The CFO (garrett) should have a similar privilege listing for the BusinessCLS.Budget table. Because of the longer line resulting from the list of column names involved with the BusinessCLS.Budget privileges, the output of that privilege listing may be a little difficult to read without increasing the width of the terminal window. The right side border is edited out and some lines are shortened to help make Figure 5.56 (as well as next in Figure 5.57) more readable.

For human resources personnel, Figure 5.57 shows the privileges for 'chu'@'localhost'. In a similar manner, we see that for the BusinessCLS. Employee table, *SELECT* and *UPDATE* privilege is associated with all columns given by their names. Likewise, for BusinessCLS.Budget, *SELECT* privilege is assigned for all columns given by their names. That way, if any columns are later added to either table, they will be default secure. Other users, except for the CEO and CFO, will have a similar privilege listing for the BusinessCLS.Budget table.

```
mysql> SHOW GRANTS FOR 'chu'@'localhost';
+----------------------------------------------------------------------------+
| Grants for chu@localhost                                                   |
+----------------------------------------------------------------------------+
| GRANT USAGE ON *.* TO `chu`@`localhost`
| GRANT SELECT (`BudgetID`, `Expenses`, `Quarter`, `Sales`, `Year`) ON `BusinessCLS`.`Budget` TO `chu`@`localhost`
| GRANT SELECT (`Address`, `DOB`, `EmpID`, `FName`, `LName`, `Office`, `SSN`, `Salary`, `Title`), INSERT, UPDATE (`Addr
ess`, `DOB`, `EmpID`, `FName`, `LName`, `Office`, `SSN`, `Salary`, `Title`), DELETE ON `BusinessCLS`.`Employee` TO `chu
`@`localhost`
| GRANT SELECT ON `BusinessTLSSplitHR`.`Budget` TO `chu`@`localhost`
| GRANT SELECT, INSERT, UPDATE, DELETE ON `BusinessTLSSplitHR`.`Employee` TO `chu`@`localhost`
| GRANT SELECT, INSERT, UPDATE, DELETE ON `BusinessTLSSplitHR`.`HR` TO `chu`@`localhost`
| GRANT SELECT ON `BusinessTLS`.`Budget` TO `chu`@`localhost`
| GRANT SELECT, INSERT, UPDATE, DELETE ON `BusinessTLS`.`Employee` TO `chu`@`localhost`
+----------------------------------------------------------------------------+
8 rows in set (0.00 sec)

mysql> []
```

FIGURE 5.57 Showing table and column-level privileges for human resources, edited for brevity.

5.8 CLS AND EVOLVING DATA ACCESS REQUIREMENTS AND DATA

In practice, data access requirements may change over time. The tasks or data access requirements of an employee may be extended to require accessibility to more data, or reduced to require accessibility to less data. In addition, new data may be introduced in the form of one or more new table columns that may or may not be accessible to certain employees. Let's consider the following changes that might occur over time within our business scenario:

1. The capability for CEO and CFO to read Salary data
2. The capability for Employees to see Address data
3. The capability for executives to keep private notes in the Budget table.

The capability for CEO and CFO to read salary data

A situation may arise where management or administration may need access to certain employee PI, such as employee salaries to determine budgets, hiring considerations, or raises. If we want to give the CEO and CFO read access to employee salaries, we only need to add a column-level privilege for the Salary column to those users. Figure 5.58 illustrates how we can do so.

```
mysql> GRANT SELECT (Salary) ON BusinessCLS.Employee TO 'roberts';
Query OK, 0 rows affected (0.08 sec)

mysql> GRANT SELECT (Salary) ON BusinessCLS.Employee TO 'garrett';
Query OK, 0 rows affected (0.06 sec)

mysql> []
```

FIGURE 5.58 Adding an additional column-level privilege for two users to read salaries.

Note that if a user already has a set of privileges for that table, we can add to (or remove from) those privileges by specifying only the *relative* change to the current privileges. In other words, we do not have to specify a complete set of privileges that includes the current privilege(s) as well as the new privilege(s).

Now both the CEO and CFO can read data in the Salary column along with the other non-confidential data. Figure 5.59 shows user roberts retrieving employee names and their salaries. We should similarly test that user garrett can do so as well.

```
mysql> SELECT FName,LName,Salary FROM BusinessCLS.Employee;
+--------+----------+--------+
| FName  | LName    | Salary |
+--------+----------+--------+
| Tom    | Roberts  | 175000 |
| Alison | Garrett  | 140000 |
| Betty  | Chu      |  80000 |
| Cindy  | Donnelly |  60000 |
| Alex   | Gardner  |  48000 |
| Miguel | Sanford  | 160000 |
+--------+----------+--------+
6 rows in set (0.00 sec)

mysql> []
```

FIGURE 5.59 User roberts reading salary data with the newly added privilege.

The capability for employees to see address data

At times, a situation may arise where certain PI may be accessed in a limited manner, such as employee addresses for mailing of cards, gifts, or other purposes. If we consider that all employees may be allowed to read address data of other employees, we can incorporate that capability by similarly adding a *SELECT* privilege to the Address column for the affected employees. Figure 5.60 illustrates the adding of this privilege to the user roberts, and we would add this privilege similarly to other employees. Note that we do not need to add that particular privilege to human resources personnel because they already have been assigned read-write access to Address. But if we did add *SELECT* privilege to a user that already has a *SELECT* privilege for that column, there would be no functional change to the user's capability to access that column.

```
mysql> GRANT SELECT (Address) ON BusinessCLS.Employee TO 'roberts';
Query OK, 0 rows affected (0.08 sec)

mysql> []
```

FIGURE 5.60 Adding a column-level privilege to read addresses.

There can be other approaches to achieve a similar data access requirement, and we will see some of those in later chapters. If the privilege is temporary, we would later have to remove that data access with the *REVOKE* statement as shown in Figure 5.61.

```
mysql> REVOKE SELECT (Address) ON BusinessCLS.Employee FROM 'roberts';
Query OK, 0 rows affected (0.10 sec)

mysql> []
```

FIGURE 5.61 Removing a column-level privilege to read addresses.

We would have to similarly issue this statement for other non-human resources personnel. Note that we would have to be careful to *not* apply this *REVOKE* statement to all employees, because if applied to human resources personnel, we would remove their capability to retrieve employee addresses.

The capability for executives to keep private notes in the budget table

Let's now consider the case where a table structure may change with the creation of new data. Suppose that the CEO and CFO wish to store private data in the Budget table that only they can read and write. No other employees are allowed even read access to that new data. We can implement this new data requirement by adding to the Budget table a column named Notes to store that confidential data, so that the Budget relation structure and its data is like that shown in Figure 5.62.

```
Budget (BudgetID, Year, Quarter, Sales, Expenses, Notes)

Budget
```

BudgetID	Year	Quarter	Sales	Expenses	Notes
B01	2021	1	1600000	1450000	(confidential)
B02	2021	2	1700000	1460000	(confidential)
B03	2021	3	1550000	1380000	(confidential)
B04	2021	4	1760000	1430000	(confidential)
B05	2022	1	1710000	1395000	(confidential)
B06	2022	2	1775000	1435000	(confidential)
B07	2022	3	1920000	1520000	(confidential)
B08	2022	4	1830000	1480000	(confidential)

FIGURE 5.62 Budget table structure and data with added column.

We can add a new column to the Budget table with the *ALTER* statement shown in Figure 5.63. For demonstration and testing purposes, we also fill in values for that new column.

```
mysql> ALTER TABLE BusinessCLS.Budget
    -> ADD Notes VARCHAR(4096);
Query OK, 0 rows affected (0.25 sec)
Records: 0  Duplicates: 0  Warnings: 0

mysql> UPDATE BusinessCLS.Budget SET Notes='(confidential)';
Query OK, 8 rows affected (0.10 sec)
Rows matched: 8  Changed: 8  Warnings: 0

mysql> []
```

FIGURE 5.63 Adding a new column and values for the confidential data.

Notice that the newly added Notes column is default secure, because we previously assigned column-level privileges to access the BusinessCLS.Budget data as opposed to table-level privileges. Referring back to Figure 5.56 we can confirm that column is secure by noticing that user roberts has *SELECT* and *UPDATE* privileges to the columns (BudgetID,Expenses,Quarter,Sales,Year), and that the new Notes column does not appear, either by name or inclusion by a Budget.* column wildcard. User garrett has a similar privilege listing for that table. Recall other users have no privileges to access the data in that table, so at this time no users have access to the new column.

We must then add to the CEO and CFO a privilege that allows them read-write access to the Notes column. Figure 5.64 shows the *GRANT* statement that adds read-write privilege to the CEO and CFO for the new column.

```
mysql> GRANT SELECT (Notes), UPDATE (Notes) ON BusinessCLS.Budget TO 'roberts';
Query OK, 0 rows affected (0.06 sec)

mysql> GRANT SELECT (Notes), UPDATE (Notes) ON BusinessCLS.Budget TO 'garrett';
Query OK, 0 rows affected (0.12 sec)

mysql> []
```

FIGURE 5.64 Adding read-write column-level privileges for confidential data.

We can confirm that users roberts and garrett now have access to the new column, as illustrated for roberts in Figure 5.65.

```
mysql> SELECT * FROM BusinessCLS.Budget WHERE BudgetID='B08';
+----------+------+---------+------------+------------+----------------+
| BudgetID | Year | Quarter | Sales      | Expenses   | Notes          |
+----------+------+---------+------------+------------+----------------+
| B08      | 2022 |       4 | 1830000.00 | 1480000.00 | (confidential) |
+----------+------+---------+------------+------------+----------------+
1 row in set (0.00 sec)

mysql> UPDATE BusinessCLS.Budget SET Notes='(new-confidential)' WHERE BudgetID='B08';
Query OK, 1 row affected (0.09 sec)
Rows matched: 1  Changed: 1  Warnings: 0

mysql> []
```

FIGURE 5.65 Testing that user roberts has successful read-write access to confidential data.

The added Notes column is an example of how we must be careful with table-level privileges in order to maintain the principle of least privilege with columns added in the future. If we had previously assigned a user read-only access to the BusinessCLS.Budget table and later added the Notes column, that user would now have read-only access to the confidential Notes column by default. However, because we previously assigned non-CEO and non-CFO users read-only privilege at the column-level by specifying all columns by name, there are no privileges for the newly added Notes column until we assign such, so the data in that new column is default secure. Consequently, by *default*, or without any additional steps, all non-CEO and non-CFO employees have no access to that column, as demonstrated and tested by user chu in Figure 5.66.

```
mysql> SELECT * FROM BusinessCLS.Budget WHERE BudgetID='B08';
ERROR 1142 (42000): SELECT command denied to user 'chu'@'localhost' for table 'Budget'
mysql> UPDATE BusinessCLS.Budget SET Notes='(non-confidential)' WHERE BudgetID='B08';
ERROR 1142 (42000): UPDATE command denied to user 'chu'@'localhost' for table 'Budget'
mysql> []
```

FIGURE 5.66 Testing that user chu has unsuccessful read-write access to confidential data.

While column-level privileges provide more detailed security management over table-level privileges, table-level privileges and splitting tables can still be helpful. First, if we can split tables so that all columns within a table share the same security requirement, we may simplify database security management by assigning privileges on a table-basis only, rather than on both a table- and column-level basis. Second, the task of specifying privileges for every necessary column by name raises the risk of omitting a column or incorrectly defining a column's privilege, either of which can potentially compromise all CIA security principles. This may result with loss of confidentiality (by improperly allowing read access to unauthorized individuals, loss of integrity (by improperly allowing write or delete access to unauthorized individuals) or loss of availability (by disallowing access to authorized individuals). Finally, while most DBMSs support column-level privileges, one may encounter a DBMS (or an earlier version of one) that may not adequately support per-column privileges, and another approach such as table-level privileges may be necessary.

5.9   ROW LEVEL SECURITY

The final dimension we will consider is row-level security. *Row-level security* (or RLS) is based on the management of data access in terms of row(s), rather than by table or column.

A common situation involving row-level security involves a table that contains data about users, such as one user per row. In that table is a column that contains personal information such as a SSN or a password that we want to keep confidential. We want to allow a user to access the data in the row(s) that corresponds to them, but disallow that user to access data in any other rows.

Implementation of RLS is not as straightforward as with TLS or CLS, and that is because DBMSs typically do not implement RLS natively or directly. Rather than specify privileges directly as we did with TLS or CLS, RLS approaches vary among DBMSs. In general, we can use views, encryption or database applications to manage RLS, and we cover those ideas more in Chapter 7.

5.10 SUMMARY

In this chapter, we described and demonstrated a number of security controls to manage user access to database components and data itself. These controls can provide a great deal of base-level security to the DBMS. The next chapter expands on this concept to describe how we may more efficiently apply these security controls to a large number of user accounts. And later chapters will add more control with managing user account access to the DBMS and its data.

CHAPTER 6

ROLES

Now that we have an understanding of implementing database security requirements with database users and privileges, let's see how we may better manage such security requirements among database users with the concept of roles. A *role* represents a set of users that have common data access requirements. Examples of a role include administration, managers, human resources personnel, users working on a certain project, and so on. Rather than assign privileges to a user directly as we did before, we instead assign privileges to a role. Then we can add (as well remove) a user to that role. A user who has been added to a role is considered to *belong* to the role or be a *member* of the role. We can alternatively add a user to the role first and then assign privileges to the role. Either way, the user then inherits the privilege(s) assigned to that role. A role can have one or multiple user members, and a user can belong to one or multiple roles.

To see how roles can streamline the management of database security requirements with privileges, consider the repetitive work that might have to be issued when assigning or removing privileges to a number of users who have similar data access requirements. As an example, in our business scenario when we previously assigned users read-only access to nonconfidential employee data, we issued a grant statement for *each* such user. Likewise, when we then added or removed columns that could be accessed read-only, we had to issue a grant or revoke statement for *each* affected user. If we had instead created a role that represented all employees and added all employees to that role, we can add or remove privileges for all employees with a *single* grant or revoke statement.

In addition to streamlining the management of privileges, roles can provide a more secure approach to privilege management. Namely, after we assign privileges to a role, we do not have to repeat the assignment of those privileges to a new user who enters that role. This can reduce the possibility of incorrectly assigning the privileges, whether by omitting a privilege—or even worse—granting more privileges than are necessary. Likewise, as a user's job responsibility changes or is removed, we can remove the user from that role, which causes the user to lose that role's privileges, and we do not risk overlooking the removal of privileges that are no longer required. In both of these examples, roles helped maintain the principle of least privilege.

The method to use database roles involves first defining which users belong to a role, as well as the data access requirements required for the role. This will later define the exact privileges a role requires. After that, we create the role or roles. In our demonstration, we then next assign privileges to a role and then add users to a role. As mentioned, we could alternatively add users to a role and then add privileges to the role, but that approach may be considered less secure, because if we incorrectly assign the role privileges, all user members have those privileges until we correct that error. However, during the evolution of the environment and data access requirements, data access requirements to a role may change, and we may add or remove privileges to a role that already has user members.

6.1 DEFINING ROLE MEMBERS AND DATA ACCESS REQUIREMENTS

To demonstrate the use of roles with privilege management, let's look at the BusinessRole database, which contains our Business scenario but will use roles. Here we have the *Employee* and original *Budget* tables (without the Notes column included) of the previous chapter but with no privileges assigned. Let's see how we can alternatively use roles to achieve and manage the data access requirements given in Table 5.5, Table 5.6 and Table 5.7. In this scenario, we can consider five roles or sets of users: a general role for all employees in the business, a role for the CEO employee(s), a role for the CFO employee(s), a role for HR employee(s), and a role for the CIO employee(s). Table 6.1 indicates the user(s) that belong in each role, with an X placed in the corresponding cell that matches a given row (user) with the role (column).

user	Role				
	AllEmployees	**CEO**	**CFO**	**HR**	**CIO**
roberts	X	X			
garrett	X		X		
chu@localhost	X			X	
gardner@192.168.2.10_	X				
donnelly@localhost	X				
donnelly@192.168.2.8	X				
sanford@localhost	X				X
sandord@192.168.2.%	X				

TABLE 6.1 Users and their roles in the business scenario.

Now let's define the TLS and/or CLS requirements for each role. Depending on the scenario, we may have only TLS requirements, only CLS requirements, or both TLS and CLS requirements. In this case we have both. Table 6.2a shows the TLS specifications for each role. Notice that we are allowing all employees to have *USAGE* privilege for both tables. Recall that *USAGE* privilege itself does not provide for specific access to a table, but rather allows a user to access a table based on other privileges, such as the CLS privileges that we will soon include. Even though certain employees will have additional table-level privileges (such as the CFO's requirement to add or delete rows in the Budget table), we still define a minimal set of privileges that is applied to all employees. If an employee is to have additional table-level privileges, we add to the minimal set of privileges by adding the user to another role that has those additional privileges. For example, even though user garrett is in the AllEmployees role and has minimal access to all tables, that user is also in the CFO role, and the CFO role includes the capability to add or remove rows of data in the Budget table. So garrett has *USAGE* privilege provided by the AllEmployees role, as well as *INSERT* and *DELETE* privileges provided by the CFO role. The HR and CIO roles also have additional privileges that are added to the privileges of the respective users who belong to those roles.

Role	Employee	Budget
AllEmployees	usage	usage
CEO	usage	usage
CFO	usage	usage,add,remove
HR	usage,add,remove	usage
CIO	usage,grant	usage,grant

TABLE 6.2A Roles and their TLS requirements that will be supplemented with CLS in the business scenario.

When we list TLS (and, as we will also soon see, CLS) requirements for roles, we may have some roles that have identical requirements. When that happens, we can either implement both roles with the identical requirements, or consolidate the roles into one role in order to implement fewer roles. Both approaches have advantages and disadvantages, and we may find that one approach is more suitable for a given scenario. For example, in Table 6.2a, the AllEmployees role and CEO role have the same TLS requirements, namely only *USAGE* privilege to the Employee and Budget tables. We can either implement both roles with the same sets of TLS privileges, or consolidate both roles into one.

If we implement both roles and their identical TLS requirements, notice that for any employee who has the CEO role, the CEO role adds no additional TLS capabilities beyond that of the AllEmployees role. That is because in this scenario, the CEO personnel also belongs to the AllEmployees role. Even though this particular situation involves only two roles and one user, the involvement of roles that add no additional privileges may accumulate and increase the overall number and complexity of roles to manage. In practice, when implementing security measures, we typically opt for the simpler and/ or smaller configuration of a security control. By doing so, we become less likely to compromise the principle of least privilege or introduce security vulnerabilities. Such concerns can especially arise if we reduce a privilege in the future for one role but overlook reducing that privilege in another role that should also have had that privilege removed. As an example, suppose that the AllEmployees and CEO roles have identical privileges that include read access to some data. But later, the data access requirements change such that we must remove read privilege of that data for all employees, including the CEO. If we remove that read privilege from the AllEmployees role but overlook removing read privilege from the CEO role, the CEO personnel would still have read privilege to that data, thus compromising the principle of least privilege.

On the other hand, if the AllEmployees and CEO roles have identical privileges to a table, suppose we instead consolidate those roles, so there is not a CEO role in the TLS requirements. Consequently, the CEO is a member of only the AllEmployees role, and removing the read privilege from the AllEmployees role now affects all employees, including the CEO. Following the idea to consolidate roles when possible, we can reduce the list of roles involved with—as well as simply the management of—TLS requirements by omitting a set of TLS privileges for the CEO role, because that set would add no additional TLS capabilities. Because the other roles do not share identical requirements, we do not consider consolidating them. Table 6.2b shows a reduced set of TLS requirements for roles, with the CEO role requirements omitted, or more accurately, consolidated with the AllEmployees role.

Role	Employee	Budget
AllEmployees	usage	usage
CFO	usage	usage,add,remove
HR	usage,add,remove	usage
CIO	usage,grant	usage,grant

TABLE 6.2B Reduced set of roles and their TLS requirements that will be supplemented with CLS in the business scenario.

Looking at the CIO role, we see the privileges for table usage as well as to manage user privileges. Recall that the CIO sanford@localhost is to have the capability to manage user privileges on both tables, however sanford@192.168.2.% is to have no such capability. We can implement that distinction by adding both users to the AllEmployees role, but only add sanford@localhost to the CIO role. That in effect allows user sanford to have the CIO role, and hence the capability to manage user privileges, only when logging directly into the DBMS. In contrast, when user sanford logs into the DBMS from another system in the 192.168.2.% network, that user is considered to be in only the AllEmployees role and does not have the capability to manage user privileges.

With the TLS requirements defined, we can now look at the CLS requirements of each table. Table 6.3a lists the CLS data access requirements for the Employee table. Here we have read-only access to nonconfidential data for all employees, but employees with the HR role additionally have read-write access to all data.

role	EmpID	FName	LName	Title	
AllEmployees	read	read	read	read	
CEO	read	read	read	read	
CFO	read	read	read	read	. . .
HR	read,write	read,write	read,write	read,write	
CIO	read	read	read	read	

(Continued)

(Continued)

	Office	Address	SSN	DOB	Salary
	read	none	none	none	none
	read	none	none	none	none
...	read	none	none	none	none
	read,write	read,write	read,write	read,write	read,write
	read	none	none	none	none

TABLE 6.3A CLS data access requirements by role for the Employee table columns.

Here we see a case that has a greater number of identical requirements between roles. Among the five roles, four of them have identical CLS requirements. We can reduce the overall set of CLS data access requirements and simplify the implementation of column-level privileges with the consolidated list given in Table 6.3b.

role	EmpID	FName	LName	Title	
AllEmployees	read	read	read	read	...
HR	read,write	read,write	read,write	read,write	

	Office	Address	SSN	DOB	Salary
...	read	none	none	none	none
	read, write	read, write	read, write	read, write	read, write

TABLE 6.3B Reduced set of CLS data access requirements by role for the Employee table columns.

In Table 6.4a, for the Budget table we also see some identical CLS data access requirements across roles. As with the Employee table, we can combine the roles that have read-only access and thus omit the HR and CIO roles.

role	BudgetID	Year	Quarter	Sales	Expenses
AllEmployees	read	read	read	read	read
CEO	read, write	read, write	read, write	read, write	read, write
CFO	read, write	read, write	read, write	read, write	read, write
HR	read	read	read	read	read
CIO	read	read	read	read	read

TABLE 6.4A CLS data access requirements by role for the Budget table columns.

Turning to the CEO and CFO roles, we also see they have identical data access requirements and can be consolidated. However, such a consolidation may create some confusion, because if we were to consolidate both roles into the CEO role, then we would have to add both roberts and garrett (the CFO employee) to the CEO role. Likewise, if we had instead consolidated both roles into the CFO role, we would have to add both roberts (the CEO) and garrett to the CFO role. Either way, we add a user to a role that does not match their actual job description.

To avoid such confusion, we may choose to create a new role (such as Financial) and consolidate the CEO and CFO roles into that. However, such a choice increases the number of roles, and we must now add both users roberts and garrett to that new role. Alternatively, we may find it simpler overall to leave both the CEO and CFO roles in this set of requirements, so each role provides the necessary privileges to their user(s). Table 6.4b follows the latter approach, omitting the roles that have identical requirements to AllEmployees but keeping the CEO and CFO roles, even though they have identical data access requirements.

role	BudgetID	Year	Quarter	Sales	Expenses
AllEmployees	read	read	read	read	read
CEO	read, write	read, write	read, write	read, write	read, write
CFO	read, write	read, write	read, write	read, write	read, write

TABLE 6.4B Reduced set of CLS data access requirements by role for the Budget table columns.

6.2 CREATING A DATABASE ROLE, SHOWING ROLE PRIVILEGES, AND REMOVING A ROLE

With the roles and their TLS and CLS data access requirements defined, we can now implement that form of database security with roles. We will first create the roles. To create a role with MySQL, MariaDB, and Oracle, we use the *CREATE ROLE* statement, whose general syntax is given in Figure 6.1.

CREATE ROLE **'role'**[**@'hostname'**];

FIGURE 6.1 General SQL syntax to create a database role.

To create one role, we specify a single role name, as we do for AllEmployees shown in Figure 6.2. A role name follows the same rules as that of a database user name, where we must enclose the name within quotes if the name contains special characters. Even though our role names do not contain special characters, we still enclose them within quotes for uniformity. We can also specify that a role is restricted to a particular host or network with the @ symbol followed by the restriction, as we did with database users. Here, we are providing no such restrictions, so these roles are recognized when a user logs in from any system.

```
mysql> CREATE ROLE 'AllEmployees';
Query OK, 0 rows affected (0.06 sec)

mysql> []
```

FIGURE 6.2 Creating a single database role.

To create multiple roles at once, we can alternatively provide a comma-separated list of role names, as shown in Figure 6.3. Here we create the remaining roles for our Business scenario.

```
mysql> CREATE ROLE 'CEO', 'CFO', 'HR', 'CIO';
Query OK, 0 rows affected (0.10 sec)

mysql> []
```

FIGURE 6.3 Creating multiple database roles.

To show the current privileges of a role, we use the *SHOW GRANTS* statement like we did to show the privileges of a database user, except that we specify the name of a role rather than a database user. Figure 6.4 shows the current privileges for the AllEmployees role, which in this case shows that by default, *USAGE* privilege exists for the tables in all databases. Because we

have not yet assigned any privileges to our roles, the other roles will currently
have a similar listing.

```
mysql> SHOW GRANTS FOR 'AllEmployees';
+---------------------------------------------+
| Grants for AllEmployees@%                   |
+---------------------------------------------+
| GRANT USAGE ON *.* TO `AllEmployees`@`%`    |
+---------------------------------------------+
1 row in set (0.00 sec)

mysql> []
```

FIGURE 6.4 Showing the current privileges of a database role.

6.3   ASSIGNING PRIVILEGES TO ROLES

Now that the roles are created, we can assign the privileges to each role.
To add a privilege to a role with MySQL, MariaDB, and Oracle, we use the
GRANT statement similar to how we add a privilege to a database user. The
general syntax of this form of *GRANT* statement is given in Figure 6.5, and
is like that of granting a privilege to a database user, except we specify a role
rather than a user.

```
GRANT privilege(s)
ON   [database(s).]table(s)
TO   role(s);
```

FIGURE 6.5 General syntax of SQL *GRANT* statement that assigns privileges to database roles.

Starting with the TLS requirements given in Table 6.2b, we can assign
USAGE privilege of the Employee and Budget tables to the AllEmployees
role, as shown in Figure 6.6. Notice that we specify each table specifically
rather than use a wildcard, to maintain the principle of least privilege in case
a table was later added to the BusinessRoles database.

```
mysql> GRANT USAGE ON BusinessRoles.Employee TO 'AllEmployees';
Query OK, 0 rows affected (0.07 sec)

mysql> GRANT USAGE ON BusinessRoles.Budget TO 'AllEmployees';
Query OK, 0 rows affected (0.07 sec)

mysql> []
```

FIGURE 6.6 Assigning table-level privileges to a database role.

With a base or minimal set of table-level privileges established to AllEmployees, we can now add table-level privileges to roles that require them. Recall the CEO role was consolidated with the AllEmployees role, so we will start with the next role in the list, namely the CFO role. The CFO role requires *USAGE* privilege for the Employee table and *USAGE, INSERT,* and *DELETE* privileges for Budget. Although *USAGE* privilege alone may already exist by default, we will add it to the Employee table anyway just to be sure. Figure 6.7 shows how we can assign these privileges to the CFO role.

```
mysql> GRANT USAGE ON BusinessRoles.Employee TO 'CFO';
Query OK, 0 rows affected (0.05 sec)

mysql> GRANT USAGE,INSERT,DELETE ON BusinessRoles.Budget TO 'CFO';
Query OK, 0 rows affected (0.05 sec)

mysql> ■
```

FIGURE 6.7 Assigning table-level privileges to the CFO role.

Moving on to the HR role, we need to assign *USAGE, INSERT,* and *DELETE* privileges for the Employee table, and only *USAGE* privilege for Budget. Figure 6.8 shows the assigning of these privileges to the HR role.

```
mysql> GRANT USAGE,INSERT,DELETE ON BusinessRoles.Employee TO 'HR';
Query OK, 0 rows affected (0.10 sec)

mysql> GRANT USAGE ON BusinessRoles.Budget TO 'HR';
Query OK, 0 rows affected (0.08 sec)

mysql> []
```

FIGURE 6.8 Assigning table-level privileges to the HR role.

We now reach the CIO role. In addition to *USAGE* privilege, the CIO role requires the capability to manage user privileges on both tables. Similar to how we granted the *WITH GRANT OPTION* privilege to database users, we can do so with roles, as shown in Figure 6.9.

```
mysql> GRANT USAGE ON BusinessRoles.Employee TO 'CIO' WITH GRANT OPTION;
Query OK, 0 rows affected (0.05 sec)

mysql> GRANT USAGE ON BusinessRoles.Budget TO 'CIO' WITH GRANT OPTION;
Query OK, 0 rows affected (0.08 sec)

mysql> []
```

FIGURE 6.9 Assigning table-level privileges to the CIO role.

Once the TLS requirements are implemented, we turn to the CLS requirements. Based on the data access requirements given in Table 6.3b, we assign column-level privileges to only the AllEmployees and HR roles for the Employee table. Figure 6.10 shows the assignment of read-only access of the nonconfidential data to the AllEmployees role. In the same way that we assign column-level privileges for a specific set of columns to a database user, we provide the names of the affected columns in a parenthetically enclosed comma-separated list immediately after the corresponding type of access.

```
mysql> GRANT SELECT (EmpID,FName,LName,Title,Office) ON BusinessRoles.Employee TO 'AllEmployees';
Query OK, 0 rows affected (0.08 sec)

mysql> []
```

FIGURE 6.10 Assigning column-level privileges of Employee data to the AllEmployees role.

For the HR role, we must assign read-write access to all columns in the Employee table. As we did with assigning access to all columns of a table with database users, we want to specify the names of all affected columns in order to maintain the principle of least privilege with any future changes. Figure 6.11 shows that assignment of read-write column-level privileges with the Employee table for the HR role. The SQL statement in this figure and in the next few are issued across multiple lines for readability.

```
mysql> GRANT SELECT (EmpID,FName,LName,Title,Office,Address,SSN,DOB,Salary),
    ->        UPDATE (EmpID,FName,LName,Title,Office,Address,SSN,DOB,Salary)
    ->        ON BusinessRoles.Employee TO 'HR';
Query OK, 0 rows affected (0.09 sec)

mysql> []
```

FIGURE 6.11 Assigning column-level privileges of all columns to the HR role.

Turning to the Budget table, Table 6.4b contains three roles for which we must assign column-level privileges. Starting with the AllEmployees role, we assign read-only privileges to all columns as shown in Figure 6.12.

```
mysql> GRANT SELECT (BudgetID,Year,Quarter,Sales,Expenses)
    ->        ON BusinessRoles.Budget TO 'AllEmployees';
Query OK, 0 rows affected (0.06 sec)

mysql> []
```

FIGURE 6.12 Assigning column-level privileges of Budget data to the AllEmployees role.

The CEO and CFO roles have identical read-write column-level privileges because we chose to keep both roles in the design. Figure 6.13 shows the two statements that each assign read-write privileges to one of those roles.

```
mysql> GRANT SELECT (BudgetID,Year,Quarter,Sales,Expenses),
    ->        UPDATE (BudgetID,Year,Quarter,Sales,Expenses)
    ->        ON BusinessRoles.Budget TO 'CEO';
Query OK, 0 rows affected (0.05 sec)

mysql> GRANT SELECT (BudgetID,Year,Quarter,Sales,Expenses),
    ->        UPDATE (BudgetID,Year,Quarter,Sales,Expenses)
    ->        ON BusinessRoles.Budget TO 'CFO';
Query OK, 0 rows affected (0.07 sec)

mysql> []
```

FIGURE 6.13 Assigning column-level privileges of Budget data to the CEO and CFO roles.

After assigning privileges to a role, it is always a good practice to review those privileges. By doing so, we can learn about incorrect privilege assignments and correct them as soon as possible. This is not only important to maintain security of users that are already members of that role, but also for users that we later add to that role. Figure 6.14 shows the current table-level and column-level privileges for the AllEmployees role. We see the AllEmployees role has *USAGE* privilege to all tables in the DBMS (by default). We also see that role has *SELECT* privilege to all columns (explicitly named) in the Budget table as well as for nonconfidential data in the Employee table.

```
mysql> SHOW GRANTS FOR 'AllEmployees';
+--------------------------------------------------------------------------------------------------------+
| Grants for AllEmployees@%                                                                              |
+--------------------------------------------------------------------------------------------------------+
| GRANT USAGE ON *.* TO `AllEmployees`@`%`                                                                |
| GRANT SELECT (`BudgetID`, `Expenses`, `Quarter`, `Sales`, `Year`) ON `BusinessRoles`.`Budget` TO `AllEmployees`@`%` |
| GRANT SELECT (`EmpID`, `Fname`, `LName`, `Office`, `Title`) ON `BusinessRoles`.`Employee` TO `AllEmployees`@`%` |
+--------------------------------------------------------------------------------------------------------+
3 rows in set (0.00 sec)

mysql>
```

FIGURE 6.14 Showing privileges for the AllEmployee role.

Figure 6.15 contains the statements to show and the resulting output of the privileges for the CEO and CFO roles. Because the output of these statements has lines that wrap, the output has been slightly edited for readability. You will notice similar listings for both roles, as they both have identical *USAGE*, *SELECT*, and *UPDATE* privileges. However, the CFO role additionally has *INSERT* and *DELETE* privileges for the Budget table because that role has the capability to add and remove rows in that table.

```
mysql> SHOW GRANTS FOR 'CEO';
+-----------------------------------------------------------------------------------+
| Grants for CEO@%                                                                  |
+-----------------------------------------------------------------------------------+
| GRANT USAGE ON *.* TO `CEO`@`%`                                                   |
| GRANT SELECT (`BudgetID`, `Expenses`, `Quarter`, `Sales`, `Year`), UPDATE (`BudgetID`, `Expenses`, `Quarter`, `Sales`, `Year`) ON `BusinessRoles`.`Budget` TO `CEO`@`%` |
+-----------------------------------------------------------------------------------+
2 rows in set (0.00 sec)

mysql> SHOW GRANTS FOR 'CFO';
+-----------------------------------------------------------------------------------+
| Grants for CFO@%                                                                  |
| GRANT USAGE ON *.* TO `CFO`@`%`                                                   |
| GRANT SELECT (`BudgetID`, `Expenses`, `Quarter`, `Sales`, `Year`), INSERT, UPDATE (`BudgetID`, `Expenses`, `Quarter`, `Sales`, `Year`), DELETE ON `BusinessRoles`.`Budget` TO `CFO`@`%` |
+-----------------------------------------------------------------------------------+
2 rows in set (0.00 sec)

mysql>
```

FIGURE 6.15 Showing privileges for the CEO and CFO roles.

Figure 6.16 shows the privileges of the HR role. This output also has wrapped lines and has been slightly edited for readability. Similar to the CFO role, the HR role has the ability to read, write, add, and remove data in the Employee table.

```
mysql> SHOW GRANTS FOR 'HR';
+-----------------------------------------------------------------------------+
| Grants for HR@%                                                             |
+-----------------------------------------------------------------------------+
| GRANT USAGE ON *.* TO `HR`@`%`                                              |
| GRANT SELECT (`Address`, `DOB`, `EmpID`, `Fname`, `LName`, `Office`, `SSN`, `Salary`, `Title`), INSERT, UPDATE (`Addr
ess`, `DOB`, `EmpID`, `Fname`, `LName`, `Office`, `SSN`, `Salary`, `Title`), DELETE ON `BusinessRoles`.`Employee` TO `H
R`@`%`                                                                       |
+-----------------------------------------------------------------------------+
2 rows in set (0.00 sec)

mysql> █
```

FIGURE 6.16 Showing privileges for the HR role.

Finally to the privileges of the CIO role. As shown in Figure 6.17, we see *USAGE* privilege similar to the AllEmployees role, with the additional capability to manage user privileges as indicated by the *WITH GRANT OPTION* privilege.

```
mysql> SHOW GRANTS FOR 'CIO';
+-----------------------------------------------------------------------------+
| Grants for CIO@%                                                            |
+-----------------------------------------------------------------------------+
| GRANT USAGE ON *.* TO `CIO`@`%`                                            |
| GRANT USAGE ON `BusinessRoles`.`Budget` TO `CIO`@`%` WITH GRANT OPTION      |
| GRANT USAGE ON `BusinessRoles`.`Employee` TO `CIO`@`%` WITH GRANT OPTION    |
+-----------------------------------------------------------------------------+
3 rows in set (0.00 sec)

mysql> █
```

FIGURE 6.17 Showing privileges for the CIO role.

If we want to remove a database role, we can issue a similar form of the *DROP* statement, with the syntax given in Figure 6.18.

DROP **role**[**@hostname**]**;**

FIGURE 6.18 General SQL syntax to remove a database role.

Reviewing the privileges that we set, if the privilege listings appear like those in Figure 6.17, they are as expected with our design. Now we can move to the last implementation step and add users to our roles.

6.4 DATABASE USERS AND ROLE

Now that we have roles created and their privileges assigned, we can add users to those roles. This will in effect allow the users to obtain the privileges of those roles.

Adding and removing a database user to a role

We add a user to a role with MySQL, MariaDB, and Oracle by using the *GRANT* statement, although in a slightly different manner than we did to assign privileges to database users or roles. Here, we specify the role or roles rather than privileges. The general syntax to add a user to a role is given in Figure 6.19.

GRANT **'role'**[@**'hostname'**]**(s)** *TO* **'user'**[@**'hostname'**]**(s);**

FIGURE 6.19 General SQL syntax to add a database user to a role.

With this form of *GRANT* statement, we can specify one or more roles of which one or more users are to be added. When specifying multiple roles or users, we provide them in a comma-separated list. We can also optionally specify the @ symbol and hostname or network restrictions for any user, and we will later see that in our Business scenario.

Based on the user and role specifications given in Table 6.1, we can begin adding users to their role or roles. Starting with the simplest form of adding a single user to a single role, let's add user 'roberts' to the CEO role. Figure 6.20 shows the *GRANT* statement to add a user to a role.

```
mysql> GRANT 'CEO' TO 'roberts';
Query OK, 0 rows affected (0.06 sec)

mysql> []
```

FIGURE 6.20 Adding a user to the CEO role.

Following the idea of adding one user to one role, let's now add user 'garrett' to the CFO role, user 'chu'@'localhost' to the HR role, and user 'sanford'@'localhost' to the CIO role. Figure 6.21 shows the three statements that each adds one of those users to their role. The first and second statement have a similar form to that in Figure 6.20. The third statement contains an additional *WITH ADMIN OPTION* clause, which will give the CIO the capability to manage (add or remove) the roles for a database user.

```
mysql> GRANT 'CFO' TO 'garrett';
Query OK, 0 rows affected (0.05 sec)

mysql> GRANT 'HR' TO 'chu'@'localhost';
Query OK, 0 rows affected (0.05 sec)

mysql> GRANT 'CIO' TO 'sanford'@'localhost' WITH ADMIN OPTION;
Query OK, 0 rows affected (0.07 sec)

mysql> []
```

FIGURE 6.21 Adding a user to each of the CFO, HR, and CIO role.

Tip: The *WITH ADMIN OPTION* privilege allows a user to manage the roles of other users.

The last addition to a role for our Business scenario involves adding all of our database users to the base AllEmployees role. This task will use the *GRANT* statement with multiple users in a comma separated list and one role, as shown in Figure 6.22. We also issue this statement across multiple lines for readability among the list of users.

```
mysql> GRANT 'AllEmployees' to 'roberts',
    ->                         'garrett',
    ->                         'chu'@'localhost',
    ->                         'donnelly'@'localhost',
    ->                         'donnelly'@'192.168.2.8',
    ->                         'gardner'@'192.168.2.10_',
    ->                         'sanford'@'localhost',
    ->                         'sanford'@'192.168.2.%';
Query OK, 0 rows affected (0.08 sec)

mysql> []
```

FIGURE 6.22 Adding multiple users to a base role.

In the event that we need to remove a user from a role, we can also do that. Such a need may arise if we incorrectly add the user to a role and must undo that action. Other situations may require the removal of a user from a role, and we will see as well as demonstrate that situation later in this chapter. The general syntax to remove a user from a role is given in Figure 6.23.

```
REVOKE 'role'[@'hostname'](s) FROM 'user'[@'hostname'](s);
```

FIGURE 6.23 General SQL syntax to remove a database user from a role.

Listing, setting, and testing a user's role

Now that we have added the users to their roles, we may wish to review the roles in which a user belongs. In a similar manner to how we previously listed a user's directly assigned privileges in Chapter 5, we can also list information about the roles to which a user belongs with the *SHOW GRANTS* statement, using the syntax given in Figure 6.24.

```
SHOW GRANTS [FOR 'user'[@'hostname'] [USING 'role'[@'hostname'](s)]];
```

FIGURE 6.24 General SQL syntax to show a user's privileges and roles.

In the simplest form of this statement, a user can review their own privileges and roles by issuing the *SHOW GRANTS* statement itself. Let's demonstrate this with user garrett. Upon logging in, suppose garrett lists their privileges and roles. Figure 6.25 shows the result. We see a listing of privileges that were assigned for other databases similar to before. We also see the roles (AllEmployees and CFO) assigned to the user, highlighted in Figure 6.25 for emphasis.

(Figure 6.25 shows all other privileges that were previously assigned to that user for other databases, because for comparison and review, we kept those databases and privileges). We will later return to other forms of the *SHOW GRANTS* syntax shown in Figure 6.24.

```
mysql> SHOW GRANTS;
+-----------------------------------------------------------------------------------+
| Grants for garrett@%                                                              |
+-----------------------------------------------------------------------------------+
| GRANT USAGE ON *.* TO `garrett`@`%`                                                |
| GRANT SELECT (`Notes`), INSERT, UPDATE (`Notes`), DELETE ON `BusinessCLS`.`Budget` TO `garrett`@`%` |
| GRANT SELECT (`EmpID`, `FName`, `Salary`) ON `BusinessCLS`.`Employee` TO `garrett`@`%` |
| GRANT SELECT, INSERT, UPDATE, DELETE ON `BusinessTLSSplitHR`.`Budget` TO `garrett`@`%` |
| GRANT SELECT ON `BusinessTLSSplitHR`.`Employee` TO `garrett`@`%`                   |
| GRANT SELECT, INSERT, UPDATE, DELETE ON `BusinessTLS`.`Budget` TO `garrett`@`%`    |
| GRANT SELECT ON `BusinessTLS`.`Employee` TO `garrett`@`%`                          |
| GRANT `AllEmployees`@`%`, `CFO`@`%` TO `garrett`@`%`                               |
+-----------------------------------------------------------------------------------+
8 rows in set (0.00 sec)

mysql> 
```

FIGURE 6.25 User garrett listing their privileges and roles after logging in.

Let's explore further with user garrett. Suppose we wish to test that user's access to the BusinessRoles database. We may be in for a surprise, because upon logging in, even though garrett has roles assigned for the BusinessRoles database, we instead experience what is illustrated in Figure 6.26.

```
mysql> USE BusinessRoles;
ERROR 1044 (42000): Access denied for user 'garrett'@'%' to database 'BusinessRoles'
mysql> SELECT * FROM BusinessRoles.Budget;
ERROR 1142 (42000): SELECT command denied to user 'garrett'@'localhost' for table 'Budget'
mysql> []
```

FIGURE 6.26 User garrett initially with no access to BusinessRoles database.

We see in Figure 6.26 that garrett is unable to access the BusinessRoles database either by choosing it with the *USE* keyword, or by retrieving data with a *SELECT*. It seems that the CFO role—and even the AllEmployees role—has no effect in regards to data access for the user, even though the roles appear when the user lists their own privileges and roles in Figure 6.25.

To understand why garrett does not have any access to the BusinessRoles database, we must consider that before a role can take effect for a user, either the user must set the role as active or change to the role, or an administrator must set the role as a default for the user. A user can make a role active or change to a role, by issuing the *SET ROLE* statement, whose general syntax is given in Figure 6.27. To interpret this syntax, the | symbol represents a logical OR that separates the alternativesin the curly {} braces. We must specify exactly one of these alternatives. In this case we follow the *SET ROLE* keywords with either a list of one or more comma-separated roles that are to be active, the keyword *ALL* (which represents to make active all roles to which the user is a member, or the keyword *NONE* (which represents that no roles are to be active).

SET ROLE {**'role'(s)** | *ALL* | *NONE*};

FIGURE 6.27 General SQL syntax for a user to set their active role(s).

Let's continue our demonstration by setting a role with user garrett. Suppose garrett makes active the AllEmployees role, and issues *SET ROLE* followed by the role name, AllEmployees, as shown in Figure 6.28.

```
mysql> SET ROLE 'AllEmployees';
Query OK, 0 rows affected (0.00 sec)

mysql> SELECT * FROM BusinessRoles.Budget WHERE BudgetID='B08';
+----------+------+---------+------------+------------+
| BudgetID | Year | Quarter | Sales      | Expenses   |
+----------+------+---------+------------+------------+
| B08      | 2022 |       4 | 1830000.00 | 1480000.00 |
+----------+------+---------+------------+------------+
1 row in set (0.00 sec)

mysql> UPDATE BusinessRoles.Budget SET Expenses=1500000.00 WHERE BudgetID='B08';
ERROR 1142 (42000): UPDATE command denied to user 'garrett'@'localhost' for table 'Budget'
mysql> []
```

FIGURE 6.28 Setting active and testing the AllEmployees role.

After setting the role, garrett successfully attempts to read the Budget table. Data access seems as expected so far. Then garrett unsuccessfully attempts to write to the Budget table. If we expected that garrett should have read-write access to the Budget table, we should consider the role that was made active allows for read-only access to Budget.

If garrett now lists their privileges and roles, we see a slightly different result than before. As shown in Figure 6.29, compared to the listing in Figure 6.25, we see the privileges provided by the active role (AllEmployees), highlighted in this figure for emphasis.

```
mysql> SHOW GRANTS;
+----------------------------------------------------------------------------------------------------------+
| Grants for garrett@%                                                                                     |
+----------------------------------------------------------------------------------------------------------+
| GRANT USAGE ON *.* TO `garrett`@`%`                                                                      |
| GRANT SELECT (`Notes`), INSERT, UPDATE (`Notes`), DELETE ON `BusinessCLS`.`Budget` TO `garrett`@`%`      |
| GRANT SELECT (`EmpID`, `FName`, `Salary`) ON `BusinessCLS`.`Employee` TO `garrett`@`%`                   |
| GRANT SELECT (`BudgetID`, `Expenses`, `Quarter`, `Sales`, `Year`) ON `BusinessRoles`.`Budget` TO `garrett`@`%` |
| GRANT SELECT (`EmpID`, `FName`, `Fname`, `LName`, `Office`, `Title`) ON `BusinessRoles`.`Employee` TO `garrett`@`%` |
| GRANT SELECT, INSERT, UPDATE, DELETE ON `BusinessTLSSplitHR`.`Budget` TO `garrett`@`%`                   |
| GRANT SELECT ON `BusinessTLSSplitHR`.`Employee` TO `garrett`@`%`                                         |
| GRANT SELECT, INSERT, UPDATE, DELETE ON `BusinessTLS`.`Budget` TO `garrett`@`%`                          |
| GRANT SELECT ON `BusinessTLS`.`Employee` TO `garrett`@`%`                                                |
| GRANT `AllEmployees`@`%`, `CFO`@`%` TO `garrett`@`%`                                                     |
+----------------------------------------------------------------------------------------------------------+
10 rows in set (0.00 sec)

mysql> █
```

FIGURE 6.29 User garrett listing their privileges and roles after changing roles to the AllEmployees role.

In order to write to Budget, garrett must make the CFO role active. Figure 6.30 illustrates garrett making the CFO role active, followed by testing for a successful read as well as write to the Budget table. Notice that garrett could have also set both roles active by specifying both roles as a comma-separated list.

```
mysql> SET ROLE 'CFO';
Query OK, 0 rows affected (0.00 sec)

mysql> SELECT * FROM BusinessRoles.Budget WHERE BudgetID='B08';
+----------+------+---------+------------+------------+
| BudgetID | Year | Quarter | Sales      | Expenses   |
+----------+------+---------+------------+------------+
| B08      | 2022 |       4 | 1830000.00 | 1480000.00 |
+----------+------+---------+------------+------------+
1 row in set (0.00 sec)

mysql> UPDATE BusinessRoles.Budget SET Expenses=1500000.00 WHERE BudgetID='B08';
Query OK, 1 row affected (0.06 sec)
Rows matched: 1  Changed: 1  Warnings: 0

mysql> []
```

FIGURE 6.30 Setting active and testing the CFO role.

If garrett were to list their privileges and roles now, we would see the CFO role privileges in effect, namely *SELECT* and *UPDATE* privileges to the Budget table. These privileges are highlighted in Figure 6.31 for emphasis, and the figure is edited for readability.

```
mysql> SHOW GRANTS;
+----------------------------------------------------------------------------------+
| Grants for garrett@%                                                             |
+----------------------------------------------------------------------------------+
| GRANT USAGE ON *.* TO `garrett`@`%`
| GRANT SELECT (`Notes`), INSERT, UPDATE (`Notes`), DELETE ON `BusinessCLS`.`Budget` TO `garrett`@`%`
| GRANT SELECT (`EmpID`, `FName`, `Salary`) ON `BusinessCLS`.`Employee` TO `garrett`@`%`
| GRANT SELECT (`BudgetID`, `Expenses`, `Quarter`, `Sales`, `Year`), INSERT, UPDATE (`BudgetID`, `Expenses`, `Quarter`, `Sales`, `Year`), DELETE ON `BusinessRoles`.`Budget` TO `garrett`@`%`
| GRANT SELECT, INSERT, UPDATE, DELETE ON `BusinessTLSSplitHR`.`Budget` TO `garrett`@`%`
| GRANT SELECT ON `BusinessTLSSplitHR`.`Employee` TO `garrett`@`%`
| GRANT SELECT, INSERT, UPDATE, DELETE ON `BusinessTLS`.`Budget` TO `garrett`@`%`
| GRANT SELECT ON `BusinessTLS`.`Employee` TO `garrett`@`%`
| GRANT `AllEmployees`@`%`, `CFO`@`%` TO `garrett`@`%`
+----------------------------------------------------------------------------------+
9 rows in set (0.00 sec)

mysql> []
```

FIGURE 6.31 User garrett listing their privileges and roles after changing roles to the CFO role.

A few notes about roles as we end this example of setting a role to be active or changing roles. First, a user can only change to or make active a role to which an administrator has assigned the user. Second, when a user issues a *SET ROLE* statement, any role that was active is no longer, unless that role is represented among the list of roles specified in the new statement.

The concept of setting a role to be active or changing roles may seem a tedious and annoying step for most users, however it serves as a security measure. The goal is to abide by the principle of least privilege as much as possible. Consider a situation where a user requires, say add, remove, and read-write access to data only at certain times, and just read-only access the remainder or much of the time. Because only read-only access is mostly needed, allowing the user to have add, remove, and read-write access at all times compromises the principle of least privilege and introduces security vulnerabilities. However, if we have read-only access active for the user in general and allow the user to change to read-write access when necessary, we maintain the principle of least privilege and reduce such security vulnerabilities. Of course, after adding, removing or writing data, the user would have to change their role back to a less privileged one in order to maintain the principle of least privilege when fewer privileges are needed. In a similar manner, setting active all roles (with the *ALL* keyword as the role name) should be used with care, but in certain cases may be necessary.

The default role

MySQL, MariaDB, and Oracle also provide a way for a user to have a default role that immediately takes effect for the user as soon as that user logs into the DBMS. A default role typically represents a minimal or baseline set of privileges that we allow a user to have immediately upon logging in. Additionally, a user must already be a member of the role that we assign as the default role for that user. Because we already specified a minimal set of privileges in the AllEmployees role and added the employees as members, we can set the AllEmployees role as their default role, so its privileges are automatically in effect when a user logs in. To assign a default role, we issue the *SET DEFAULT ROLE* statement, which has a similar syntax to granting a role to a user and is given in Figure 6.32.

SET DEFAULT ROLE {`'role'(s)` | *ALL* | *NONE*} *TO* `'user'[@'hostname'](s);`

FIGURE 6.32 General SQL syntax to set a user's default role.

Figure 6.33 shows how we can set a default role of AllEmployees to all of the users in the Business scenario. This statement is issued across multiple lines here for readability among the list of users.

```
mysql> SET DEFAULT ROLE 'AllEmployees' to 'roberts',
    ->                                     'garrett',
    ->                                     'chu'@'localhost',
    ->                                     'donnelly'@'localhost',
    ->                                     'donnelly'@'192.168.2.8',
    ->                                     'gardner'@'192.168.2.10_',
    ->                                     'sanford'@'localhost',
    ->                                     'sanford'@'192.168.2.%';
Query OK, 0 rows affected (0.09 sec)

mysql> []
```

FIGURE 6.33 Adding the default role to users.

> **Tip:** Before a role can affect a user's data access, the user must first make the role active, or an administrator must set the role as a default role for the user.

Now one of those users, such as user chu, can log in and have the effect of the AllEmployees role immediately active without any additional steps. Figure 6.34 shows user chu, after logging in, with a successful read attempt of nonconfidential data on the Employee table, and an unsuccessful attempt with confidential data. If chu were to list their privileges and grants, we would see *SELECT* privilege is allowed for nonconfidential Employee data, because of the default AllEmployees role that is active.

```
mysql> SELECT FName,LName FROM BusinessRoles.Employee WHERE EmpID='E05';
+-------+---------+
| FName | LName   |
+-------+---------+
| Alex  | Gardner |
+-------+---------+
1 row in set (0.00 sec)

mysql> SELECT DOB FROM BusinessRoles.Employee WHERE EmpID='E05';
ERROR 1143 (42000): SELECT command denied to user 'chu'@'localhost' for column 'DOB' in table 'Employee'
mysql> []
```

FIGURE 6.34 Testing the default role.

If user chu needs to access confidential Employee data, as well as to add or remove data, the user must make the HR role active. Figure 6.35 shows chu making the HR role active and accessing confidential data.

```
mysql> SET ROLE 'HR';
Query OK, 0 rows affected (0.00 sec)

mysql> SELECT DOB FROM BusinessRoles.Employee WHERE EmpID='E05';
+------------+
| DOB        |
+------------+
| 1982-10-16 |
+------------+
1 row in set (0.00 sec)

mysql> []
```

FIGURE 6.35 Setting active and testing the HR role.

Listing privileges and roles revisited

The inclusion of roles may increase the complexity of reviewing and recognizing a user's data access capabilities with privileges and roles, but we will see later how roles can simplify the management of such data access. To describe the methods by which a user as well as an administrator can review a user's privileges and roles, let's return to other forms of the *SHOW GRANTS* statement whose syntax was given back in Figure 6.24. For this discussion, we will see the different ways in which we can see the privileges and roles for user roberts.

We mentioned that the simplest form of the *SHOW GRANTS* command is where a user lists their own privileges and roles, and we did so previously with user garrett. Figure 6.36a and Figure 6.36b (both edited for readability) show what user roberts sees when showing their own privileges and roles. Figure 6.36a shows the directly assigned privileges, the names of assigned roles (highlighted for emphasis), as well as the privileges of the default role that were made active upon logging in.

```
mysql> SHOW GRANTS;
+-------------------------------------------------------------------------------------------------------+
| Grants for roberts@%                                                                                   |
+-------------------------------------------------------------------------------------------------------+
| GRANT USAGE ON *.* TO `roberts`@`%`                                                                    |
| GRANT ALL PRIVILEGES ON `BusinessTLS`.* TO `roberts`@`%`                                               |
| GRANT SELECT (`BudgetID`, `Expenses`, `Notes`, `Quarter`, `Sales`, `Year`), UPDATE (`BudgetID`, `Expenses`, `Notes`,
`Quarter`, `Sales`, `Year`) ON `BusinessCLS`.`Budget` TO `roberts`@`%`                                  |
| GRANT SELECT (`EmpID`, `FName`, `LName`, `Office`, `Salary`, `Title`) ON `BusinessCLS`.`Employee` TO `roberts`@`%` |
| GRANT SELECT (`BudgetID`, `Expenses`, `Quarter`, `Sales`, `Year`) ON `BusinessRoles`.`Budget` TO `roberts`@`%`  |
| GRANT SELECT (`EmpID`, `FName`, `Fname`, `LName`, `Office`, `Title`) ON `BusinessRoles`.`Employee` TO `roberts`@`%` |
| GRANT SELECT, UPDATE ON `BusinessTLSSplitHR`.`Budget` TO `roberts`@`%`                                 |
| GRANT SELECT ON `BusinessTLSSplitHR`.`Employee` TO `roberts`@`%`                                       |
| GRANT SELECT, UPDATE ON `BusinessTLS`.`Budget` TO `roberts`@`%`                                        |
| GRANT SELECT ON `BusinessTLS`.`Employee` TO `roberts`@`%`                                              |
| GRANT `AllEmployees`@`%`, `CEO`@`%` TO `roberts`@`%`                                                   |
+-------------------------------------------------------------------------------------------------------+
11 rows in set (0.00 sec)

mysql> █
```

FIGURE 6.36A A user showing their privileges and roles, with assigned roles highlighted.

Figure 6.36b shows the same listing but highlights the privileges provided by the default role.

```
mysql> SHOW GRANTS;
+----------------------------------------------------------------------------+
| Grants for roberts@%                                                        |
+----------------------------------------------------------------------------+
| GRANT USAGE ON *.* TO `roberts`@`%`                                         |
| GRANT ALL PRIVILEGES ON `BusinessTLS`.* TO `roberts`@`%`                    |
| GRANT SELECT (`BudgetID`, `Expenses`, `Notes`, `Quarter`, `Sales`, `Year`), UPDATE (`BudgetID`, `Expenses`, `Notes`, |
| `Quarter`, `Sales`, `Year`) ON `BusinessCLS`.`Budget` TO `roberts`@`%`      |
| GRANT SELECT (`EmpID`, `FName`, `LName`, `Office`, `Salary`, `Title`) ON `BusinessCLS`.`Employee` TO `roberts`@`%`   |
| GRANT SELECT (`BudgetID`, `Expenses`, `Quarter`, `Sales`, `Year`) ON `BusinessRoles`.`Budget` TO `roberts`@`%`      |
| GRANT SELECT (`EmpID`, `FName`, `Fname`, `LName`, `Office`, `Title`) ON `BusinessRoles`.`Employee` TO `roberts`@`%`  |
| GRANT SELECT, UPDATE ON `BusinessTLSSplitHR`.`Budget` TO `roberts`@`%`      |
| GRANT SELECT ON `BusinessTLSSplitHR`.`Employee` TO `roberts`@`%`            |
| GRANT SELECT, UPDATE ON `BusinessTLS`.`Budget` TO `roberts`@`%`             |
| GRANT SELECT ON `BusinessTLS`.`Employee` TO `roberts`@`%`                   |
| GRANT `AllEmployees`@`%`,`CEO`@`%` TO `roberts`@`%`                         |
+----------------------------------------------------------------------------+
11 rows in set (0.00 sec)

mysql> []
```

FIGURE 6.36B A user showing their privileges and roles, with privileges of default role highlighted.

The purpose of showing both listings describes how a user can review their assigned roles and the privileges of the active role(s). roberts can make active or change to the roles highlighted in Figure 6.36a, and after that, the privileges provided by the active role(s) will appear in a manner like that in Figure 6.36b.

From a user's or administrator's perspective, we can show a user's privileges and roles using the *SHOW GRANTS* statement like we did in Chapter 5. This approach allows an administrator to review a user's privileges, roles, and privileges provided by roles. This approach also allows a user to do the same, provided the user is assigned to the roles specified. Figure 6.37 (edited for readability) shows how roberts or the administrator can list the privileges and roles assigned to roberts. The assigned roles are highlighted for emphasis. Notice no privileges are listed for the BusinessRoles database, not even those for the default role.

```
mysql> SHOW GRANTS FOR 'roberts';
+----------------------------------------------------------------------------+
| Grants for roberts@%                                                        |
+----------------------------------------------------------------------------+
| GRANT USAGE ON *.* TO `roberts`@`%`                                         |
| GRANT ALL PRIVILEGES ON `BusinessTLS`.* TO `roberts`@`%`                    |
| GRANT SELECT (`BudgetID`, `Expenses`, `Notes`, `Quarter`, `Sales`, `Year`), UPDATE (`BudgetID`, `Expenses`, `Notes`, |
| `Quarter`, `Sales`, `Year`) ON `BusinessCLS`.`Budget` TO `roberts`@`%`      |
| GRANT SELECT (`EmpID`, `FName`, `LName`, `Office`, `Salary`, `Title`) ON `BusinessCLS`.`Employee` TO `roberts`@`%`   |
| GRANT SELECT, UPDATE ON `BusinessTLSSplitHR`.`Budget` TO `roberts`@`%`      |
| GRANT SELECT ON `BusinessTLSSplitHR`.`Employee` TO `roberts`@`%`            |
| GRANT SELECT, UPDATE ON `BusinessTLS`.`Budget` TO `roberts`@`%`             |
| GRANT SELECT ON `BusinessTLS`.`Employee` TO `roberts`@`%`                   |
| GRANT `AllEmployees`@`%`,`CEO`@`%` TO `roberts`@`%`                         |
+----------------------------------------------------------------------------+
9 rows in set (0.00 sec)

mysql> []
```

FIGURE 6.37 Administrator listing of a user's privileges and roles.

An administrator can also see a more comprehensive listing of a user's privileges provided by one or more roles. This approach uses an extended form of the *SHOW GRANTS* that includes a *USING* clause which contains a list of one or more roles. As before, a role may have an optional host or network restriction, and multiple roles are given in a comma-separated list. For each role specified, the privileges provided by that role are included in the output. Figure 6.38 shows how we can obtain a comprehensive listing of privileges for user roberts and the role AllEmployees (the output is edited for readability).

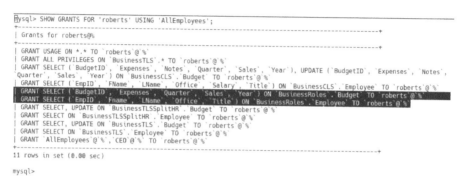

```
mysql> SHOW GRANTS FOR 'roberts' USING 'AllEmployees';
+-----------------------------------------------------------------------------------+
| Grants for roberts@%                                                              |
+-----------------------------------------------------------------------------------+
| GRANT USAGE ON *.* TO `roberts`@`%`                                               |
| GRANT ALL PRIVILEGES ON `BusinessTLS`.* TO `roberts`@`%`                          |
| GRANT SELECT (`BudgetID`, `Expenses`, `Notes`, `Quarter`, `Sales`, `Year`), UPDATE (`BudgetID`, `Expenses`, `Notes`, |
| `Quarter`, `Sales`, `Year`) ON `BusinessCLS`.`Budget` TO `roberts`@`%`            |
| GRANT SELECT (`EmpID`, `FName`, `LName`, `Office`, `Salary`, `Title`) ON `BusinessCLS`.`Employee` TO `roberts`@`%`   |
| GRANT SELECT (`BudgetID`, `Expenses`, `Quarter`, `Sales`, `Year`) ON `BusinessRoles`.`Budget` TO `roberts`@`%`       |
| GRANT SELECT (`EmpID`, `Fname`, `LName`, `Office`, `Title`) ON `BusinessRoles`.`Employee` TO `roberts`@`%`           |
| GRANT SELECT, UPDATE ON `BusinessTLSSplitHR`.`Budget` TO `roberts`@`%`            |
| GRANT SELECT ON `BusinessTLSSplitHR`.`Employee` TO `roberts`@`%`                  |
| GRANT SELECT, UPDATE ON `BusinessTLS`.`Budget` TO `roberts`@`%`                   |
| GRANT SELECT ON `BusinessTLS`.`Employee` TO `roberts`@`%`                         |
| GRANT `AllEmployees`@`%`,`CEO`@`%` TO `roberts`@`%`                               |
+-----------------------------------------------------------------------------------+
11 rows in set (0.00 sec)

mysql>
```

FIGURE 6.38 Showing a user's comprehensive privileges with the Employees role.

Compared to the output in Figure 6.37, we see in addition a listing of indirectly assigned privileges provided by the AllEmployees role to the Employee and Budget tables in the BusinessRoles database. This additional output contains the BusinessRoles database name and is highlighted in Figure 6.38 for emphasis. Namely, in the two highlighted rows, we see *SELECT* privilege for the nonconfidential data in the Employee table as well as for all columns (specified by name) in the Budget table. Notice the indirectly assigned privileges provided in this comprehensive listing is similar to the privilege listing of the AllEmployees role, that was shown in Figure 6.14.

We can obtain other comprehensive privilege listings for a user by specifying another role or multiple roles for that user. For example, to see the privileges for roberts provided by the CEO role, roberts or an administrator can issue the *SHOW GRANTS* statement shown in Figure 6.39. The figure, edited for readability, highlights the privileges provided by the CEO role.

```
mysql> SHOW GRANTS FOR 'roberts' USING 'CEO';
+----------------------------------------------------------------------------------------+
| Grants for roberts@%                                                                   |
+----------------------------------------------------------------------------------------+
| GRANT USAGE ON *.* TO `roberts`@`%`                                                    |
| GRANT ALL PRIVILEGES ON `BusinessTLS`.* TO `roberts`@`%`                               |
| GRANT SELECT (`BudgetID`, `Expenses`, `Notes`, `Quarter`, `Sales`, `Year`), UPDATE (`BudgetID`, `Expenses`, `Notes`, |
| `Quarter`, `Sales`, `Year`) ON `BusinessCLS`.`Budget` TO `roberts`@`%`                 |
| GRANT SELECT (`EmpID`, `FName`, `LName`, `Office`, `Salary`, `Title`) ON `BusinessCLS`.`Employee` TO `roberts`@`%`  |
| GRANT SELECT (`BudgetID`, `Expenses`, `Quarter`, `Sales`, `Year`), UPDATE (`BudgetID`, `Expenses`, `Quarter`, `Sales`, |
| `Year`) ON `BusinessRoles`.`Budget` TO `roberts`@`%`                                   |
| GRANT SELECT, UPDATE ON `BusinessTLSSplitHR`.`Budget` TO `roberts`@`%`                 |
| GRANT SELECT ON `BusinessTLSSplitHR`.`Employee` TO `roberts`@`%`                       |
| GRANT SELECT, UPDATE ON `BusinessTLS`.`Budget` TO `roberts`@`%`                        |
| GRANT SELECT ON `BusinessTLS`.`Employee` TO `roberts`@`%`                              |
| GRANT `AllEmployees`@`%`,`CEO`@`%` TO `roberts`@`%`                                    |
+----------------------------------------------------------------------------------------+
10 rows in set (0.00 sec)

mysql> []
```

FIGURE 6.39 Showing a user's comprehensive privileges with the CEO role.

If we wish to have a fully comprehensive listing of privileges for user roberts and all the roles to which that user belongs (AllEmployees and CEO), we can issue the statement shown in Figure 6.40. The output is edited for readability, and the privileges provided by both roles is highlighted in this figure for emphasis.

```
mysql> SHOW GRANTS FOR 'roberts' USING 'AllEmployees','CEO';
+----------------------------------------------------------------------------------------+
| Grants for roberts@%                                                                   |
+----------------------------------------------------------------------------------------+
| GRANT USAGE ON *.* TO `roberts`@`%`                                                    |
| GRANT ALL PRIVILEGES ON `BusinessTLS`.* TO `roberts`@`%`                               |
| GRANT SELECT (`BudgetID`, `Expenses`, `Notes`, `Quarter`, `Sales`, `Year`), UPDATE (`BudgetID`, `Expenses`, `Notes`, |
| `Quarter`, `Sales`, `Year`) ON `BusinessCLS`.`Budget` TO `roberts`@`%`                 |
| GRANT SELECT (`EmpID`, `FName`, `LName`, `Office`, `Salary`, `Title`) ON `BusinessCLS`.`Employee` TO `roberts`@`%`  |
| GRANT SELECT (`BudgetID`, `Expenses`, `Quarter`, `Sales`, `Year`), UPDATE (`BudgetID`, `Expenses`, `Quarter`, `Sales`, |
| `Year`) ON `BusinessRoles`.`Budget` TO `roberts`@`%`                                   |
| GRANT SELECT (`EmpID`, `Fname`, `LName`, `Office`, `Title`) ON `BusinessRoles`.`Employee` TO `roberts`@`%`          |
| GRANT SELECT, UPDATE ON `BusinessTLSSplitHR`.`Budget` TO `roberts`@`%`                 |
| GRANT SELECT ON `BusinessTLSSplitHR`.`Employee` TO `roberts`@`%`                       |
| GRANT SELECT, UPDATE ON `BusinessTLS`.`Budget` TO `roberts`@`%`                        |
| GRANT SELECT ON `BusinessTLS`.`Employee` TO `roberts`@`%`                              |
| GRANT `AllEmployees`@`%`,`CEO`@`%` TO `roberts`@`%`                                    |
+----------------------------------------------------------------------------------------+
11 rows in set (0.00 sec)

mysql> []
```

FIGURE 6.40 Showing a user's comprehensive privileges and roles.

As with implementing any changes to the configuration of security controls that manage access to data, we should issue various tests and confirm whether the results are as expected. Namely, to evaluate the database security provided by roles, we should verify that a user has their expected data access requirements and nothing more. As examples, we should confirm that in regard to the Employee table, non-human resources employees can access only nonconfidential Employee data, while human resources employees can also access confidential data. And in regards to the Budget table, only the CEO and CFO personnel have read-write access to the Budget data but everyone else has read access (recall we do not have the Notes column in the BusinessRoles.Budget table at this time).

6.5   ROLES AND EVOLUTION

In Chapter 5, we assigned privileges directly to a database user as an effective implementation with a database security control to manage a user's access to data. In this chapter, we used database roles as another effective way to indirectly assign privileges to database users. However, the use of roles requires us to additionally create and assign roles and may appear to involve more work than if we directly assigned privileges. That may be the case at first; however, once established, roles can greatly ease the management of user data access requirements. To observe the differences between both approaches and the benefits that roles can provide, let's consider the following events that may likely happen in practice over the evolution of an organization:

1. A new employee is hired

2. An employee moves from one position to another

3. An employee leaves their position or the organization

A new employee is hired

When a new employee is hired and begins work at a position, we will have to manage the security controls to provide the necessary data access requirements for that user. We may take an approach to assign such privileges directly to the user as we did in Chapter 5. However, as we have seen, we may have to grant a number of privileges and/or specify a number of column names. Not only may this be a tedious and time-consuming task, but with the more steps and detail involved, we increase the possibility of introducing a security vulnerability with confidentiality or integrity by incorrectly including more privileges than needed, or with availability by incorrectly omitting necessary privileges.

Let's consider a new employee that is hired to start in human resources. The new employee, with a username of smalls@localhost, has the same TLS and CLS data access requirements for the other human resources employee chu@localhost, that we defined in Chapter 5. If we create a new user account and directly assign privileges to that user, we would have to issue the following steps:

- create the user account;
- grant *SELECT, UPDATE, INSERT, DELETE* privileges to the Employee table, specifying all columns by name;
- grant *SELECT* privilege to the Budget table, specifying all necessary columns by name.

The statements to carry out these steps are given in Figure 6.41. Notice that we are assigning these direct privileges for the BusinessCLS database, because we are not using roles here. We will use roles and the BusinessRoles database shortly.

```
mysql> CREATE USER 'smalls'@'localhost' IDENTIFIED BY 'passsmalls';
Query OK, 0 rows affected (0.07 sec)

mysql> GRANT INSERT,DELETE ON BusinessCLS.Employee TO 'smalls'@'localhost';
Query OK, 0 rows affected (0.06 sec)

mysql> GRANT SELECT (EmpID,FName,LName,Title,Office,Address,SSN,DOB,Salary),
    ->        UPDATE (EmpID,FName,LName,Title,Office,Address,SSN,DOB,Salary)
    ->        ON BusinessCLS.Employee TO 'smalls'@'localhost';
Query OK, 0 rows affected (0.08 sec)

mysql> GRANT SELECT (BudgetID, Year, Quarter, Sales, Expenses) ON BusinessCLS.Budget TO 'smalls'@'localhost';
Query OK, 0 rows affected (0.09 sec)

mysql> []
```

FIGURE 6.41 Adding a new user and directly assigning privileges.

As you may envision, this task may be time consuming and error prone, especially if we were to have a number of new hires or frequently hire new employees. On the other hand, if we have roles established, after we create the new user's account we only have to add the AllEmployees and HR roles, and then set the default role, as outlined in these steps.

- create the user account;
- add the user to the AllEmployees and HR roles;
- set AllEmployees as the default role.

While the number of steps is the same, the statements and details are fewer and easier compared to if we assign privileges directly. Figure 6.42 shows the statements to carry out those steps with roles.

```
mysql> CREATE USER 'smalls'@'localhost' IDENTIFIED BY 'passsmalls';
Query OK, 0 rows affected (0.09 sec)

mysql> GRANT AllEmployees,HR TO 'smalls'@'localhost';
Query OK, 0 rows affected (0.05 sec)

mysql> SET DEFAULT ROLE 'AllEmployees' TO 'smalls'@'localhost';
Query OK, 0 rows affected (0.08 sec)

mysql> █
```

FIGURE 6.42 Adding a new user and assigning roles.

Now the new human resources user can login and immediately have access according to the AllEmployees role. Should the new user require HR role access, the user can make active the HR role.

An employee adds a role or moves to another role

As other changes that may occur within an organization, an employee may have responsibilities added, in which case the employee takes on another role. Similarly, an employee may change responsibilities altogether and move from one role to another. Let's demonstrate each case with the new user account. We will also focus on management with roles only rather than privileges. Suppose user smalls is to assist with CFO responsibilities and needs the access to do so. We can add the CFO role to the user, as shown in Figure 6.43.

```
mysql> GRANT 'CFO' TO 'smalls'@'localhost';
Query OK, 0 rows affected (0.06 sec)

mysql> []
```

FIGURE 6.43 Adding another role to a user.

The user can show their privileges and roles to see the role added to them. Figure 6.44 illustrates the user showing their updated privileges and roles. This figure suggests the AllEmployees role is active, but if the user were to make the HR or CEO role active, those privileges would also appear.

```
mysql> SHOW GRANTS;
+-----------------------------------------------------------------------------------------+
| Grants for smalls@localhost                                                             |
+-----------------------------------------------------------------------------------------+
| GRANT USAGE ON *.* TO `smalls`@`localhost`                                              |
| GRANT SELECT (`BudgetID`, `Expenses`, `Quarter`, `Sales`, `Year`) ON `BusinessRoles`.`Budget` TO `smalls`@`localhost` |
| GRANT SELECT (`EmpID`, `FName`, `LName`, `Office`, `Title`) ON `BusinessRoles`.`Employee` TO `smalls`@`localhost` |
| GRANT `AllEmployees`@`%`, `CFO`@`%`, `HR`@`%` TO `smalls`@`localhost`                    |
+-----------------------------------------------------------------------------------------+
4 rows in set (0.00 sec)

mysql> []
```

FIGURE 6.44 A user showing their added roles.

If an employee is moving from one role to another, we would follow the addition of the new role with the removal of the former role. The next event describes that process.

An employee leaves a role or the organization

As part of moving from one role to another, having responsibilities reduced, or leaving the organization altogether (offboarded), we may have to remove a user from one or more roles. To remove a user from a role, we use the *REVOKE* statement, in a similar manner as we did to remove a user's privileges.

Suppose user user smalls is moving from the HR to the CFO role. In addition to adding the CFO role to that user, we must remove the user from the HR role, as shown in Figure 6.45.

```
mysql> REVOKE 'HR' FROM 'smalls'@'localhost';
Query OK, 0 rows affected (0.08 sec)

mysql>
```

FIGURE 6.45 Removing a role from a user.

User smalls or the administrator should now see the move of role assignments from HR to CFO complete. The user or administrator can confirm that by reshowing the user's privileges and roles. Figure 6.46 illustrates the administrator showing the user's current privileges and roles.

```
mysql> SHOW GRANTS FOR 'smalls'@'localhost';
+-----------------------------------------------------------------+
| Grants for smalls@localhost                                     |
+-----------------------------------------------------------------+
| GRANT USAGE ON *.* TO `smalls`@`localhost`                      |
| GRANT `AllEmployees`@`%`,`CFO`@`%` TO `smalls`@`localhost`      |
+-----------------------------------------------------------------+
2 rows in set (0.00 sec)

mysql>
```

FIGURE 6.46 Administrator showing a user's changed roles.

Organizations will have different procedures regarding employee offboarding. For example, an organization's policy for employee offboarding may involve simply disabling the employee's account(s), or may instead or additionally involve removal of roles or privileges from the employee account(s).

To remove the user from all roles and privileges, or certain roles or privileges, we can use *REVOKE* statements like the one in Figure 6.44. In order to ensure applicable privileges and roles are removed, the administrator should list the user's privileges and roles to see those that are assigned and revoke them. The administrator should list the user's privileges and roles to confirm the applicable ones have been removed.

Should we actually want to remove a database user account and/or a role, we can do so with the *DROP* statement. We described in Chapter 4 how to remove a database user's account in this manner. Removing a database user account also removes any privileges and role that were assigned to that account. Care should be taken when removing a database user and/or a role, because data that was managed by that user or role may require a certain set of privileges. And removing the account and/or role may complicate or introduce challenges with accessing that data in the future.

6.6   SUMMARY

In this chapter, we looked at the use of roles to manage a large number of users more easily and efficiently. We also described and demonstrated a number of concerns that may affect the security that we want especially in an evolving environment. We also described the principle of least privilege and put it to use to help mitigate those concerns. In the next chapter we continue with various security mechanisms that can provide confidentiality for user accounts and data.

7

DATABASE SECURITY CONTROLS FOR CONFIDENTIALITY

So far, we have covered a range of database security controls and measures, including database design and the use of database users, roles, and privileges. In addition to those security controls and measures, we have other mechanisms that we can employ to provide a greater degree of security to a database and its data. In this chapter, we explore a variety of these mechanisms.

7.1 VIEWS

In many situations, we may want to allow or deny access to certain data for viewing, insert, modification, or delete purposes. By doing so, we can impose additional data allowances or restrictions to specify what data a user may see or access for a given database operation. The concept of a *database view* is a flexible way to implement this concept.

Concept of a view

While the idea of a database view to allow or deny a user's ability to access data by table, column, or row may seem similar to that of table-level, column-level, and/or row-level privileges, database views also provide additional features. First, a database view can additionally process data into an aggregated form that we can present to the user, rather than present the raw data itself.

By hiding the raw data in this manner, a view can provide confidentiality or anonymity of an individual associated with a particular data value.

To illustrate this idea, consider a case example for a class of students that take an exam, and afterwards each student receives their own exam score. The instructor then wishes to share information about all exam scores to all those students. Of course, if the instructor were to release a list of scores and names associated with each score, a student would know the grade of another student. But even if the instructor withholds the names and releases only a list of exam scores, we still have a risk of compromising confidentiality or anonymity because a student may still be able to derive the score of another student. To see how, suppose two rival students often have the highest scores and wish to keep their scores confidential from each other. One of these students obtains a 99 out of 100, and the other obtains a 91. Even if only scores were shared to all students, the student that received the score of 99 could infer the other student obtained a score of 91, and the student that received the 91 could infer the other student obtained a 99. Instead, if the instructor were to aggregate the scores and release only the average or median score, then one could not infer the score of the other (that is, provided there are three or more students that took the exam). Thus, confidentiality of scores and anonymity of who is associated with a particular score is upheld.

As another case example, consider a medical patient data scenario that includes social security number (SSN), first name, last name, date of birth, weight, height, blood pressure, cholesterol level, and COVID vaccination status of fully vaccinated, partially vaccinated, or unvaccinated. Even without SSN and names included in the data, a release of that data in raw form may still allow one to associate an individual as one of those patients. For example, if one knows a person who has the same date of birth, weight, and height as that of one of the patients in that data, one might infer that person has the blood pressure, cholesterol level, and vaccination status of that patient. As a result, we have a potential compromise to the anonymity of the patient to whom the data belongs, as well as the confidentiality of the patient's protected health information or personal health information. On the other hand, if we were to portray only information about COVID vaccinations among patient age groups, we could create a view that portrays the percentages of fully vaccinated, partially vaccinated, and unvaccinated patients within the defined age groups.

In these and similar cases, we can specify that a database view will portray a sum, average, count, or other aggregate calculation of the data, and not the actual raw data values. Thus, confidentiality and anonymity are maintained.

Such a distinction between portraying the data values in raw form or a processed form is not possible with only the use of database table-, column-, and/or row-level privileges.

To demonstrate the security risks and to demonstrate the solutions we can provide with views in our medical patient data scenario, suppose we have the data to a set of patients as shown in Figure 7.1.

PatientId	SSN	FName	LName	Address	DOB	Height	Weight	Systolic	Diastolic	Cholesterol	VaccinationStatus
P01	000-102-4045	Bob	Smith	344 Maple Ave	1960-04-02	74	230	130	82	280	Full
P02	000-302-5045	Sally	Smith	344 Maple Ave	1962-05-05	68	150	124	80	245	Full
P03	000-455-6301	Sonny	Garcia	77 Circle Rd	1980-10-14	69	170	122	82	270	Full
P04	000-776-5785	Helen	Garcia	77 Circle Rd	1980-09-02	63	135	120	76	265	Full
P05	000-341-6021	Manny	Garcia	77 Circle Rd	2006-04-02	63	125	116	72	210	Full
P06	000-877-0812	Steve	Redmond	3212 Oak Ave	1978-12-02	72	210	130	78	240	None
P07	000-609-2311	Alice	Redmond	3212 Oak Ave	1979-02-24	67	155	122	76	214	Full
P08	000-452-7885	Joseph	Redmond	3212 Oak Ave	2007-04-19	65	140	112	72	205	None
P09	000-890-1201	Camille	Redmond	3212 Oak Ave	2009-06-02	62	108	120	72	215	Full
P10	000-122-9242	Barbara	Chow	421 Liberty Ave	1984-07-12	56	135	122	80	190	Full
P11	000-605-4877	Sammy	Chow	421 Liberty Ave	2008-11-09	63	120	115	72	180	Partial
P12	000-803-4732	Sandra	Chow	421 Liberty Ave	2015-01-24	61	98	110	70	180	Unknown
P13	000-554-3345	Janet	Cruz	781 Spring Ave	1995-04-02	66	130	108	68	175	Full
P14	000-784-4300	Perry	Dobson	123 Rockford Ct	1998-04-02	70	185	120	80	210	Unknown
P15	000-677-8091	Elise	Zuzka	990 East Main	1987-05-01	62	115	116	82	225	Full

FIGURE 7.1 Patient data for our medical case study.

As you may already notice, Figure 7.1 contains quite a bit of personal and medical information. Such information is considered personally identifiable information (PII) as well as protected or personal health information (PHI). Both types of information should have limited access to preserve their confidentiality. There are a number of security solutions that we can implement to limit access of that information to only that required for a particular task. For example, based on the actual need, we may process and portray data related to only blood pressure, cholesterol levels, and/or vaccination status and keep the remainder of the data confidential. We can also consider whether we want to process and portray information about a collection of data, say for all ages, or only within certain age groups. Let's begin with the latter scenario and suppose that we want to permit processing and portrayal of data for only adult patients (18 years of age or older) or for only minor patients (below 18 years of age).

Creating a view

To allow processing and portrayal of only the data for adult patients, we can create a view that allows a database user to only see or access Patient table rows that correspond to an age of 18 years or older. If we want to allow access to all of the columns of the Patient table but only for those certain rows, we can define a view like that given in Figure 7.2. In Figure 7.2, we use the *CREATE VIEW* statement, followed by the name to use for that view, the *AS* keyword, and finally the SQL statement that specifies what data the view is to access and contain. In our case, we are specifying all columns for the rows that have a calculated age of 18 or greater. Also notice that we first choose the MedicalCaseStudy database, which has a Patient table that contains the data in Figure 7.1.

```
mysql> USE MedicalCaseStudy;
Database changed
mysql> CREATE VIEW PatientAdult AS
    -> SELECT * FROM Patient WHERE timestampdiff(YEAR,DOB,CURDATE()) >= 18;
Query OK, 0 rows affected (0.18 sec)

mysql> []
```

FIGURE 7.2 Creating a database view to access only rows of adult patients.

We can show all of the data allowed by the view by issuing the *SELECT* statement given in Figure 7.3. Here, we are issuing this statement as the root or database administrator user (we will soon explain what is needed to allow a view to be used by a nonadministrative user). Note that we simply provide the name of the defined view rather than the name of the table from which the data is derived.

```
 File   Edit   View   Bookmarks   Settings   Help
mysql> SELECT * FROM PatientAdult;
+-----------+---------------+-----------+----------+--------------+--------+--------+----------------+----------+-----------+
| PatientID | SSN           | FName     | LName    | DOB          | Height | Weight | Address        | Systolic | Diastolic |
| Cholesterol | VaccinationStatus |
+-----------+---------------+-----------+----------+--------------+--------+--------+----------------+----------+-----------+
| P01       | 000-102-4045  | Bob       | Smith    | 1960-04-02   |   74   |  230   | 344 Maple Ave  |   130    |    82     |
|       280 | Full          |
| P02       | 000-302-5045  | Sally     | Smith    | 1962-05-05   |   68   |  150   | 344 Maple Ave  |   124    |    80     |
|       245 | Full          |
| P03       | 000-455-6301  | Sonny     | Garcia   | 1980-10-14   |   69   |  170   | 77 Circle Rd   |   122    |    82     |
|       270 | Full          |
| P04       | 000-776-5785  | Helen     | Garcia   | 1980-09-02   |   63   |  135   | 77 Circle Rd   |   120    |    76     |
|       265 | Full          |
| P06       | 000-877-0812  | Steve     | Redmond  | 1978-12-02   |   72   |  210   | 3212 Oak Ave   |   130    |    78     |
|       240 | None          |
| P07       | 000-609-2311  | Alice     | Redmond  | 1979-02-24   |   67   |  155   | 3212 Oak Ave   |   122    |    76     |
|       214 | Full          |
| P10       | 000-122-9242  | Barbara   | Chow     | 1984-07-12   |   56   |  135   | 4212 Libery Ave |  122    |    80     |
|       190 | Full          |
| P13       | 000-554-3345  | Janet     | Cruz     | 1995-04-02   |   66   |  130   | 781 Spring Ave |   108    |    68     |
|       175 | Full          |
| P14       | 000-784-4300  | Perry     | Dobson   | 1998-04-02   |   70   |  185   | 123 Rockford Ct |  120    |    80     |
|       210 | Unknown       |
| P15       | 000-677-8091  | Elise     | Zuzka    | 1987-05-01   |   62   |  115   | 990 East Main  |   116    |    82     |
|       225 | Full          |
+-----------+---------------+-----------+----------+--------------+--------+--------+----------------+----------+-----------+
10 rows in set (0.00 sec)

mysql> []
```

FIGURE 7.3 Using the PatientAdult view to show only rows of adult patients.

The general syntax to create a view is given in Figure 7.4. By default, a view shows the columns specified in the *SELECT* list with column names that are the same as those in the table. On the other hand, if we want the view to show alternative column names for the table columns, we can specify after the view name an optional list of column names that are to be presented in the view. Such column renaming can be helpful if we want to represent a column's value or values with a certain context or more accurate description of the data. We demonstrate this later then we process the data in a column, and the data in the result of the processing has a different context than that of the original column name.

```
CREATE [OR REPLACE] VIEW view_name [(column_list)]
AS select_statement;
```

FIGURE 7.4 General syntax to create a database view.

Showing a list of views and a view definition

To see the actual definition of a view, we can issue the *SHOW CREATE* statement, as demonstrated in Figure 7.5 for the PatientAdult view. Figure 7.5 is edited for brevity, and your actual output may contain other lines or information than that portrayed here.

```
mysql> SHOW CREATE VIEW PatientAdult;

| PatientAdult | CREATE VIEW `PatientAdult` AS select `Patient`.`PatientID` AS `PatientID`,`Patient`.`SSN` AS `SSN`,`Pati
ent`.`FName` AS `FName`,`Patient`.`LName` AS `LName`,`Patient`.`DOB` AS `DOB`,`Patient`.`Height` AS `Height`,`Patient`.`W
eight` AS `Weight`,`Patient`.`Address` AS `Address`,`Patient`.`Systolic` AS `Systolic`,`Patient`.`Diastolic` AS `Diastoli
c`,`Patient`.`Cholesterol` AS `Cholesterol`,`Patient`.`VaccinationStatus` AS `VaccinationStatus` from `Patient` where (ti
mestampdiff(YEAR,`Patient`.`DOB`,curdate()) >= 18)

1 row in set (0.00 sec)

mysql> []
```

FIGURE 7.5 Showing a database view definition.

If we want to obtain a list of views by name, there are two general approaches. The first approach is to see only a list of names to defined views (and not of tables) for the currently selected database. In Figure 7.6, we issue a *SHOW FULL TABLES* statement to do just that. Note the where clause limits the result to contain only views.

```
mysql> SHOW FULL TABLES WHERE table_type = 'VIEW';
+-----------------------------+-------------+
| Tables_in_MedicalCaseStudy  | Table_type  |
+-----------------------------+-------------+
| PatientAdult                | VIEW        |
+-----------------------------+-------------+
1 row in set (0.00 sec)

mysql> []
```

FIGURE 7.6 Showing a list of views in the current database.

The second approach to list the names of views is to use the familiar SQL command that shows a list of names to tables in the current database, as shown in Figure 7.7. The resulting list contains the names of views as well as tables in the current database.

```
mysql> SHOW TABLES;
+---------------------------+
| Tables_in_MedicalCaseStudy |
+---------------------------+
| Patient                    |
| PatientAdult               |
+---------------------------+
2 rows in set (0.01 sec)

mysql> []
```

FIGURE 7.7 Showing a list of views and tables in the current database.

Accessing the data of a view

You may wonder why views are listed with tables in Figure 7.7. The reason is that in a relational database system, both tables and views both have the properties of a relation and technically are relations. With that idea in mind, we can access a view in the same manner as we can a table. We can even assign or restrict user and role privileges to a view, just as we can for a table! To demonstrate the assignment of a privilege to a view, in Figure 7.8 we create a new user 'sally'@'localhost' and then assign sally only the ability to issue a *SELECT* operation that can retrieve data in the PatientAdult view.

```
mysql> CREATE USER 'sally'@'localhost' IDENTIFIED BY 'passsally';
Query OK, 0 rows affected (0.10 sec)

mysql> GRANT SELECT ON PatientAdult to 'sally'@'localhost';
Query OK, 0 rows affected (0.11 sec)

mysql> []
```

FIGURE 7.8 Creating a new database user and assigning a privilege to access a view.

Now user sally can log into the DBMS locally, and retrieve data from the PatientAdult view, as demonstrated in Figure 7.9.

```
mysql> USE MedicalCaseStudy;
Reading table information for completion of table and column names
You can turn off this feature to get a quicker startup with -A

Database changed
mysql> SELECT * FROM PatientAdult;
+-----------+--------------+---------+----------+------------+--------+--------+------------------+----------+-----------+
-----------+-------------------+
| PatientID | SSN          | FName   | LName    | DOB        | Height | Weight | Address          | Systolic | Diastolic |
Cholesterol | VaccinationStatus |
+-----------+--------------+---------+----------+------------+--------+--------+------------------+----------+-----------+
-----------+-------------------+
| P01       | 000-102-4045 | Bob     | Smith    | 1960-04-02 |   74   |   230  | 344 Maple Ave    |   130    |    82     |
        280 | Full              |
| P02       | 000-302-5045 | Sally   | Smith    | 1962-05-05 |   68   |   150  | 344 Maple Ave    |   124    |    80     |
        245 | Full              |
| P03       | 000-455-6301 | Sonny   | Garcia   | 1980-10-14 |   69   |   170  | 77 Circle Rd     |   122    |    82     |
        270 | Full              |
| P04       | 000-776-5785 | Helen   | Garcia   | 1980-09-02 |   63   |   135  | 77 Circle Rd     |   120    |    76     |
        265 | Full              |
| P06       | 000-877-0812 | Steve   | Redmond  | 1978-12-02 |   72   |   210  | 3212 Oak Ave     |   130    |    78     |
        240 | None              |
| P07       | 000-609-2311 | Alice   | Redmond  | 1979-02-24 |   67   |   155  | 3212 Oak Ave     |   122    |    76     |
        214 | Full              |
| P10       | 000-122-9242 | Barbara | Chow     | 1984-07-12 |   56   |   135  | 4212 Libery Ave  |   122    |    80     |
        190 | Full              |
| P13       | 000-554-3345 | Janet   | Cruz     | 1995-04-02 |   66   |   130  | 781 Spring Ave   |   108    |    68     |
        175 | Full              |
| P14       | 000-784-4300 | Perry   | Dobson   | 1998-04-02 |   70   |   185  | 123 Rockford Ct  |   120    |    80     |
        210 | Unknown           |
| P15       | 000-677-8091 | Elise   | Zuzka    | 1987-05-01 |   62   |   115  | 990 East Main    |   116    |    82     |
        225 | Full              |
+-----------+--------------+---------+----------+------------+--------+--------+------------------+----------+-----------+
-----------+-------------------+
10 rows in set (0.00 sec)

mysql> []
```

FIGURE 7.9 Demonstration of allowed privileges with a view.

However, sally has no other privileges for other operations such changing, adding, or removing data. Figure 7.10 illustrates the restriction of those types of accesses to the data provided by the view.

```
mysql> UPDATE PatientAdult SET VaccinationStatus='None' WHERE PatientID = 'P15';
ERROR 1142 (42000): UPDATE command denied to user 'sally'@'localhost' for table 'PatientAdult'
mysql> DELETE FROM PatientAdult WHERE PatientID = 'P15';
ERROR 1142 (42000): DELETE command denied to user 'sally'@'localhost' for table 'PatientAdult'
mysql> INSERT INTO PatientAdult VALUES ('P16','000-000-0000','Bobby','Tappert','1984-02-06',56,150,'123 Main',120,80,210,
'Unknown');
ERROR 1064 (42000): You have an error in your SQL syntax; check the manual that corresponds to your MySQL server version
for the right syntax to use near 'Main',120,80,210,'Unknown')' at line 1
mysql> []
```

FIGURE 7.10 Demonstration of restricted privileges with a view.

Also note that while user sally has restricted access to the data provided by the PatientAdult view, sally has no access whatsoever to the Patient table and its data, maintaining security of that data through confidentiality. Figure 7.11 shows an attempt by sally to retrieve data from the Patient table. Other operations to add, change, or delete data are similarly denied.

```
mysql> SELECT * FROM Patient;
ERROR 1142 (42000): SELECT command denied to user 'sally'@'localhost' for table 'Patient'
mysql> []
```

FIGURE 7.11 Demonstration of disallowed access to a view's table.

Security considerations of a view

Before we proceed with defining a similar view to process and portray only patient data for those under the age of 18, let's consider a possible security concern with our PatientAdult view that was just created. The security concern involves the use of the * wildcard in the *SELECT* list, which gives the view access to all columns in the table. Even though we may want to allow a view to have access to all columns, as in this case, we should still specify in the *SELECT* list all of the columns by their names instead. By doing so we can avoid the risk of compromising confidentiality that inadvertently allows access to newly added columns that actually should be inaccessible to the view.

To demonstrate this security concern, suppose that after we received the requirements for the adult and minor patient views, a new column is added to the Patient table. Let's say this column is named nInfections and maintains a count of the number of COVID infections for a patient. However, this number of infections is *not* to be processed or portrayed by the PatientAdult or soon-to-be created PatientMinor views. Because we created the PatientAdult view before we add the new column, we specified the * wildcard with the belief that all those columns in the Patient table (at least, at that time), are to be accessible by the view. But if we were to create a view with the * wildcard *after* the new column is added, the new view will contain the new column that we really want to keep confidential. To illustrate this concern, let's say that a database administrator adds the nInfections column with the statement given in Figure 7.12.

```
mysql> ALTER TABLE Patient ADD nInfections INT;
Query OK, 0 rows affected (0.81 sec)
Records: 0  Duplicates: 0  Warnings: 0

mysql>
```

FIGURE 7.12 Adding a new column to the Patient table.

Afterwards, the (possibly other) user that is creating the views defines the view for patients under the age of 18—that is, for minor patients—as given in Figure 7.13.

```
mysql> CREATE VIEW PatientMinor AS
    -> SELECT * FROM Patient WHERE TIMESTAMPDIFF(YEAR,DOB,CURDATE()) < 18;
Query OK, 0 rows affected (0.16 sec)

mysql> []
```

FIGURE 7.13 Creating a database view to access only rows of minor patients.

Running both views that we now have, we see that the view created before the column is added does not contain the new column, which is what we want, but the view created afterwards does. Figure 7.14 shows the data portrayed by the PatientAdult view. Notice the absence of the nInfections column with the PatientAdult view.

```
mysql> SELECT * FROM PatientAdult;
+-----------+--------------+--------+---------+------------+--------+--------+----------------+----------+-----------+-
-----------+------------------+
| PatientID | SSN          | FName  | LName   | DOB        | Height | Weight | Address        | Systolic | Diastolic |
Cholesterol | VaccinationStatus |
+-----------+--------------+--------+---------+------------+--------+--------+----------------+----------+-----------+-
-----------+------------------+
| P01       | 000-102-4045 | Bob    | Smith   | 1960-04-02 |   74 |    230 | 344 Maple Ave  |    130 |      82 |
       280 | Full             |
| P02       | 000-302-5045 | Sally  | Smith   | 1962-05-05 |   68 |    150 | 344 Maple Ave  |    124 |      80 |
       245 | Full             |
| P03       | 000-455-6301 | Sonny  | Garcia  | 1980-10-14 |   69 |    170 | 77 Circle Rd   |    122 |      82 |
       270 | Full             |
| P04       | 000-776-5785 | Helen  | Garcia  | 1980-09-02 |   63 |    135 | 77 Circle Rd   |    120 |      76 |
       265 | Full             |
| P06       | 000-877-0812 | Steve  | Redmond | 1978-12-02 |   72 |    210 | 3212 Oak Ave   |    130 |      78 |
       240 | None             |
| P07       | 000-609-2311 | Alice  | Redmond | 1979-02-24 |   67 |    155 | 3212 Oak Ave   |    122 |      76 |
       214 | Full             |
| P10       | 000-122-9242 | Barbara| Chow    | 1984-07-12 |   56 |    135 | 4212 Libery Ave |   122 |      80 |
       190 | Full             |
| P13       | 000-554-3345 | Janet  | Cruz    | 1995-04-02 |   66 |    130 | 781 Spring Ave |    108 |      68 |
       175 | Full             |
| P14       | 000-784-4300 | Perry  | Dobson  | 1998-04-02 |   70 |    185 | 123 Rockford Ct |   120 |      80 |
       210 | Unknown          |
| P15       | 000-677-8091 | Elise  | Zuzka   | 1987-05-01 |   62 |    115 | 990 East Main  |    116 |      82 |
       225 | Full             |
+-----------+--------------+--------+---------+------------+--------+--------+----------------+----------+-----------+-
-----------+------------------+
10 rows in set (0.00 sec)

mysql> []
```

FIGURE 7.14 The data of the PatientAdult view after adding a new column.

Similarly, Figure 7.15 shows the data portrayed by the PatientMinor view. Notice the inclusion of the nInfections column.

```
mysql> SELECT * FROM PatientMinor;
+-----------+-------------+----------+----------+------------+--------+--------+----------------+----------+-----------+-
------------+-------------------+-------------+
| PatientID | SSN         | FName    | LName    | DOB        | Height | Weight | Address        | Systolic | Diastolic |
Cholesterol | VaccinationStatus | nInfections |
+-----------+-------------+----------+----------+------------+--------+--------+----------------+----------+-----------+-
------------+-------------------+-------------+
| P05       | 000-341-6021| Manny    | Garcia   | 2006-04-02 |    63  |   125  | 77 Circle Rd   |    116   |     72    |
        210 | Full              |    NULL     |
| P08       | 000-452-7885| Joseph   | Redmond  | 2007-04-19 |    65  |   140  | 3212 Oak Ave   |    112   |     72    |
        205 | None              |    NULL     |
| P09       | 000-898-1201| Camille  | Redmond  | 2009-06-02 |    62  |   108  | 3212 Oak Ave   |    120   |     72    |
        215 | Full              |    NULL     |
| P11       | 000-605-4877| Sammy    | Chow     | 2008-11-09 |    63  |   120  | 4212 Libery Ave|    115   |     72    |
        180 | Partial           |    NULL     |
| P12       | 000-803-4732| Sandra   | Chow     | 2015-01-24 |    61  |    98  | 4212 Libery Ave|    110   |     70    |
        180 | Unknown           |    NULL     |
+-----------+-------------+----------+----------+------------+--------+--------+----------------+----------+-----------+-
------------+-------------------+-------------+
5 rows in set (0.00 sec)

mysql> ▯
```

FIGURE 7.15 The data of the PatientMinor view after adding a new column.

We can also illustrate the inadvertent inclusion of the nInfections column with the PatientMinor view by showing its view definition. Figure 7.16 shows the PatientMinor view definition, with the output edited for brevity.

```
mysql> SHOW CREATE VIEW PatientMinor;

| PatientMinor | CREATE VIEW `PatientMinor` AS select `Patient`.`PatientID` AS `PatientID`,`Patient`.`SSN` AS `SSN`,`Pati
ent`.`FName` AS `FName`,`Patient`.`LName` AS `LName`,`Patient`.`DOB` AS `DOB`,`Patient`.`Height` AS `Height`,`Patient`.`W
eight` AS `Weight`,`Patient`.`Address` AS `Address`,`Patient`.`Systolic` AS `Systolic`,`Patient`.`Diastolic` AS `Diastoli
c`,`Patient`.`Cholesterol` AS `Cholesterol`,`Patient`.`VaccinationStatus` AS `VaccinationStatus`,`Patient`.`nInfections`
AS `nInfections` from `Patient` where (timestampdiff(YEAR,`Patient`.`DOB`,curdate()) < 18)

1 row in set (0.00 sec)

mysql> ▯
```

FIGURE 7.16 Showing the definition of the PatientMinor view.

Consequently, by creating a view with the * column wildcard, we run the risk of compromising the confidentiality of newly added columns, as well as having an inconsistent access of data by similar views (that is, one view accessing one set of columns and the other view accessing another set).

As another reason to avoid the use of the * wildcard when defining the columns to be accessible in a view, consider that we create another security vulnerability—this time with availability—if any columns are later removed that were originally included by the * wildcard. In particular, when a view is defined with a * column wildcard, the names of all of the columns are implicitly added to the view. If a column is later removed from the table and the view is accessed, the view will attempt to access the removed column, which generates a failure and lack of availability to the contents of the view.

To illustrate this introduced vulnerability of availability, in Figure 7.17 we drop the nInfections column, and then (unsuccessfully) attempt to access the contents of the PatientMinor view. Note, however, that the PatientAdult view is not affected by the removal of that particular column because PatientAdult was created before the nInfections column existed. But if we were to drop a column that is part of the PatientAdult view definition, we will introduce a similar vulnerability of availability for that view.

```
mysql> ALTER TABLE Patient DROP nInfections;
Query OK, 0 rows affected (1.88 sec)
Records: 0  Duplicates: 0  Warnings: 0

mysql> SELECT * FROM PatientMinor;
ERROR 1356 (HY000): View 'MedicalCaseStudy.PatientMinor' references invalid table(s) or column(s) or function(s) or defin
er/invoker of view lack rights to use them
mysql> ▯
```

FIGURE 7.17 Removing a column and compromising view availability.

In both cases, if we were to have initially defined the views with explicit column lists rather than column wildcards, then we can avoid such issues. In the first case, we could later add columns to the table without creating a security vulnerability of compromising their confidentiality when those columns are not to be accessible by the views. In the second case, if we were to drop a column that was not in the column list for the view, then we will also not risk availability when accessing that view.

As another example of the security vulnerabilities that can be introduced by defining a view with a * wildcard, suppose we now need to keep data about patient revaccinations and add a column for that purpose in the Patient table. We then create a view to access all the other Patient table columns (not the revaccination data) for patients 65 years of age or older, but happen to specify a * column wildcard. As before, we introduce a security vulnerability of confidentiality by allowing inadvertent access to the revaccination data. On top of that, we then change our decision about keeping revaccination data and later remove that column. Now when that view is accessed, it will attempt to access all of the Patient columns that existed at the time the view was created. Because the revaccination data column existed at the time that view was created, that column is part of the view. However, because that column no longer exists, the view is incomplete, causing an error within the DBMS system. In Figure 7.18, we add a RevaccinationStatus column to the Patient table and create a new view of all Patient columns with the * wildcard. We then remove the RevaccinationStatus column and access the view, which in turn accesses the removed column and generates an error. We then remove the now incomplete view.

```
mysql> ALTER TABLE Patient ADD RevaccinationStatus ENUM ('Yes','No','Unknown');
Query OK, 0 rows affected (0.81 sec)
Records: 0  Duplicates: 0  Warnings: 0

mysql> CREATE VIEW PatientSenior AS
    -> SELECT * FROM Patient WHERE TIMESTAMPDIFF(YEAR,DOB,CURDATE()) >= 65;
Query OK, 0 rows affected (0.14 sec)

mysql> ALTER TABLE Patient DROP RevaccinationStatus;
Query OK, 0 rows affected (1.56 sec)
Records: 0  Duplicates: 0  Warnings: 0

mysql> SELECT * FROM PatientSenior;
ERROR 1356 (HY000): View 'MedicalCaseStudy.PatientSenior' references invalid table(s) or column(s) or function(s) or defi
ner/invoker of view lack rights to use them
mysql> []
```

FIGURE 7.18 An Introduced security vulnerability involving availability.

Deleting and redefining views

To show the proper way to define these views and to demonstrate how they mitigate the risks we mentioned, let's define the PatientAdult and PatientMinor views with a list of specific column names. Because we already have views defined with those names, we can either delete the views and then recreate them or replace an existing view with a new definition. Let's describe both approaches, starting with deleting and recreating the views. To delete or drop the views, we can use the *DROP VIEW* statements given in Figure 7.19. For security measures, we should also consider dropping the PatientSenior view to prevent any future access potential, even though it currently fails.

```
mysql> DROP VIEW PatientAdult;
Query OK, 0 rows affected (0.13 sec)

mysql> DROP VIEW PatientMinor;
Query OK, 0 rows affected (0.15 sec)

mysql> []
```

FIGURE 7.19 Deleting views.

We can then properly define the views with the original view names like before, but this time to have a higher degree of security by specifying a list of allowed columns by name, as given in Figure 7.20.

```
mysql> CREATE VIEW PatientAdult AS
    -> SELECT PatientId, SSN, FName, LName, DOB, Height, Weight, Address, Systolic, Diastolic, Cholesterol, VaccinationSt
atus
    -> FROM Patient
    -> WHERE TIMESTAMPDIFF(YEAR,DOB,CURDATE()) >= 18;
Query OK, 0 rows affected (0.18 sec)

mysql> CREATE VIEW PatientMinor AS
    -> SELECT PatientId, SSN, FName, LName, DOB, Height, Weight, Address, Systolic, Diastolic, Cholesterol, VaccinationSt
atus
    -> FROM Patient
    -> WHERE TIMESTAMPDIFF(YEAR,DOB,CURDATE()) < 18;
Query OK, 0 rows affected (0.14 sec)

mysql> []
```

FIGURE 7.20 Properly defining views with a column name list.

Alternatively, we can also redefine an existing view without first deleting the view by using a variation of the *CREATE VIEW* statement, as shown in Figure 7.21. Here we use the *CREATE OR REPLACE VIEW* statement, to replace the existing definition of the PatientAdult and PatientMinor views with the definition that follows. When using this statement, if a view does not already exist with that name, the statement effectively creates a view with that name and definition.

```
mysql> CREATE OR REPLACE VIEW PatientAdult AS
    -> SELECT PatientId, SSN, FName, LName, DOB, Height, Weight, Address, Systolic, Diastolic, Cholesterol, VaccinationSt
atus
    -> FROM Patient
    -> WHERE TIMESTAMPDIFF(YEAR,DOB,CURDATE()) >= 18;
Query OK, 0 rows affected (0.15 sec)

mysql> CREATE OR REPLACE VIEW PatientMinor AS
    -> SELECT PatientId, SSN, FName, LName, DOB, Height, Weight, Address, Systolic, Diastolic, Cholesterol, VaccinationSt
atus
    -> FROM Patient
    -> WHERE TIMESTAMPDIFF(YEAR,DOB,CURDATE()) < 18;
Query OK, 0 rows affected (0.17 sec)

mysql> []
```

FIGURE 7.21 Replacing an existing view's definition.

You will now notice that neither view specifies the nInfections column. Thus, the nInfections data is not accessible with these views, maintaining confidentiality of that data if the column were to be later added to the Patient table. Figure 7.22 repeats the demonstration of adding the nInfections column and showing the data of those views, but now both views do not include the nInfections column and thus maintains that confidentiality. For brevity, the statements that access both views retrieve only one row and the result edited.

```
mysql> SELECT * FROM PatientAdult WHERE PatientId = 'P01';
| PatientId | SSN        | FName | LName | DOB        | Height | Weight | Address      | Systolic | Diastolic | Choles
terol | VaccinationStatus |
+-----------+------------+-------+-------+------------+--------+--------+--------------+----------+-----------+-------
------+-------------------+
| P01       | 000-102-4045 | Bob   | Smith | 1960-04-02 |     74 |    230 | 344 Maple Ave |      130 |        82 |
  280 | Full              |
1 row in set (0.00 sec)

mysql> SELECT * FROM PatientMinor WHERE PatientId = 'P05';
| PatientId | SSN        | FName | LName  | DOB        | Height | Weight | Address     | Systolic | Diastolic | Choles
terol | VaccinationStatus |
+-----------+------------+-------+--------+------------+--------+--------+-------------+----------+-----------+-------
------+-------------------+
| P05       | 000-341-6021 | Manny | Garcia | 2006-04-02 |     63 |    125 | 77 Circle Rd |      116 |        72 |
  210 | Full              |
1 row in set (0.00 sec)

mysql> []
```

FIGURE 7.22 Adding a column and maintaining its confidentiality.

Furthermore, if there is a future data change that involves removing the nInfections column, we can now safely remove that column without adversely affecting the functionality of our two views, as shown in Figure 7.23. For brevity, we likewise retrieve only one row in Figure 7.23 and edit the resulting output to remove extra lines.

```
mysql> SELECT * FROM PatientAdult WHERE PatientId = 'P01';
| PatientId | SSN        | FName | LName | DOB        | Height | Weight | Address      | Systolic | Diastolic | Choles
terol | VaccinationStatus |
+-----------+------------+-------+-------+------------+--------+--------+--------------+----------+-----------+-------
------+-------------------+
| P01       | 000-102-4045 | Bob   | Smith | 1960-04-02 |     74 |    230 | 344 Maple Ave |      130 |        82 |
  280 | Full              |
1 row in set (0.00 sec)

mysql> SELECT * FROM PatientMinor WHERE PatientId = 'P05';
| PatientId | SSN        | FName | LName  | DOB        | Height | Weight | Address     | Systolic | Diastolic | Choles
terol | VaccinationStatus |
+-----------+------------+-------+--------+------------+--------+--------+-------------+----------+-----------+-------
------+-------------------+
| P05       | 000-341-6021 | Manny | Garcia | 2006-04-02 |     63 |    125 | 77 Circle Rd |      116 |        72 |
  210 | Full              |
1 row in set (0.00 sec)

mysql> []
```

FIGURE 7.23 Removing a column and maintaining view availability.

Consequently, even though specifying columns by name rather than wildcard when defining a view may be tedious and increase the length of the defining SQL statement, we must keep in mind the risk of compromising the principle of least privilege that occurs when using a wildcard for all columns. Recall that we encountered a similar concern when defining access to all table columns with column-level privileges in Chapter 6.

Views and multiple data access requirements

As another example of limiting data access with views, let's consider a situation where we may have multiple access requirements for the same data. Suppose that we want a user to access only certain patient data, such as first and last name, but not their vaccination status, in order to keep a certain patient's vaccination status confidential to the user. In addition, suppose that we do want to allow that user to have access to the percentage of patients that are fully vaccinated but not other PII or PHI. In other words, we do not want the user to have direct access to the VaccinationStatus column, but the user will have to be able to access the VaccinationStatus column somehow to obtain the percentage of fully vaccinated patients. If we were to consider database column-level privileges for this situation, we could satisfy one requirement but deny the other. More specifically, we would either deny access to the VaccinationStatus column (which would fulfill the first data access requirement but not the second) or allow access to the VaccinationStatus column (which would fulfill the second data access requirement but not the first). However, with the use of database views, we can fulfill both data access requirements!

To accomplish both data access requirements, we will define two views: one that provides the first requirement and another that provides the second. The first view will allow access to the patient FName and LName only. The second view will access the VaccinationStatus column to calculate the percentage of patients that are fully vaccinated. Figure 7.24 shows how these two views may be created. Notice that we define the FullVaccinatedPercentage view to show the result with a descriptive column name of PercentageFullyVaccinated.

```
mysql> CREATE VIEW PatientNames AS
    -> SELECT FName, LName FROM Patient;
Query OK, 0 rows affected (0.12 sec)

mysql> CREATE VIEW FullyVaccinatedPercentage(PercentageFullyVaccinated) AS
    -> SELECT AVG (VaccinationStatus='Full') FROM Patient;
Query OK, 0 rows affected (0.16 sec)

mysql> []
```

FIGURE 7.24 Creating two views to support multiple data requirements to the same data.

As shown in Figure 7.25, now the user can access both views and obtain the necessary information for a given purpose without compromising any other data.

```
mysql> SELECT * FROM PatientNames;
+---------+---------+
| FName   | LName   |
+---------+---------+
| Bob     | Smith   |
| Sally   | Smith   |
| Sonny   | Garcia  |
| Helen   | Garcia  |
| Manny   | Garcia  |
| Steve   | Redmond |
| Alice   | Redmond |
| Joseph  | Redmond |
| Camille | Redmond |
| Barbara | Chow    |
| Sammy   | Chow    |
| Sandra  | Chow    |
| Janet   | Cruz    |
| Perry   | Dobson  |
| Elise   | Zuzka   |
+---------+---------+
15 rows in set (0.01 sec)

mysql> SELECT * FROM FullyVaccinatedPercentage;
+---------------------------+
| PercentageFullyVaccinated |
+---------------------------+
|                    0.6667 |
+---------------------------+
1 row in set (0.01 sec)

mysql> []
```

FIGURE 7.25 Demonstrating multiple access requirements to the same data.

As another example of limiting data access with views, let's consider that we want to access information about vaccinations without compromising anonymity or confidentiality. In other words, we want to permit access to the Vaccination column but not to the SSN, FName, LName, DOB, Height, Weight, Systolic, Diastolic and Cholesterol columns. We can define that limited access with one or more views that process rows by DOB and limit what is accessible and portrayed from that data.

While this use of views to restrict access to certain columns may also seem similar to using column-level database privileges, consider that privileges are specified for users and roles. As we saw in the last example, a user or role may require access to certain data one context but should be denied access to that same data in another context. The use of views allows that flexibility whereas user and role privileges cannot.

Views should be considered a supplement, rather than an alternative, to user and role table-level, column-level, and even row-level privileges. User and role privileges can establish necessary access but views can refine that access and provide more options and capabilities of accessing data while keeping data secure. Additionally, a view can restrict access to columns or rows of data in a DBMS that does not have full column-level or row-level privileges.

7.2 ENCRYPTION, DECRYPTION, AND HASHING

At times, we may have situations where we must store data in a table but also we want to keep that data confidential, even if one has access to retrieve that data. As an example, say we need to store a user's credit card number. If we were to store the number, any user, role, or view that has access to that data can access the stored credit card number. We cannot rely on user or role column-level privileges alone for a security measure here, because we need to allow each user access to the column in order to access their credit card column value; therefore, we cannot completely deny a user access to that column. Additionally, we want to protect the confidential data in the event of a compromised privileged account or a malicious user that is able to obtain privilege to access and see the data.

In these situations, we cannot store the data in raw or *plaintext* form, otherwise a user, role, or view that has access to the data can clearly see the confidential data. If we were to store the credit card number in plaintext form, any user, role, or view that has access to that data can clearly see the stored number. We need a way in which we can employ confidentiality so that, should an unauthorized user or role gains access to the credit card data, we *do not* want the number to be revealed. But if an authorized user or role does access the credit card data, we *do* want the number revealed.

Encryption

The typical solution to this confidentiality problem is to employ encryption or techniques that scramble the data into *ciphertext*, or a form that seems undecipherable to the plaintext, and store that instead. That way, if one were to look at the stored ciphertext, they could not determine the original plaintext. However, with the proper credentials, one could decrypt or convert the ciphertext back to its plaintext and then obtain the plaintext content.

Typically, we use passwords or passphrases as the credential to encrypt the plaintext into ciphertext and decrypt the ciphertext into plaintext. There are two forms of encryption: symmetric key and asymmetric key. Both forms are supported by MySQL, MariaDB, and Oracle DBMSs. *Symmetric key* (or *shared key*) encryption uses the same key (such as a password or passphrase) to encrypt as well as decrypt. In other words, for the decryption of ciphertext to be successful, one must provide the same key that was used to encrypt that ciphertext. On the other hand, with *asymmetric* (or *public key*) encryption, one key is used for encryption and another key must be used for decryption. The two keys are generated beforehand as a key pair, such that one key encrypts and other decrypts. Our examples use symmetric key encryption, although the same approaches can be used for asymmetric key encryption by using one key (typically a user's public key) to encrypt and the corresponding other key (typically the same user's private key) to decrypt.

We will demonstrate encryption and decryption using the advanced encryption standard (AES), which is widely accepted as the most secure encryption approach because AES ciphertext is virtually impossible to convert back to plaintext without the proper key. To encrypt data in our DBMS, we use the *AES_ENCRYPT* function, whose basic syntax is given in Figure 7.26. The first argument is the plaintext data in string form, and the second argument is the encryption key, such as a password or passphrase. The function returns the generated ciphertext.

$$AES\_ENCRYPT(\texttt{plaintext,key});$$

FIGURE 7.26 Basic syntax to encrypt with AES.

To obtain a better understanding of how we can encrypt and decrypt data, let's go through a standalone example before looking at data that is stored in a database. We will use symmetric encryption to encrypt some plaintext (in this case "my secret data") with a simple password (in this case "mykey"), as shown in Figure 7.27.

```
mysql> SELECT (AES_ENCRYPT('my secret data','mykey'));
+---------------------------------------------------------------------------+
| (AES_ENCRYPT('my secret data','mykey'))                                   |
+---------------------------------------------------------------------------+
| 0xFB8CDE1E80A0E90D73A1F639A6653BF2                                        |
+---------------------------------------------------------------------------+
1 row in set (0.00 sec)

mysql> []
```

FIGURE 7.27 Encrypting with AES and showing the generated ciphertext.

The *AES_ENCRYPT* function returns the ciphertext as a binary string or a sequence of byte values, not a character string. This is because some of the AES ciphertext may not be representable as alphanumeric symbols. As such, the *SELECT* statement in Figure 7.27 shows the ciphertext in hexadecimal or base 16 format. We don't need to explain hexadecimal in depth for our purposes—just consider that a hexadecimal symbol consists of the digits 0 to 9 as well as the letters A to F, allowing 16 possible values per symbol, or base 16. Two hexadecimal symbols together represent one byte value, which is in the range of 0 to 255 decimal. So in Figure 7.27, after the 0x prefix that indicates a hexadecimal value follows, the 32 hexadecimal symbols represent 16 bytes of ciphertext.

Decryption

To decrypt the ciphertext back to the original plaintext, we can use the *AES_DECRYPT* function, whose basic syntax to decrypt is given in Figure 7.28.

$$AES\_DECRYPT(\texttt{ciphertext,key});$$

FIGURE 7.28 Basic syntax to decrypt with AES.

The distinction between the ciphertext as a binary string and a character is important, because we must provide that ciphertext as a binary string to properly decrypt back to the original plaintext. One way we can do that is to provide the given ciphertext hexadecimal representation with the 0x prefix but no quotes, which is the approach we will use to decrypt. In this manner, we can decrypt the ciphertext that we just created and see the resulting plaintext, by issuing the *SELECT* statement given in Figure 7.29.

```
mysql> SELECT CAST((AES_DECRYPT(0xFB8CDE1E80A0E90D73A1F639A6653BF2,'mykey')) AS CHAR);
+----------------------------------------------------------------------+
| CAST((AES_DECRYPT(0xFB8CDE1E80A0E90D73A1F639A6653BF2,'mykey')) AS CHAR) |
+----------------------------------------------------------------------+
| my secret data                                                       |
+----------------------------------------------------------------------+
1 row in set (0.00 sec)

mysql> []
```

FIGURE 7.29 Decrypting with AES and showing the generated plaintext.

AES_DECRYPT also returns a binary string and not a character string, so in order to see the character representation of the resulting plaintext, we must convert the result into a character format. We can accomplish that task with the *CAST* function, which in this situation takes as an argument the binary string result generated by *AES_DECRYPT*, and then we specify *AS CHAR* to convert that argument into a character format.

Hashing

While we can provide a password or passphrase as the key for *AES_ENCRYPT* or *AES_DECRYPT*, it is considered more secure to pass a hashed form (or more simply called, hash) of the password or passphrase instead. A *hash* is a scrambled representation of data, which may sound like encryption but rather is a *one-way* scrambling, in that a hash cannot be unscrambled back to the original data. By providing a hash form of the password or passphrase during encryption, we can encrypt with an additional level of security compared to encrypting with the password or passphrase alone. This further protects the encrypted ciphertext (password or passphrase) against attacks that involve password guessing or password cracking.

There are a number of hashing methods that we can use, although the one considered to be most secure is the secure hash algorithm (SHA). There are actually three SHA versions: SHA1 (sometimes called just SHA), SHA2, and SHA3. Currently Oracle, MySQL, and MariaDB natively support SHA1 and SHA2. SHA2 is more secure than SHA1 and, of these two, should be used when available. We can generate an SHA2 hash into 256, 384, or 512 bits (or 64, 128 hexadecimal symbols), and we can represent that as SHA-256, SHA-384, or SHA-512, respectively. The larger the number of bits, the more secure the hash value against two different plaintext data sets hashing to the same value (known as a *collision*), as well as against reversing the hash value back to the plaintext. At this time, SHA-256 is considered secure (and U.S. government agencies even require hashes to be generated with SHA-256), though SHA-384 and SHA-512 can provide even higher security against collisions or reversing.

To generate an SHA2 hash of 256 bits, we can issue the *SHA2* function with two arguments. The first argument is the plaintext and the second argument is the number of bits for the hash, in this case 256. Figure 7.30 generates and shows the SHA2 hash value of 256 bits for the plaintext "myplaintext". In this example, the hash value is the sequence of 64 hexadecimal symbols that starts with 8cde. Because *SHA2* returns a character string and not a binary string, the result is not prefixed with 0x.

```
mysql> SELECT SHA2('myplaintext',256);
+------------------------------------------------------------------+
| SHA2('myplaintext',256)                                          |
+------------------------------------------------------------------+
| 8cde7860d9453f6dc628615c0da5e981882878aefbac4d34573e95a17988d73b |
+------------------------------------------------------------------+
1 row in set (0.00 sec)

mysql> []
```

FIGURE 7.30 Generating and showing an SHA2 hash.

To see the resulting ciphertext that combines SHA2 256 bit hashing with a key to make the previous encryption example more secure, we can issue the statement given in Figure 7.31. Notice that we are providing the hash value of the key rather than the key itself. And recall that *AES_ENCRYPT* returns a binary string, hence the resulting ciphertext is prefixed with 0x.

```
mysql> SELECT (AES_ENCRYPT('my secret data',SHA2('mykey',256)));
+------------------------------------------------------------------------------------------+
| (AES_ENCRYPT('my secret data',SHA2('mykey',256)))                                        |
+------------------------------------------------------------------------------------------+
| 0x6DE8E9BB22D57D0CBA096BD9E0CDFF5A                                                        |
+------------------------------------------------------------------------------------------+
1 row in set (0.00 sec)

mysql> []
```

FIGURE 7.31 Generating and showing ciphertext encrypted with an SHA2 hash.

To decrypt ciphertext that was encrypted with a hashed key, we must also provide that same hashed key as the decrypt key. Figure 7.32 demonstrates how we can decrypt the ciphertext that we just encrypted with the hashed key and see the resulting plaintext.

```
mysql> SELECT CAST((AES_DECRYPT(0x6DE8E9BB22D57D0CBA096BD9E0CDFF5A,SHA2('mykey',256))) AS CHAR);
+----------------------------------------------------------------------------------+
| CAST((AES_DECRYPT(0x6DE8E9BB22D57D0CBA096BD9E0CDFF5A,SHA2('mykey',256))) AS CHAR) |
+----------------------------------------------------------------------------------+
| my secret data                                                                   |
+----------------------------------------------------------------------------------+
1 row in set (0.00 sec)

mysql> []
```

FIGURE 7.32 Decrypting with an SHA2 hash and showing the result.

Now to actually storing and using the encrypted ciphertext in a database. To store ciphertext in a table column, we must use a binary data type for that column. Typical DBMS binary data types for this purpose include *VARBINARY*, *TINYBLOB*, *BLOB*, *MEDIUMBLOB*, and *LARGEBLOB*. When using the *VARBINARY* type, to determine the column size using AES, we take the length of the plaintext and round up to the next higher multiple of 16. As examples, for plaintext lengths of 0 to 15 bytes, the AES ciphertext is exactly 16 bytes. For plaintext lengths of 16 to 31 bytes, the AES ciphertext is exactly 32 bytes, and so on. *BLOB* is short for Binary Large OBject, and its variations define the maximum size of the binary data. Specifically, *TINYBLOB* can store up to 255 bytes, *BLOB* up to 64KB-1 bytes, *MEDIUMBLOB* up to 16MB-1 bytes, and *LARGEBLOB* up to 4GB-1 bytes of binary data or ciphertext.

To demonstrate the use of stored encrypted data, as well as the storing of a password credential and its use for authorization, suppose we have a PatientCredentials table that contains three columns: PatientId, CreditCardNo, and one for the user password. We have the CreditCardNo data type defined as *VARBINARY*(32), because we are assuming a typical credit card number of 16 character digits without dashes, and 19 characters if three dashes separate the number in xxxx-xxxx-xxxx-xxxx format. With those assumptions, the next higher multiple of 16 is 32. We will get to the data type for the password later.

Suppose we want to encrypt a patient's credit card number with that patient's password and store the resulting ciphertext. If patient P01 has a credit card number of 1111-2222-3333-4444 and a password of 'P01StrongPassword', we can store the hashed, encrypted credit card number with a statement like that given in Figure 7.33.

```
mysql> UPDATE PatientCredentials
    -> SET CreditCardNo=AES_ENCRYPT('1111-2222-3333-4444',SHA2('P01StrongPassword',256))
    -> WHERE PatientID='P01';
Query OK, 1 row affected (0.06 sec)
Rows matched: 1  Changed: 1  Warnings: 0

mysql> []
```

FIGURE 7.33 Storing an encrypted credit card number.

Later, if we need to access and reveal the credit card number, we can prompt the user for the password to decrypt and reveal the credit card number. To decrypt the patient's stored credit card number to access and show its plaintext value, we can issue a statement like that given in Figure 7.34.

```
mysql> SELECT CAST(AES_DECRYPT(CreditCardNo,SHA2('P01StrongPassword',256)) AS CHAR)
    -> FROM PatientCredentials
    -> WHERE PatientId='P01';
+------------------------------------------------------------------+
| CAST(AES_DECRYPT(CreditCardNo,SHA2('P01StrongPassword',256)) AS CHAR) |
+------------------------------------------------------------------+
| 1111-2222-3333-4444                                              |
+------------------------------------------------------------------+
1 row in set (0.00 sec)

mysql> []
```

FIGURE 7.34 Decrypting a stored credit card number.

Turning to the stored password, let's assume the user previously provided that password for future authentication purposes. As such, we can later authenticate that user by asking the user for their password and comparing the response with the stored password. If the comparison is successful, we consider the user to be authenticated. However, we cannot store a password in plaintext form, or any user, role, or view that has access to that column can clearly see the password itself. As with the credit card number example, we cannot rely on user or role privileges alone for a security measure either. Consequently, we must store the password in a form other than plaintext for confidentiality purposes. Notice that encryption is *not* a good solution for this purpose, because if we use encryption and the key that encrypts the password is compromised, that password (as well as possibly all other passwords in the system) is also compromised. For example, if a system were to use a single key to encrypt all user passwords and then decrypt a password for authentication purposes, we have a huge security vulnerability. Namely, if that key is compromised, *all* user passwords can be decrypted and are thus compromised.

It turns out that hashing is a typical solution to securely store a password in a nonplaintext form. A given hashing method will generate a hash of a fixed number of bytes. As a result, when using the same hash method, any password's hash value will be the same length, regardless of the length of the password itself. Hence, one cannot determine the possible length of the password based on the length of the hashed password. Consequently, a malicious user that attempts to compromise a password gains no clue about the length of the password by looking at the hashed password.

However, because a hash is a one-way scrambling of plaintext data into its hashed form, we can convert plaintext data into a hashed form, but we cannot convert a hashed form back into the original plaintext. We can solve this matter by asking an authenticating user for the proper password, hash that provided password, and then compare that result against the stored hashed password. If both hashes match, we consider the password provided for authentication matches the initial password that was hashed and stored, and thus authentication is successful. If the hashes do not match, then we can say the password provided for authentication does not match the previously hashed and stored password, and authentication was unsuccessful.

To see this approach in action, consider that the user with UserId P01 is providing the password 'P01StrongPassword' in Figure 7.35 for future authentication. Here we store the hashed password in a column appropriately named HashedPassword. The column has a data type of 64 characters to hold the 64 hexadecimal characters that represent the 256 bit hash value.

```
mysql> UPDATE PatientCredentials
    -> SET HashedPassword=SHA2('P01StrongPassword',256)
    -> WHERE PatientID='P01';
Query OK, 0 rows affected (0.00 sec)
Rows matched: 1  Changed: 0  Warnings: 0

mysql> []
```

FIGURE 7.35 Storing a hashed password.

We can later authenticate that user by asking them for the correct password, hashing that, and comparing the hashed result against the stored hash. Figure 7.36 shows the two hashed values for comparison purposes, starting with the hashed result of the user-provided password 'P01StrongPassword' and then the stored hash.

```
mysql> SELECT SHA2('P01StrongPassword',256);
+------------------------------------------------------------------+
| SHA2('P01StrongPassword',256)                                    |
+------------------------------------------------------------------+
| 8e2978ad2460839ef7597186f2af9d34293ed95933d24eb77659702d94f08dac |
+------------------------------------------------------------------+
1 row in set (0.00 sec)

mysql> SELECT HashedPassword FROM PatientCredentials WHERE PatientId='P01';
+------------------------------------------------------------------+
| HashedPassword                                                   |
+------------------------------------------------------------------+
| 8e2978ad2460839ef7597186f2af9d34293ed95933d24eb77659702d94f08dac |
+------------------------------------------------------------------+
1 row in set (0.00 sec)

mysql> []
```

FIGURE 7.36 Hashing an authenticating password and showing the stored hash of the previously set password for a match and successful authentication.

To illustrate an unsuccessful authentication attempt, suppose the user provides 'P01WrongPassword' as the authenticating password. Figure 7.37 shows the generated hash of that password, which in this case is different than the stored hash.

```
mysql> SELECT SHA2('P01WrongPassword',256);
+------------------------------------------------------------------+
| SHA2('P01WrongPassword',256)                                     |
+------------------------------------------------------------------+
| 7daae6631b79644e6cd11ef2dc99fde53298c62c9fd65d777b83ca07ceed40e6 |
+------------------------------------------------------------------+
1 row in set (0.00 sec)

mysql> SELECT HashedPassword FROM PatientCredentials WHERE PatientId='P01';
+------------------------------------------------------------------+
| HashedPassword                                                   |
+------------------------------------------------------------------+
| 8e2978ad2460839ef7597186f2af9d34293ed95933d24eb77659702d94f08dac |
+------------------------------------------------------------------+
1 row in set (0.00 sec)

mysql> []
```

FIGURE 7.37 Hashing an authenticating password and showing the stored hash of the previously set password for an unsuccessful authentication.

Salting

Many password-based mechanisms use an additional security control that helps make the password less susceptible to certain password attacks. This control, called *salt*, essentially strengthens the password by making it longer in a unique manner. One benefit provided with password salt is that when two users use the same password, the stored password hash is different among them. Such a difference in hash values does not give an attacker any clue when the two users use the same password. So if the attacker were to somehow obtain a list of a system's stored password hashes, and somehow compromise the password of one of those two users, the visual difference in hash values does not indicate that password would authenticate the second user. A second benefit is that password salt makes a password stronger, so even a less-than-ideal password can be made stronger and less susceptible to various password cracking attempts. Another benefit with password salt is that a password can become very resistant to *rainbow table attacks*, where an attacker attempts to speed up the process of password cracking by comparing a hashed password against a precomputed list of hash values based on password guesses. The inclusion of an arbitrary salt value means that an attacker must also include that salt value when precomputing a list of hash values for that attack. Otherwise, the precomputed list will be of no use with compromising that password.

To demonstrate the use of password in our current example, suppose that patient P02 sets their password also to 'P01StrongPassword'. Figure 7.38 issues a statement to set that password.

```
mysql> UPDATE PatientCredentials
    -> SET HashedPassword=SHA2('P01StrongPassword',256)
    -> WHERE PatientID='P02';
Query OK, 1 row affected (0.09 sec)
Rows matched: 1  Changed: 1  Warnings: 0

mysql> []
```

FIGURE 7.38 Setting the same password for another user.

Now, if an attacker was to get access to the stored password hashes, the attacker could realize that the passwords for patients P01 and P02 are the same, because their password hashes are identical. Figure 7.39 illustrates this observation. For a full comparison, Figure 7.39 shows different stored password hashes for all the other users, indicating they each have a unique password. In setting up this example we previously set the password for patient Pxx to 'PxxStrongPassword', so that patient P03 has the password 'P03StrongPassword', patient P04 has 'P04StrongPassword', and so on, up to patient P15 with 'P15StrongPassword'. Horizontal line separators have been removed from 7.39 to shorten it.

```
mysql> SELECT * FROM PatientCredentials;
| PatientID | CreditCardNo                                             | Password
| P01       | 0x759AE8669124CE90475A7A61E268DB52EC2F4276C8604171D94E2C0951009BFC | 0x3865323937386164323436303833339656637
353937313836663261663964333432393365643935393333364323465623737363539373032643934663038646163 |
| P02       | NULL                                                     | 0x3865323937386164323436303833339656637
353937313836663261663964333432393365643935393333364323465623737363539373032643934663038646163 |
| P03       | NULL                                                     | 0x37323539353961363230336163331633131636330
663065663323962366134626365376665636464656363313564643732363439366338376430376335616231353833 |
| P04       | NULL                                                     | 0x6531623231373062234663334326266636639
666637613665616466837303562233062363237383838323333666132306264363864326365616330663393061341 |
| P05       | NULL                                                     | 0x3838633930643337366665633535330333634
3562623531316339356138373038653764346433653162633438646361655613166638623632383635164623732 |
| P06       | NULL                                                     | 0x63333231383134643464461383731306233336
6362396164366661393337393633373665363534326239316431613035303333306162396663535663066334666462 |
| P07       | NULL                                                     | 0x6631623532353038353343931653465613363
34616335613734346336653316130346531666430346232330666666632393632303063313342383763331346656231 |
| P08       | NULL                                                     | 0x66356236343262230663432303232643663663
6634363165393738333316630373031326534653936326636373564393264356365303338373336437643734313136 |
| P09       | NULL                                                     | 0x39316564386135333656362633935531613262
313164313537396231613262643762616133861643435346338053773361663063343861656339316563665376563 |
| P10       | NULL                                                     | 0x39366363031623366323037373365363431
363462303264346435383236386563635353463330356166353965343437633333461333038326534623436434566437 |
| P11       | NULL                                                     | 0x62633362653303463376266638616239643031
363533663566637653862376231303236313365383830653535363326234373634376538646338303630632356564 |
| P12       | NULL                                                     | 0x6136633436313434623564396435303739362
37663136622353865376532383361346163353436663034663761333263353343333383562383236616336666616132 |
| P13       | NULL                                                     | 0x3061333431626335303662396616376616639
663631626338363566386135331663137396331316363823831626461631335373138383030393731346237666561 |
| P14       | NULL                                                     | 0x6165346339373131316613931316230336338
653365316636383430363133396434613213130366638653336626136303162636313263334386464535383235353666 |
| P15       | NULL                                                     | 0x62653234373332356438336566603035653535
3235623635303231663564335366362386430343030346138313564343266643334373131363931396537366535 |
15 rows in set (0.00 sec)

mysql>
```

FIGURE 7.39 Showing stored user password hashes.

To add salt to a password, we must first have a unique value associated with each user. Often this value is a number generated by the system as a random, unique value during creation of that user's account or—as a more secure measure—each time a user changes their password. In our case, we will add a column named Salt to the PatientCredentials table, as in Figure 7.40.

```
mysql> ALTER TABLE PatientCredentials ADD Salt CHAR(64);
Query OK, 0 rows affected (0.36 sec)
Records: 0  Duplicates: 0  Warnings: 0

mysql> []
```

FIGURE 7.40 Adding a column to store a patient's salt value.

We chose for the Salt column a character type of 32 bytes, as we will use SHA2 hashing against the system clock to create a virtually unique 256 bit value. While 256 bits may seem overkill, as many systems use only a 32 bit salt, it is often recommended to use a salt of the same size generated by the hashing method.[1]

Now to add the salt values for each user. In Figure 7.41, we add the salt for Patient P01 by obtaining the system clock with a resolution down to microseconds with the NOW(6) function, then hashing that result with SHA2 to generate a 256 bit hash. The argument of 6 that we provide to the NOW function specifies 6 digits of precision, thus giving us microsecond resolution. We then store that hash result as a 32 byte (or 64 hex symbol) text string.

```
mysql> UPDATE PatientCredentials
    -> SET Salt=SHA2(NOW(6),256)
    -> WHERE PatientID='P01';
Query OK, 1 row affected (0.07 sec)
Rows matched: 1  Changed: 1  Warnings: 0

mysql> []
```

FIGURE 7.41 Setting the salt value for a user, in this case Patient P01.

We then want to repeat that operation for all of the other users. In Figure 7.42, we reissue that same statement for Patient P02. To illustrate the generated salt values, we then show the salt values generated thus far in the PatientCredentials table. Notice that because the salt value is based on the system clock, the salt values shown in Figure 7.42 will most likely not match the ones you obtain.

---

[1]While there may be other means available to generate a salt value with a truly (or more truly) random value and with a larger range, we use the system clock for a more simple and straightforward example.

```
mysql> UPDATE PatientCredentials SET Salt=SHA2(NOW(6),256) WHERE PatientID='P02';
Query OK, 1 row affected (0.07 sec)
Rows matched: 1  Changed: 1  Warnings: 0

mysql> SELECT PatientId,Salt FROM PatientCredentials;
+-----------+-------------------------------------------------------------------+
| PatientId | Salt                                                              |
+-----------+-------------------------------------------------------------------+
| P01       | a73f84408f51a8d95354cd680f18e30f17401327d4c3019a349dffd919a70f67 |
| P02       | 2f615fc0237e3aa7b29344c2f4612bb9b1628b111dbd19af68bc9a6feacc7e29 |
| P03       | NULL                                                              |
| P04       | NULL                                                              |
| P05       | NULL                                                              |
| P06       | NULL                                                              |
| P07       | NULL                                                              |
| P08       | NULL                                                              |
| P09       | NULL                                                              |
| P10       | NULL                                                              |
| P11       | NULL                                                              |
| P12       | NULL                                                              |
| P13       | NULL                                                              |
| P14       | NULL                                                              |
| P15       | NULL                                                              |
+-----------+-------------------------------------------------------------------+
15 rows in set (0.00 sec)

mysql> []
```

FIGURE 7.42 Setting the salt value for Patient P02 and showing the two salt values.

Using the generated salt values with the user password, we can then hash the salted passwords and store that result in the Patient Credentials table. In Figure 7.43, we store the hashed salted password of Patient P01 by first concatenating the patient's salt value with their plaintext password. Concatenating essentially adds two strings together to create a third string that consists of the first string immediately followed by the second. We then generate the SHA2 hash of the concatenated strings and store that hash value in the patient's password column.

```
mysql> UPDATE PatientCredentials
    -> SET HashedPassword=SHA2(CONCAT(Salt,'P01StrongPassword'),256)
    -> WHERE PatientID='P01';
Query OK, 1 row affected (0.07 sec)
Rows matched: 1  Changed: 1  Warnings: 0

mysql> []
```

FIGURE 7.43 Generating and storing a hashed salted password.

We repeat that statement to store the passwords of the other users. In Figure 7.44, we do so for Patient P02 with the same password as that for patient P01. Even though patient P02 may likely have a different password, we wanted to use the same to illustrate that the stored hashed salted passwords will be different. Figure 7.44 follows by doing just that. Note that because your patient salt values are likely different from those generated here, your stored, hashed, salted passwords will likely be different than those shown in Figure 7.44. Also notice that the stored hash values are different, even when both users set the same password.

```
mysql> UPDATE PatientCredentials
    -> SET HashedPassword=SHA2(CONCAT(Salt,'P01StrongPassword'),256)
    -> WHERE PatientID='P02';
Query OK, 1 row affected (0.06 sec)
Rows matched: 1  Changed: 1  Warnings: 0

mysql> SELECT PatientId,HashedPassword FROM PatientCredentials WHERE PatientId BETWEEN 'P01' AND 'P02';
+-----------+------------------------------------------------------------------+
| PatientId | HashedPassword                                                   |
+-----------+------------------------------------------------------------------+
| P01       | 759a6f371e5405d80639aae665d92785647486e253030587cde957e577592a8c |
| P02       | dc23153fb1d2904a717d910e663d69a480943f150ce4ce56cacc898472087e2c |
+-----------+------------------------------------------------------------------+
2 rows in set (0.00 sec)

mysql> []
```

FIGURE 7.44 Generating and storing another hashed salted password, then comparing against the first stored password.

Password-based security is a very common, practical and effective authentication mechanism. However, depending on the DBMS and other system hardware, other authentication mechanisms may be available and more appropriate or secure for a given environment. Many environments now use multifactor authentication, where two or more authentication mechanisms are involved during the authentication process of a user. As examples, a common approach is to use password authentication along with possession of a certain device. However, password-based authentication involves approaches like those presented here, and one could use these approaches in all or part of an authentication scheme.

As a side note, in these examples we showed the actual hashed passwords, salt values, and ciphertext for visual, demonstrative purposes only. In a practical implementation, we would neatly and more securely implement such functionality in a database application or stored function, as we do with password lookup and comparison in the next section.

7.3 STORED ROUTINES

As described in the previous section, a view can provide a useful and effective security measure limiting what data a user can *access*. But a view itself may not be able to limit what a user *does* with that accessible data. As a result, we often may have to consider additional security measures for a comprehensive security implementation.

A security vulnerability of a view is that a malicious user may still be able to derive unauthorized information with the accessible data in the view. As an example of such a security vulnerability, consider that in our medical case study, a user needs to calculate a percentage of fully vaccinated patients within an age range, and the age range can vary. If we were to create a view that allows the user to access only a patient's date of birth and vaccination status to calculate the percentage, that will reduce but not eliminate the risk of compromising confidentiality or anonymity. That is because the user may still be able to correlate a date of birth from the view with a specific patient, and the view would also reveal that patient's vaccination status. Thus, we risk compromising the identity of that patient. To demonstrate this risk, let's create a view named AgeVaccination that accesses only a patient's date of birth and vaccination status. Then as the database root or administrative user, we give user sally access to see the data of the view, as demonstrated in Figure 7.45.

```
mysql> CREATE VIEW AgeVaccination AS SELECT DOB,VaccinationStatus FROM Patient;
Query OK, 0 rows affected (0.10 sec)

mysql> GRANT SELECT ON AgeVaccination to 'sally'@'localhost';
Query OK, 0 rows affected (0.10 sec)

mysql> []
```

FIGURE 7.45 A view with a confidentiality vulnerability.

User sally can now access this view to determine the percentage of patients within a certain age range that are fully vaccinated. Figure 7.46 shows one way that sally can obtain that percentage for patients within the ages of 18 to 30 by issuing a *SELECT* statement on that view.

```
mysql> SELECT AVG (VaccinationStatus='Full') FROM AgeVaccination
    -> WHERE TIMESTAMPDIFF(YEAR,DOB,CURDATE()) BETWEEN 18 AND 30;
+------------------------------+
| AVG (VaccinationStatus='Full') |
+------------------------------+
|                       0.5000 |
+------------------------------+
1 row in set (0.00 sec)

mysql> []
```

FIGURE 7.46 Accessing the limited patient data to calculate a percentage.

While the view restricts most PHI and PII for calculation purposes, a malicious user can still access the remaining PHI and PII for a confidentiality compromise. In particular, sally can use this view to see any or all of the data in view, as illustrated in Figure 7.47. We show the data for the same age range used in the previous calculation, although sally can also see similar data for all ages.

```
mysql> SELECT * FROM AgeVaccination
    -> WHERE TIMESTAMPDIFF(YEAR,DOB,CURDATE()) BETWEEN 18 AND 30;
+------------+-------------------+
| DOB        | VaccinationStatus |
+------------+-------------------+
| 1995-04-02 | Full              |
| 1998-04-02 | Unknown           |
+------------+-------------------+
2 rows in set (0.00 sec)

mysql> []
```

FIGURE 7.47 Accessing all of the view data to compromise confidentiality.

Because PII is available as the date of birth, a patient's confidentiality of vaccination status is at risk of compromise. To maintain that confidentiality, we need a way to prevent user sally from misusing the data in the view. Specifically, we need to allow sally to obtain an average without seeing the data itself.

Even though we previously created the view FullyVaccinatedPercentage to calculate and yield the percentage of fully vaccinated patients without showing any of the source data, we cannot create a view for that purpose in this scenario because the age range is not fixed and can vary. For example, FullyVaccinatedPercentage involves all ages. While we can create a similar restricted view that contains only ages between 18 to 30, that does not solve the problem if we need to work with any other age range, such as 18 to 40. It may be impractical or (nearly) impossible to create a view for each possible age range. Consequently, we may need to consider other security mechanisms to maintain confidentiality of the PII while still allowing any age range to be accessed for the purposes of calculations only. A solution to this problem is to define a *stored routine* that specifies exactly which data is to be accessed as well as how that data is to be used. We then allow the user to invoke or call that routine. In this manner, the user cannot access data outside of the scope by which the routine operates, thus maintaining security for the data we wish to keep confidential. We will look at two forms of stored routines: *stored functions* and *stored procedures*.

Stored functions

A stored function defines a set of data accesses that returns a single value. As such, a function can serve as a solution to this case well because we want to obtain a single value, namely the average.

In Figure 7.48, we give the definition of a stored function that calculates the percentage of fully vaccinated persons whose age is within a given range. As part of this definition, we first define a new temporary *alternative delimiter* that marks the end of an SQL statement. This alternative delimiter is necessary because the semi-colon ';' symbol normally marks the end of an SQL statement, and when the DBMS scans a statement and sees a semicolon, the DBMS processes everything scanned up to that point as a complete statement. Because we have semicolons in the function definition, we do not want the DBMS to read one of those semicolons and think the statement we are expressing (the entire function definition in this case) is complete and process that. If that were to happen, the DBMS would in effect process part of the function definition and at the very least give an error that the statement is incomplete. Instead, we want the DBMS to scan and process the statement for the function definition in its entirety, so we need an alternative delimiter that can indicate the end of the function definition.

We can specify an alternative delimiter with the *DELIMITER* statement. The sequence of characters or symbols that follow will become the new statement delimiter, so that the DBMS will now consider an SQL statement to be ended with that new delimiter. Here we choose $$$ as the alternative delimiter, although you can choose any character sequence as long as the sequence does not appear within the function definition, which would still cause the DBMS to prematurely process the definition.

```
mysql> DELIMITER $$$
mysql> CREATE FUNCTION PercentByAgeRange(min INT, max INT)
    -> RETURNS DECIMAL(3,2)
    -> DETERMINISTIC
    -> BEGIN
    -> DECLARE average DECIMAL(3,2);
    -> SELECT AVG (VaccinationStatus='Full') INTO average FROM AgeVaccination
    -> WHERE TIMESTAMPDIFF(YEAR,DOB,CURDATE()) BETWEEN min AND max;
    -> RETURN average;
    -> END
    -> $$$
Query OK, 0 rows affected (0.10 sec)

mysql> DELIMITER ;
mysql> []
```

FIGURE 7.48 Definition of a stored function that limits data access.

Next, the *CREATE FUNCTION* keywords start the function definition, followed by the function name and its parameters as a list within parenthesis. The parameter list contains the names of variables that will receive the values provided as arguments when the function is called or invoked. Each parameter is defined with a name and data type. The function will reference the value passed to that parameter by the parameter name and recognize the value as that data type. If more than one parameter is defined, we comma separate each parameter definition as we do here.

We then define the data type of the value the function will return back to the caller with the *RETURN* keyword, followed by that returned data type. After that we provide the keyword *DETERMINISTIC*, which specifies the function will return the same value given the same input values and same data in the database. Because our result is based on the stored data and values given by the caller, we expect the same result to be generated if a user calls the function repeatedly with the same stored data and same age values. Hence our function is deterministic. In contrast, a nondeterministic function may generate and return a different result when given that same criteria. Usually such behavior occurs when the function bases the returned value on other data that can change across calls to the function, such as time.

The *BEGIN* keyword indicates the body of statements that execute in the function follows. In this function, we first create a data variable to hold the calculated value with the *DECLARE* statement, followed by the variable name and the variable data type. We then use a form of the *SELECT* statement to calculate the percentage of fully vaccinated patients whose age is within the given age range. Unlike a typical *SELECT* statement that processes and shows data, this form stores a result into a variable. Notice the *INTO* keyword that follows the *SELECT* list. The *INTO* keyword is followed by a variable name, and specifies that the result of the *SELECT* statement is to be stored in that variable.

We conclude the function body with the *RETURN* keyword that specifies the value or variable to return, in this case the value in the variable named average. The *END* keyword indicates the end of the function body and definition. We then specify the alternative delimiter to let the DBMS know that it can now process what we have given up to that point as a single statement. You may notice at that point, the DBMS acknowledges the processing of the entire function. Finally, we use the *DELIMITER* keyword again, this time to set the delimiter back to its normal semicolon.

Once the stored function is defined, we also need to assign the ability for the appropriate user (sally in this case) to execute the function, as we similarly did so with views. The database root or administrative user would issue a form of the *GRANT* statement as shown in Figure 7.49. Here we add *EXECUTE* privilege for the given user or role. The *FUNCTION* keyword indicates that we are assigning that privilege to a stored function name of the name that follows.

```
mysql> GRANT EXECUTE ON FUNCTION PercentByAgeRange to 'sally'@'localhost';
Query OK, 0 rows affected (0.10 sec)

mysql> []
```

FIGURE 7.49 Assigning execute privilege for a stored function.

To enforce security through confidentiality and anonymity of the PII in this scenario, we also remove the ability for user sally to directly access the AgeVaccination view, as shown in Figure 7.50. Note that even though we have now disallowed sally to directly access the AgeVaccination view, sally can still execute the PercentByAgeRange function, which does access the AgeVaccination view. Because that function accesses that view and returns information in a specific, controlled manner, sally cannot deviate beyond what the function does, and thus cannot obtain any other data beyond what the function returns or what sally is normally allowed to access.

```
mysql> REVOKE SELECT ON AgeVaccination FROM 'sally'@'localhost';
Query OK, 0 rows affected (0.06 sec)

mysql> []
```

FIGURE 7.50 Removing direct access from the view used by the function.

Now user sally can invoke or call the function by specifying the function name in a *SELECT* list, followed by the starting and ending age range in parenthesis, as shown in Figure 7.51. Here sally invokes the function for the age ranges of 18 to 30 and 18 to 40 to obtain the calculated percentages.

```
mysql> SELECT PercentByAgeRange(18,30);
+--------------------------+
| PercentByAgeRange(18,30) |
+--------------------------+
|                     0.50 |
+--------------------------+
1 row in set (0.01 sec)

mysql> SELECT PercentByAgeRange(18,40);
+--------------------------+
| PercentByAgeRange(18,40) |
+--------------------------+
|                     0.75 |
+--------------------------+
1 row in set (0.01 sec)

mysql> []
```

FIGURE 7.51 Invoking the stored function.

Notice that user sally can only access a calculated percentage of those vaccinated and has no other access to the age or vaccination data. Figure 7.52 shows that sally would be denied access to any other data of that view if sally were to directly access the view now.

```
mysql> SELECT * FROM AgeVaccination;
ERROR 1142 (42000): SELECT command denied to user 'sally'@'localhost' for table 'AgeVaccination'
mysql> []
```

FIGURE 7.52 Denied direct access of the patient data.

If we need to delete a defined function, we can issue the *DROP* statement as shown in Figure 7.53 for the PercentByAgeRangeFunction. This can be helpful if we no longer need the services of a function or need to recreate it.

```
mysql> DROP FUNCTION PercentByAgeRange;
Query OK, 0 rows affected (0.11 sec)

mysql> []
```

FIGURE 7.53 Deleting a stored function.

Stored procedures

We can similarly define a stored procedure to define what data is to be accessed and how that data will be accessed. The main difference between a stored function and procedure is that a function returns a single value with a *RETURN* statement to the caller via the function name. In contrast, a procedure cannot return a value via the procedure name and hence has no *RETURN* statement. However, unlike a function, a procedure can return one or more values via the parameters.

To demonstrate how we can define a stored procedure to provide security by specifying which data is to be accessed and how, let's comparatively create one to calculate the percentage of full vaccinations among a given age range. As shown in Figure 7.54, the definition is similar to that of the stored function with a few differences. The first difference is that we specify the *PROCEDURE* (rather than *FUNCTION*) keyword, indicating this is a stored procedure definition. For the second difference between the definition of a stored function and that of a stored procedure, we specify in the parameter list whether each parameter is only sending a data value into the procedure, only sending a value back to the caller, or doing both. We accomplish that by prefacing each parameter with *IN*, *OUT*, or *INOUT*, respectively. For the third difference, we must add a parameter for each value that is being sent back to the caller and not into the procedure. In this example, we have three parameters for the stored procedure, whereas the function implementation had two parameters. The first two parameters send into the procedure the age beginning and end range, respectively, and the third parameter sends out the calculated average to the caller. We preface the first two parameters with the *IN* keyword and the third with the *OUT* keyword. As the last difference between the function and procedure definitions, the procedure does not have a *RETURN* statement.

```
mysql> DELIMITER $$$
mysql> CREATE PROCEDURE PercentByAgeRangeProc(IN min INT, IN max INT, OUT average DECIMAL(3,2))
    -> DETERMINISTIC
    -> BEGIN
    -> SELECT AVG (VaccinationStatus='Full') INTO average FROM AgeVaccination
    -> WHERE TIMESTAMPDIFF(YEAR,DOB,CURDATE()) BETWEEN min AND max;
    -> END
    -> $$$
Query OK, 0 rows affected (0.12 sec)

mysql> DELIMITER ;
mysql> []
```

FIGURE 7.54 Defining a stored procedure to limit data access.

As with the function implementation, for user sally to have the ability to execute this procedure, the database root or administrative user must issue a *GRANT* statement like that in Figure 7.55. The only difference than before is that we specify the *PROCEDURE* keyword instead of *FUNCTION* to indicate we are managing privileges on a procedure.

```
mysql> GRANT EXECUTE ON PROCEDURE PercentByAgeRangeProc to 'sally'@'localhost';
Query OK, 0 rows affected (0.07 sec)

mysql> []
```

FIGURE 7.55 Assigning execute privilege for a stored procedure.

To invoke the procedure, the user can now issue a *CALL* statement such as that in Figure 7.56. In the *CALL* statement, we specify the procedure name followed by a parenthetically enclosed list of comma separated arguments. The last argument is a variable that will receive the value sent back by the procedure by the *OUT* parameter, the last parameter defined in the procedure. The @ symbol that appears before the variable avg indicates the name of a *session variable*, which in this case holds the value sent back by the *OUT* parameter. The use of a session variable allows the user that called the procedure to later access the value in that variable, as the session variable exists for the duration of the login session in which the variable is created. To simply show the result in the session variable, we can issue the *SELECT* statement that follows.

```
mysql> SELECT @avg AS PercentByRange;
+----------------+
| PercentByRange |
+----------------+
|           0.50 |
+----------------+
1 row in set (0.01 sec)

mysql> []
```

FIGURE 7.56 Calling a stored procedure.

Revisiting the password authentication implementation

To wrap up a number of concepts in this chapter, let's return to the password authentication task described in Section 7.2. While we showed the steps visually for demonstrative purposes, in reality, we would want to automate those steps and comparisons, not only for ease of use and speed, but also for security purposes. A security risk of a compromised password arises if we allow hashed passwords to be exposed. Namely, if an attacker were to obtain a list of password hashes, the attacker could attempt various password attacks to compromise those passwords.

We can mitigate that risk by using the concept of stored functions and procedures to limit the types of access to data. Given a user id and password, a password authentication mechanism should simply confirm whether or not the password matches the one previously set by the user. A stored function can provide that ability to return that single yes/no or true/false value. In Figure 7.57, we define a stored function named PasswordAuthenticated that accepts a user id, password given for authentication, and returns the character string "true" if the password matches the one set by the user, or "false" otherwise.

```
mysql> DELIMITER $$$
mysql> CREATE FUNCTION PasswordAuthenticated(id VARCHAR(6),attemptedpw VARCHAR(255))
    -> RETURNS VARCHAR(5)
    -> DETERMINISTIC
    -> BEGIN
    -> DECLARE storedpw, storedsalt CHAR(64);
    -> SELECT HashedPassword,Salt INTO storedpw,storedsalt FROM PatientCredentials WHERE PatientId = id;
    -> IF storedpw = SHA2(CONCAT(storedsalt,attemptedpw),256) THEN
    ->     RETURN 'true';
    -> ELSE
    ->     RETURN 'false';
    -> END IF;
    -> END
    -> $$$
Query OK, 0 rows affected (0.12 sec)

mysql> DELIMITER ;
mysql> []
```

FIGURE 7.57 A stored function implementation of password authentication.

In the function parameter list, we define the first parameter named id with a data type that matches that of a PatientId. We then the second parameter named attemptedpw to receive the password provided to authenticate, set to a maximum size of 255 characters. The function returns an up to five-character value, namely "true" or "false".

Inside the body of the function, we declare local variables storedpw and storedsalt of exactly 64 characters each. We then retrieve the hashed password and salt values for the user id from the PatientCredentials table, and store those values in those local variables. Finally, we compare the stored hashed salted password with the computed hash value of the salt and password provided. If they are identical, the function returns "true", otherwise the function returns "false".

To use the PasswordAuthenticated function, a user with the appropriate execution privilege issues a *SELECT* statement on the function and provides two arguments: the patient id and the attempted or authenticating password. Figure 7.58 shows an example of calling the function to authenticate patient P01 with the password "P01StrongPassword", and receiving "true" for a successful authentication.

```
mysql> SELECT PasswordAuthenticated('P01','P01StrongPassword');
+---------------------------------------------------+
| PasswordAuthenticated('P01','P01StrongPassword')  |
+---------------------------------------------------+
| true                                              |
+---------------------------------------------------+
1 row in set (0.00 sec)

mysql> []
```

FIGURE 7.58 Successful password authentication.

On the other hand, if the password is not a match for that user id, the function returns "false" for an unsuccessful authentication, as shown in Figure 7.59.

```
mysql> SELECT PasswordAuthenticated('P01','P01WrongPassword');
+--------------------------------------------------+
| PasswordAuthenticated('P01','P01WrongPassword')  |
+--------------------------------------------------+
| false                                            |
+--------------------------------------------------+
1 row in set (0.00 sec)

mysql> []
```

FIGURE 7.59 Unsuccessful password authentication.

7.4   SUMMARY

The database security concepts described in this chapter can supplement and add to other security concepts that are presented in the preceding chapters. By employing multiple security controls, we can achieve a layered security implementation for a more comprehensive security solution in a given environment.

CHAPTER 8

TRANSACTIONS FOR DATA INTEGRITY

So far we have looked at data tasks that involved one database access or operation (such as a single *SELECT*, *INSERT*, *UPDATE*, or *DELETE* statement). We may also have scenarios where a data task involves multiple database accesses or operations, such as two *INSERT* statements, two *UPDATE* statements, or any combination of *SELECT*, *INSERT*, *UPDATE*, and *DELETE* statements. As an example of a single data task that involves multiple database accesses or operations, consider a banking or other financial system that contains data about account balances, like the sample data given in Figure 8.1. We also include in Figure 8.1 the definition of the table—named Account—that stores this data.

```
CREATE TABLE IF NOT EXISTS Account (
        AccountID CHAR(6),
        Balance DECIMAL(14,2)
        PRIMARY KEY (AccountID)
);
```

AccountID	Balance
A00001	$10,000.00
A00002	$5,000.00
A00003	$120,000.00
A00004	$400,000.00
A00005	$325,000.00
A00006	$25,000.00

FIGURE 8.1 Sample data of a banking or financial scenario.

In this scenario, we want to issue a financial transfer from one account to another. We may consider the transfer itself as one data task, even though in reality that task involves multiple database operations. At a minimum, we have two *UPDATE* statements: one to reduce the first account by the transfer amount, and another to increase the second account by the transfer amount. In reality we may also involve other database operations for that transfer task, such as one or more *INSERT* statements to track or log the transfer activity, but we will keep this first scenario simple and just consider just the two *UPDATE* statements.

8.1   COMMITS, ROLLBACKS, AND AUTOMATIC COMMITS

Because the transfer task in our example involves two *UPDATE* statements to be carried out, we consider the overall task to be successful only if *both* *UPDATE* statements are successfully carried out. If we determine that both *UPDATE* statements are successfully carried out, only then do we want the overall transfer task to be considered successful and made permanent in the database as well as visible to other user or application *sessions*. We consider a session to be the period of time in which a user or application is logged into a DBMS for their work. So in general, if we consider all of the individual operations of a given task to be successful, we can make those individual operations—and the task—permanent and visible to other sessions by issuing an SQL *COMMIT* statement.

We do not want—and should not have—an outcome or result where only some, and not all, of those database accesses are successfully carried out. As examples of such outcomes, suppose the first *UPDATE* statement that reduces an account by the transfer amount results with a negative account balance, and business rules or data constraints do not permit negative balances. We do not want an end result where the other operation that adds the transfer amount completes. As another example, suppose the first *UPDATE* statement that reduces the balance of one account is successful, yielding a valid, positive balance. However, the second *UPDATE* statement that adds the transfer amount to the other account fails, say, because of an invalid account number or an external freeze placed on that account to prevent further activity with that account. We similarly do not want an end result where the first *UPDATE* that reduced one account has completed but the second has not. In both cases, and any such situation where one of the operations is unsuccessful, we want the end result to be as if the transfer was never started in the first place, and both accounts have the same original amounts. This means that we may have to undo, or *rollback*, the database access statements that were successful in that transfer task. We can undo those changes by issuing an SQL *ROLLBACK* statement.

When we consider a set of database accesses, each as part of a larger task such as the financial transfer, we formally refer to that task as a *database transaction*. Let's also consider that we want the transaction to either complete in full or appear to not have occurred at all, that is, in the event that one of the database accesses resulted in an error or condition that prevents us from wanting to make the transaction results permanent and visible to others. As such, we want the resulting effect that either all of the transaction's individual data accesses to appear to have completed or appear to not have occurred at all. This *all-or-nothing* concept, where all data accesses appear to have completed if the transaction is successful, or none of the data accesses appear to have completed if the transaction fails, means that the transaction is considered *atomic*. Such a transaction is known as an *atomic transaction*.

Before we demonstrate the use of commits and rollbacks with database transactions, let's first discuss the concept of when changes to data are made permanent to the database and are visible to other users or applications that operate on that database. When we issue a database operation that changes data (such with an *INSERT*, *UPDATE*, or *DELETE* statement), that change is generally considered *not* visible to other database users or applications until the change is *committed* to the database. Such a commit can either be specified *explicitly* as an SQL statement, or be *implicit* or *automatic* where, immediately after such a change occurs, the DBMS automatically issues a commit. MySQL, MariaDB, and Oracle have **autocommit** enabled by default, so when we issue an operation that changes the data in a database, the DBMS automatically commits that change to the database, whether or not that operation is part of a larger task that still has other data operations to issue.

Because we may need to assess the outcome of a set of database operations involved in a task before we can decide whether or not to commit or rollback the data changes issued with that task, we may need to first turn off, or disable, autocommit mode. This allows us to later issue a commit or rollback to data changes once we can make that decision. We can disable—as well as enable—autocommit mode explicitly in MySQL, MariaDB, and Oracle by changing the value of the *autocommit* variable. To explicitly disable automatic commitments in this manner, we simply set the value of **autocommit** to 0, as shown in Figure 8.2.

```
mysql> SET autocommit=0;
Query OK, 0 rows affected (0.00 sec)

mysql> []
```

FIGURE 8.2 Disabling automatic database commitments.

Now operations that change data in a database are in general not immediately visible to other users or applications that interact with that data.[1]

With automatic commits disabled, the effects of certain database operations may not be immediately made permanent or visible in the database. To make the effects of those operations permanent and visible, we can issue a *COMMIT* statement. On the other hand, we may decide that we do not want to keep those changes, say if the changes result with an invalid data value or some other error. In that case, we may wish to undo or reverse those data changes in order to return the database back to a state or set of values that are valid and not in error. To carry out that undoing or reversal of operations, we can issue a *ROLLBACK* statement. The resulting effect of a *ROLLBACK* is that those data changes are not permanent nor visible, as if those operations never occurred. It is important to keep in mind that, with automatic commits disabled, a *COMMIT* or *ROLLBACK* statement can affect only the database operations issued since the last *COMMIT* or *ROLLBACK* statement.

Should we later need to reenable automatic commitments (or wish to enable them if initially disabled), we can do so by changing the **autocommit** variable value to 1, as shown in Figure 8.3.

Note that when automatic commits are enabled, a *ROLLBACK* has no effect. More specifically, if we issue a *ROLLBACK* in that case, there are not any data changes to undo because the changes have already been

[1]There may be certain rules or data access methods in effect that can affect when changes to data are seen by a given user or application. In general, consider that a user or application can usually see data changes that it issues, but other users or applications cannot until the changes are committed.

automatically committed. Once a database operation has been committed, it cannot be undone with a *ROLLBACK*. The same goes for a database operation that has been undone with a *ROLLBACK*—we cannot reapply it with a *COMMIT* statement alone.

```
mysql> SET autocommit=1;
Query OK, 0 rows affected (0.00 sec)

mysql> []
```

FIGURE 8.3 Enabling automatic database commitments.

8.2 BEGINNING A TRANSACTION WITH *COMMIT* OR *ROLLBACK*

Now that we have an overview of database *COMMIT* and *ROLLBACK* mechanisms, let's discuss the two general approaches by which we can implement transactions. In the first approach, we must first explicitly disable automatic commitments—if they are enabled—as we did in Figure 8.2.

Once automatic commits are disabled, we can then issue a *COMMIT* or *ROLLBACK* statement to begin a transaction. While we often associate a *COMMIT* or *ROLLBACK* operation with the end of a transaction, we will consider that in this first approach, a transaction spans from one *COMMIT* or *ROLLBACK* statement to the next *COMMIT* or *ROLLBACK* statement. More precisely, by issuing a *COMMIT* or *ROLLBACK* statement, we either make a set of previous changes available (with a *COMMIT*) or we undo those changes to not make them available (with a *ROLLBACK*). Either way, we can consider that we have a starting point by which a new transaction can begin, and we can then issue the data operations involved in the new transaction. After those operations, we decide whether to apply or undo those changes (by some set of conditions) and issue a *COMMIT* or *ROLLBACK* statement, respectively. That final *COMMIT* or *ROLLBACK* statement effectively ends that transaction in an atomic manner. Notice that the final statement also begins another transaction, so we can immediately issue one transaction after another if we wish.

To demonstrate this first approach to implement a transaction, let's refer to the banking scenario and data shown in Figure 8.1. For now, we will presume that at a given time, only one user or application session is accessing the database at a given time (Chapter 9 explains additional considerations if multiple user or application sessions access the database at the same time). Suppose we want to transfer $10000.00 from account A00003 to account A00002. If we were to issue these operations directly, we would have a series of statements like that shown in Figure 8.4. Here we first explicitly disable automatic commits. We then apply an *UPDATE* statement to subtract the transfer amount from the source account and a second *UPDATE* statement to add the transfer amount to the destination account. After confirming that both account balances remain in a valid, positive, state, we then *COMMIT* the transaction. Finally, we reenable automatic commits.

```
mysql> set autocommit=0;
Query OK, 0 rows affected (0.00 sec)

mysql> COMMIT;
Query OK, 0 rows affected (0.00 sec)

mysql> UPDATE Account SET Balance=Balance-10000.00 WHERE AccountID='A00003';
Query OK, 1 row affected (0.00 sec)
Rows matched: 1  Changed: 1  Warnings: 0

mysql> UPDATE Account SET Balance=Balance+10000.00 WHERE AccountID='A00002';
Query OK, 1 row affected (0.00 sec)
Rows matched: 1  Changed: 1  Warnings: 0

mysql> COMMIT;
Query OK, 0 rows affected (0.05 sec)

mysql> set autocommit=1;
Query OK, 0 rows affected (0.00 sec)

mysql> []
```

FIGURE 8.4 A database transaction starting with *COMMIT* or *ROLLBACK* and ending with a *COMMIT*.

If we show the account balances after the *COMMIT*, we would see that the transfer operations completed, as shown in Figure 8.5. Compared to Figure 8.1, we see that 10000.00 has been transferred from account A00003 to account A00002.

```
mysql> SELECT * FROM Account;
+-----------+-----------+
| AccountID | Balance   |
+-----------+-----------+
| A00001    |  10000.00 |
| A00002    |  15000.00 |
| A00003    | 110000.00 |
| A00004    | 400000.00 |
| A00005    | 325000.00 |
| A00006    |  25000.00 |
+-----------+-----------+
6 rows in set (0.00 sec)

mysql> []
```

FIGURE 8.5 The result after a COMMIT.

However, certain transfers may result with a less desirable outcome. Let's demonstrate one such transfer that yields an account with a negative—or invalid—balance. If we were to now transfer 15000.00 from account A00001 to account A00002, that would leave A00001 with a negative balance. To confirm that, we also show the resulting account balances as seen by the session that issues the transfer, which typically sees the changes that it issued even though other user or application sessions may not see those changes at that time. Figure 8.6 shows that series of steps with the resulting balances.

```
mysql> set autocommit=0;
Query OK, 0 rows affected (0.01 sec)

mysql> COMMIT;
Query OK, 0 rows affected (0.00 sec)

mysql> UPDATE Account SET Balance=Balance-15000.00 WHERE AccountID='A00001';
Query OK, 1 row affected (0.00 sec)
Rows matched: 1  Changed: 1  Warnings: 0

mysql> UPDATE Account SET Balance=Balance+15000.00 WHERE AccountID='A00002';
Query OK, 1 row affected (0.00 sec)
Rows matched: 1  Changed: 1  Warnings: 0

mysql> SELECT * FROM Account;
+-----------+-----------+
| AccountID | Balance   |
+-----------+-----------+
| A00001    |  -5000.00 |
| A00002    |  30000.00 |
| A00003    | 110000.00 |
| A00004    | 400000.00 |
| A00005    | 325000.00 |
| A00006    |  25000.00 |
+-----------+-----------+
6 rows in set (0.00 sec)

mysql> []
```

FIGURE 8.6 A database transaction starting with *COMMIT* or *ROLLBACK* and resulting with invalid data.

At this point we consider that because we have an invalid balance, we do not want to make the changes permanent and visible, but rather want to undo them, so we issue a *ROLLBACK*. If we show the account balances after the *ROLLBACK*, we would see that neither of the transfer operations appear, as shown in Figure 8.7. Compared to Figure 8.5, we see no change to the balances, as if the transfer never occurred, which is exactly what we want in this situation: we do not want a result with an invalid set of data, but would rather return to the previous set of data that was valid. Note that we did not have to show the balances in Figure 8.6 before issuing the *ROLLBACK*—we showed the balances to help illustrate the before and after effect of the *ROLLBACK*.

```
mysql> ROLLBACK;
Query OK, 0 rows affected (0.03 sec)

mysql> set autocommit=1;
Query OK, 0 rows affected (0.00 sec)

mysql> SELECT * FROM Account;
+-----------+-----------+
| AccountID | Balance   |
+-----------+-----------+
| A00001    |  10000.00 |
| A00002    |  15000.00 |
| A00003    | 110000.00 |
| A00004    | 400000.00 |
| A00005    | 325000.00 |
| A00006    |  25000.00 |
+-----------+-----------+
6 rows in set (0.00 sec)

mysql>
```

FIGURE 8.7 The result after a *ROLLBACK*.

8.3 BEGINNING A TRANSACTION WITH *START TRANSACTION*

The second approach by which we can implement a transaction is by issuing a *START TRANSACTION* statement to begin the transaction. *START TRANSACTION* accomplishes two things. First, it implicitly—and temporarily—disables automatic commits, so that subsequently issued data changes (up to the next *COMMIT* or *ROLLBACK* statement) are not immediately seen by others. This means that we do not have to disable automatic commits, if they happen to be enabled. Secondly, *START TRANSACTION* also defines a point by which subsequent data operations are included in that transaction. As such, after we have issued the operations for the transaction, we must follow with either a *COMMIT* statement to make those changes permanent and visible in the database, or a *ROLLBACK* statement to undo those changes. After that *COMMIT* or *ROLLBACK* statement, the DBMS reenables automatic commits if that is the default mode or last explicitly set mode. Similar to the first transaction implementation approach, the effect is that all of the data changes involved in a transaction are atomic.

Using the second transaction implementation approach with where we left off in the financial scenario, let's transfer 10000.00 from account A00002 back to account A00003. To issue that directly with the second transaction implementation approach, we have a series of steps like those shown in Figure 8.8.

```
mysql> START TRANSACTION;
Query OK, 0 rows affected (0.00 sec)

mysql> UPDATE Account SET Balance=Balance-10000.00 WHERE AccountID='A00002';
Query OK, 1 row affected (0.00 sec)
Rows matched: 1  Changed: 1  Warnings: 0

mysql> UPDATE Account SET Balance=Balance+10000.00 WHERE AccountID='A00003';
Query OK, 1 row affected (0.00 sec)
Rows matched: 1  Changed: 1  Warnings: 0

mysql> COMMIT;
Query OK, 0 rows affected (0.06 sec)

mysql> []
```

FIGURE 8.8 A database transaction starting with *START TRANSACTION* and ending with a *COMMIT*.

You will immediately notice that this approach has fewer steps than the approach illustrated in Figure 8.4. This is because we do not have to disable and reenable automatic commits. The *START TRANSACTION* and *COMMIT* statements take care of that for us! If we were now to show the account balances, we would see the transfer completed, as shown in Figure 8.9.

```
mysql> SELECT * FROM Account;
+-----------+-----------+
| AccountID | Balance   |
+-----------+-----------+
| A00001    |  10000.00 |
| A00002    |   5000.00 |
| A00003    | 120000.00 |
| A00004    | 400000.00 |
| A00005    | 325000.00 |
| A00006    |  25000.00 |
+-----------+-----------+
6 rows in set (0.00 sec)

mysql> []
```

FIGURE 8.9 The result after a *COMMIT*.

Similarly, if we were to use *START TRANSACTION* to initiate a transfer that leaves the source account with a negative balance, we would want to conclude the transaction with a *ROLLBACK*. Figure 8.10 shows the series of steps with an invalid transfer of 200000.00 from account A00006 to account A00001.

```
mysql> START TRANSACTION;
Query OK, 0 rows affected (0.00 sec)

mysql> UPDATE Account SET Balance=Balance-200000.00 WHERE AccountID='A00006';
Query OK, 1 row affected (0.00 sec)
Rows matched: 1  Changed: 1  Warnings: 0

mysql> UPDATE Account SET Balance=Balance+200000.00 WHERE AccountID='A00001';
Query OK, 1 row affected (0.00 sec)
Rows matched: 1  Changed: 1  Warnings: 0

mysql> ROLLBACK;
Query OK, 0 rows affected (0.02 sec)

mysql> []
```

FIGURE 8.10 A database transaction starting with *START TRANSACTION* and ending with a *ROLLBACK*.

In Figure 8.10, we did not show the account balances with the negative balance before issuing the *ROLLBACK* as we did in Figure 8.6.

The showing of a negative balance is technically not necessary before we issue the *ROLLBACK*, but you may do so if you wish to confirm a negative balance before issuing the *ROLLBACK* (we actually use a similar approach in Section 8.4 to confirm the resulting account balance). If we were to show the account balances after the *ROLLBACK*, we would see the transfer did not occur, as illustrated in Figure 8.11.

```
mysql> SELECT * FROM Account;
+-----------+-----------+
| AccountID | Balance   |
+-----------+-----------+
| A00001    |  10000.00 |
| A00002    |   5000.00 |
| A00003    | 120000.00 |
| A00004    | 400000.00 |
| A00005    | 325000.00 |
| A00006    |  25000.00 |
+-----------+-----------+
6 rows in set (0.00 sec)

mysql> []
```

FIGURE 8.11 The result after a *ROLLBACK*.

While we can effectively implement transactions with either approach, the use of *START TRANSACTION* to begin a transaction is often preferable for a few reasons. First, the use of a distinct statement to begin a transaction helps us more clearly recognize the point where a given transaction begins and exists. Second, *START TRANSACTION* can be issued to begin a transaction whether or not automatic commitments are enabled. Hence, we do not have to be concerned whether automatic commitments are enabled and disable them before the transaction, as well as be concerned whether or not to reenable automatic commitments after the transaction is finished. As such, the remaining discussion with transactions will use a convention of using *START TRANSACTION* to begin a transaction.

Tip: We can issue *START TRANSACTION* to begin a transaction whether or not automatic commits are enabled.

8.4 CONDITION ISSUED *COMMIT* OR *ROLLBACK*

For demonstration purposes, the previous transaction examples—like many transaction examples found in other documentation and resources—involved a set of database operations that concluded with an explicit *COMMIT* or *ROLLBACK*. In other words, the logic or decision-making involved with deciding whether to keep or undo the changes is only explained and not actually carried out by code or SQL statements, and we simply issue a *COMMIT* or *ROLLBACK* at the end of the transaction. While such examples can easily illustrate the resulting effect of a *COMMIT* or *ROLLBACK*, they do not provide a comprehensive picture of how we can more thoroughly implement transactions with an automated decision involved as to whether to conclude the transaction with a *COMMIT* or *ROLLBACK*.

To provide such a more complete transaction implementation, we follow up the financial scenario and demonstrate another approach that does involve an automated decision whether to conclude the transaction with a *COMMIT* or *ROLLBACK*. This example also stores in variables the values of information that will vary from transaction to transaction (such as account identifiers and transfer amount), rather than using fixed values. Thus we have an example that can generally handle any transaction and is a more accurate representation of an actual implementation. Here, we issue the *UPDATE* statements for the transfer like we did before, but instead refer to variables for the account identifiers and transfer amount. We then issue a *SELECT* statement to obtain the balance of the source account and store that balance in the local variable srcBalance. We then determine whether srcBalance is nonnegative, and if so, we presume everything is valid and issue a *COMMIT* to save those transfer changes and make them visible. Otherwise, srcBalance is negative, and we presume an invalid transfer and issue a *ROLLBACK* to undo the transfer changes. Figure 8.12 shows how we may define that set of steps in a stored procedure named AccountTransferIF. AccountTransferIF accepts three parameters, in order: source account identifier, destination account identifier, and transfer amount. The remainder of the procedure follows the steps that we just outlined.

```
mysql> DELIMITER $$$
mysql> CREATE PROCEDURE AccountTransferIF(IN srcAcctID CHAR(6), IN dstAcctID CHAR(6), IN amount DECIMAL(14.2))
    -> BEGIN
    ->    DECLARE srcBalance DECIMAL(14,2);
    ->    START TRANSACTION;
    ->    UPDATE Account SET Balance=Balance-amount WHERE AccountID=srcAcctID;
    ->    UPDATE Account SET Balance=Balance+amount WHERE AccountID=dstAcctID;
    ->    SELECT Balance INTO srcBalance FROM Account WHERE AccountID=srcAcctID;
    ->    IF (srcBalance >= 0) THEN
    ->        COMMIT;
    ->    ELSE
    ->        ROLLBACK;
    ->    END IF;
    -> END;
    -> $$$
Query OK, 0 rows affected (0.10 sec)

mysql> DELIMITER ;
mysql> []
```

FIGURE 8.12 A database transaction implemented with conditional *COMMIT* or *ROLLBACK*.

By defining those steps in a stored procedure, we are able to use a familiar *IF-THEN-ELSE* statement, as well as invoke the transaction with a single *CALL* statement. Figure 8.13 demonstrates how we can invoke AccountTransferIF to transfer 25000.00 from account A00005 to account A00006. Afterwards, we show the account balances to observe the transfer was successfully completed.

```
mysql> call AccountTransferIF('A00005','A00006',25000.00);
Query OK, 0 rows affected, 2 warnings (0.08 sec)

mysql> SELECT * FROM Account;
+-----------+-----------+
| AccountID | Balance   |
+-----------+-----------+
| A00001    |  10000.00 |
| A00002    |   5000.00 |
| A00003    | 120000.00 |
| A00004    | 400000.00 |
| A00005    | 300000.00 |
| A00006    |  50000.00 |
+-----------+-----------+
6 rows in set (0.00 sec)

mysql> []
```

FIGURE 8.13 Calling a stored procedure of a database transaction implemented with conditional *COMMIT* or *ROLLBACK* and a *COMMIT* result.

If we were to call AccountTransferIF with transfer argument values that would leave an account with a negative balance, the procedure would end with a *ROLLBACK* to undo the operations. Figure 8.14 demonstrates an invalid transfer of 20000 from account A00001 to account A00006, as well as the resulting account balances, which remain unchanged from the previous successful transfer and indicate that those transfer operations were undone.

```
mysql> call AccountTransferIF('A00001','A00006',20000.00);
Query OK, 0 rows affected (0.00 sec)

mysql> SELECT * FROM Account;
+-----------+-----------+
| AccountID | Balance   |
+-----------+-----------+
| A00001    |  10000.00 |
| A00002    |   5000.00 |
| A00003    | 120000.00 |
| A00004    | 400000.00 |
| A00005    | 300000.00 |
| A00006    |  50000.00 |
+-----------+-----------+
6 rows in set (0.01 sec)

mysql> []
```

FIGURE 8.14 Calling a stored procedure of a database transaction implemented with conditional *COMMIT* or *ROLLBACK* and a *ROLLBACK* result.

8.5   EXCEPTION ISSUED *ROLLBACK*

As we just demonstrated, a condition issued *COMMIT* or *ROLLBACK* is one approach by which a set of SQL statements or an application can determine whether to conclude a transaction with a *COMMIT* or *ROLLBACK*. Still, we may have other approaches that can more seamlessly—and thoroughly—handle the decision whether to issue a *COMMIT* or *ROLLBACK*. One such approach involves the use of *exceptions*, which are mechanisms that involve the raising of a condition or signal to indicate that a special case occurred. An exception can be handled automatically by some entity, such as a system, application, or even code that we write. A number of programming languages, such as C++, Java, and PHP allow us to write code to handle exceptions and define the exact actions to take when an exception occurs. Let's now see how we can use SQL to define the actions to take when an exception occurs.

We will refine the transaction solution presented in Section 8.4 to use an exception—rather than a condition—in the determination of a *COMMIT* or *ROLLBACK*. To generate an exception, we will involve the use of check constraints to enforce data integrity, as we described in Chapter 3. The Financial database contains a table named AccountCC, which is identical to the original Account table, but additionally has a built-in check constraint to confirm an account's balance is nonnegative. AccountCC contains the same original data values as that of the Account table given in Figure 8.1. Figure 8.15 shows the AccountCC table definition with data values.

```
CREATE TABLE IF NOT EXISTS AccountCC (
        AccountID CHAR(6),
        Balance DECIMAL(14,2) CHECK (Balance >= 0.0)
        PRIMARY KEY (AccountID)
);
```

AccountID	Balance
A00001	$10,000.00
A00002	$5,000.00
A00003	$120,000.00
A00004	$400,000.00
A00005	$325,000.00
A00006	$25,000.00

FIGURE 8.15 AccountCC table definition with check constraint and data.

With that check constraint in place, when an account's balance becomes negative, the DBMS will automatically generate an exception. If no mechanism is in place to handle—or *catch*—such an exception, the DBMS will simply handle the exception by reporting it, as we demonstrated in Chapter 3. For reference, we show in Figure 8.16 how the DBMS may report an exception raised by this new check constraint, should we reduce the balance of account A00001 in table AccountCC by more than $10,000.00.

```
mysql> UPDATE AccountCC SET Balance=Balance-10001 WHERE AccountID='A00001';
ERROR 3819 (HY000): Check constraint 'AccountCC_chk_1' is violated.
mysql> []
```

FIGURE 8.16 Example of DBMS reported check constraint exception.

However, if we implement application code, a stored procedure or stored function to catch such an exception, we can define what action(s) to take. In our case, if an operation that is part of a transaction causes a check constraint-based exception, we want to undo the operations that have occurred in that transaction. Hence, we can define that the action to take is a *ROLLBACK*.

By doing so, when a data integrity condition occurs and requires the reversal of a transaction's operations that have occurred so far, we can have a *ROLLBACK* operation issued in an automated manner to undo those changes. Figure 8.17 shows how we may implement an exception-based *ROLLBACK* approach in a stored procedure named AccountTransferExc.

```
mysql> DELIMITER $$$
mysql> CREATE PROCEDURE AccountTransferExc(IN SrcAcct CHAR(6), IN DstAcct CHAR(6), IN Amount DECIMAL(14.2))
    -> BEGIN
    ->
    ->     DECLARE exit handler for sqlexception
    ->     BEGIN
    ->        ROLLBACK;
    ->     END;
    ->
    ->     START TRANSACTION;
    ->     UPDATE AccountCC SET Balance=Balance-Amount WHERE AccountID=SrcAcct;
    ->     UPDATE AccountCC SET Balance=Balance+Amount WHERE AccountID=DstAcct;
    ->     COMMIT;
    -> END;
    -> $$$
Query OK, 0 rows affected (0.11 sec)

mysql> DELIMITER ;
mysql> █
```

FIGURE 8.17 A database transaction implemented with exception-based *ROLLBACK*.

You will notice a few differences between this implementation and the conditional one given in Figure 8.12. Here, we must define a handler for the exception. In a manner similar to declaring a local variable, we declare a handler for sqlexception, which is the type of exception generated by a check constraint. We do not specify a name for the handler, but rather what type or category of exception or signal the handler is to catch. We then define between a set of *BEGIN* and *END* keywords the statements the handler is to execute, like we would with a stored procedure or function. In this case, we only need the exception handler to issue a *ROLLBACK*.[2]

---

[2]If using a language such as C++, Java or PHP, we could implement the exception handler in the "catch" portion of a "try . . . catch" block. The "try" block would issue statements (including the concluding commit) in a similar manner as our stored procedure implementation. The "catch" block would issue a rollback.

After defining the exception handler, we have the statements for the stored procedure itself. Similar to the one in Section 8.4 but simpler, for this procedure, we have the two *UPDATE* statements involved in the transfer followed by a *COMMIT*. Notice that we do not have an explicit condition or other confirmation that the transfer operations were successful before issuing the *COMMIT*. Rather, we specify in a straightforward manner what steps to carry out, as if everything will be successful. Should something go wrong, the check constraint and exception handler will automatically go into action and issue the *ROLLBACK*.

We can invoke our refined account transfer procedure similar to how we did so with the previous one. Figure 8.18 shows a call to AccountTransferExc that successfully transfers 10000.00 from account A00003 to account A00001, as well as the account balances afterwards.

```
mysql> SELECT * from AccountCC;
+-----------+-----------+
| AccountID | Balance   |
+-----------+-----------+
| A00001    |  20000.00 |
| A00002    |   5000.00 |
| A00003    | 110000.00 |
| A00004    | 400000.00 |
| A00005    | 325000.00 |
| A00006    |  25000.00 |
+-----------+-----------+
6 rows in set (0.07 sec)

mysql> []
```

FIGURE 8.18 Calling a stored procedure of a database transaction implemented with exception-based *ROLLBACK*.

For comparison, let's issue a transfer that would leave an account with a negative balance. We will observe that the exception is "quietly" handled by the handler, which issues the *ROLLBACK*, rather than allows the exception to be simply reported to the user. Figure 8.19 shows the outcome if we were to attempt a transfer of 50000.00 from Account A00001 to account A00002. If we are following these demonstrations in the sequence presented, we observe the effect that the exception handler initiated a *ROLLBACK*, and we still have the same balances that we left off with in Figure 8.18.

```
mysql> call AccountTransferExc('A00001','A00002',50000.00);
Query OK, 0 rows affected (0.00 sec)

mysql> SELECT * from AccountCC;
+-----------+-----------+
| AccountID | Balance   |
+-----------+-----------+
| A00001    |  20000.00 |
| A00002    |   5000.00 |
| A00003    | 110000.00 |
| A00004    | 400000.00 |
| A00005    | 325000.00 |
| A00006    |  25000.00 |
+-----------+-----------+
6 rows in set (0.00 sec)

mysql> []
```

FIGURE 8.19 Calling a stored procedure of a database transaction implemented with exception-based *ROLLBACK* occurring.

Such "quiet" handling of exceptions is a benefit of exception handlers, where we want an action to be automatically carried out rather than simply report the occurrence. However, in practice we may want to also record the occurrence of the exception as well as carry out the action. One way we can do both is to include in the exception handler an *INSERT* statement that adds a relevant row to a table that holds logs or error-related events. That way information about the exception is recorded so that we can refer back to it in the future. Figure 8.20 gives an example of how we may implement a revised stored procedure named AccountTransferExcLog to log information about an exception into a table named Logs, which has also been included with the Financial database.

```
mysql> DELIMITER $$$
mysql> CREATE PROCEDURE AccountTransferExcLog(IN srcAcctID CHAR(6), IN dstAcctID CHAR(6), IN amount DECIMAL(14.2))
    -> BEGIN
    ->
    ->    DECLARE exit handler for sqlexception
    ->    BEGIN
    ->       ROLLBACK;
    ->       INSERT INTO Logs(SourceAccountID,DestinationAccountID,Amount) VALUES (srcAcctID,dstAcctID,amount);
    ->    END;
    ->
    ->    START TRANSACTION;
    ->    UPDATE AccountCC SET Balance=Balance-Amount WHERE AccountID=SrcAcct;
    ->    UPDATE AccountCC SET Balance=Balance+Amount WHERE AccountID=DstAcct;
    ->    COMMIT;
    -> END;
    -> $$$
Query OK, 0 rows affected (0.11 sec)

mysql> DELIMITER ;
mysql> []
```

FIGURE 8.20 A database transaction implemented with exception-based *ROLLBACK* and logging.

If we were to repeat the previous transfer attempt of Figure 8.19, we would now additionally have the exception occurrence recorded in the Log table, as shown in Figure 8.21.

```
mysql> call AccountTransferExcLog('A00001','A00002',50000.00);
Query OK, 1 row affected, 2 warnings (0.10 sec)

mysql> SELECT * from Logs;
+-----------------+----------------------+----------+
| SourceAccountID | DestinationAccountID | Amount   |
+-----------------+----------------------+----------+
| A00001          | A00002               | 50000.00 |
+-----------------+----------------------+----------+
1 row in set (0.00 sec)

mysql> []
```

FIGURE 8.21 Showing the log entry added by exception-based *ROLLBACK*.

In addition to data integrity-based exceptions, we may also need to consider other types of error-related events that may occur—such as an error or inability to add or delete a row. Identifying a list of such errors, as well as detecting these errors with database statements or code, can be challenging, tedious, require a significant amount of SQL statements or code, and slow down activity with the extra processing. Fortunately many such events typically generate an exception that can also be handled with an exception handler like the one we just defined. And the action to take would most likely be a *ROLLBACK* of the transaction operations. Consequently, the use of an exception handler like we demonstrated to issue a *ROLLBACK* can catch or handle a variety of errors that we may not completely anticipate, and all with the same handler, so we may not have to implement additional coding or other processing. Furthermore, other types of exceptions (such as sqlwarning) may be generated by certain events. As we did for sqlexception, we can similarly define handlers for those types of exceptions if necessary.

8.6   A LARGER DEMONSTRATION OF TRANSACTIONS

As another, more comprehensive demonstration of transactions to uphold data integrity, let's consider an e-commerce scenario, where customers purchase items online.[3]

---

[3]There are various implementations to the functionality, browsing, selecting, and purchasing activities in an e-commerce system. This demonstration considers one of those implementations.

In a common e-commerce scenario, a user browses items whose data—such as description, cost, and number of that item available—is stored in a database. The user selects (or places in a "cart") the items they wish to purchase. Information about the user selections or cart contents may be stored either on the user's system or in the database itself. Either way, when the user continues with the purchase of those items, a number of database accesses will occur. At the very least, we must store information in the database about the order itself and items involved, as well as reduce the numbers of those items in stock or available for other purchases. We will consider those database accesses involved with the purchasing task as a database transaction.

If all of those database accesses are considered successful, we will have all the necessary information for the order created and item counts reduced accordingly. However, we must consider that one of those individual database accesses in the purchasing transaction may yield an error or invalid outcome. For example, suppose the number available of a particular item is *smaller* than the number requested in the order. If we were to reduce the number available by the ordered number, we would then have a negative number available, which may be considered invalid and/or a data constraint violation. An e-commerce application may handle such an outcome in a variety of ways. Perhaps the application may proceed with the purchase and include in the order only those items in which there are enough available. Alternatively, the application may interrupt the purchase altogether, allow the user to make corrections or adjustments to items and their number ordered, and retry the purchase. For our transaction scenario, we will consider the latter implementation, where the application wants to cancel that transaction, allow the user to make adjustments, and retry the purchase.

A business scenario that may fit this particular e-commerce behavior is one for a restaurant's online ordering system. A customer who, say, places an order for a dinner or event may need to make corrections immediately if an item is not available in the number desired. Let's consider a restaurant for which we are to implement online ordering of their products for customer pickup. The table definitions for the database to support this need are given in Figure 8.22 and the table data in Figure 8.23. Here, we have one table named Item that stores information about the items a customer may add to their order, and another table named CustomerOrder that stores information about all customer orders. Because we have a many-to-many relationship between the Item and CustomerOrder tables, the implementation also involves an intersection table named OrderItem that stores information about a particular order's items. The presence of a CustomerID field in the CustOrder table implies that we also have a Customer table, but for brevity we do not show that table, as it is not involved in this transaction example. Also, to keep this example more focused on the transaction process, we will assume the items that a user selects are stored on the user's system or device while the user browses and makes their order selections. When the user completes the purchase and places the order, the order information is then added to the database and the item counts are reduced accordingly.

```
CREATE TABLE IF NOT EXISTS Item (
        ItemID CHAR(4),
        Description VARCHAR(256),
        Price DECIMAL(5,2),
        Available INT CHECK (Available >= 0),
        CONSTRAINT ItemPK PRIMARY KEY (ItemID)
);

CREATE TABLE IF NOT EXISTS CustOrder (
        OrderID CHAR(4),
        CustomerID CHAR(4),
        PickupTime TIME,
        CONSTRAINT OrderPK PRIMARY KEY (OrderID)
);

CREATE TABLE IF NOT EXISTS OrderItem (
        OrderID CHAR(4),
        ItemID CHAR(4),
        Quantity INT,
        CONSTRAINT OrderItemPK PRIMARY KEY (OrderID,ItemID)
);
```

FIGURE 8.22 Table definitions for an e-commerce restaurant scenario.

ITEM

ItemID	Description	Price	Available
I001	Smoked Chicken (whole, 3 lbs)	$12.00	16
I002	Smoked Chicken (half, 1.5 lbs)	$8.00	23
I003	Smoked Baby Back Ribs (full rack)	$16.00	2
I004	Smoked Baby Back Ribs (half rack)	$10.00	5
I005	Smoked Brisket (1 lbs)	$6.00	8
I006	Smoked Butt (1 lb)	$5.00	9
I007	Hamburger (1/4 lb)	$4.50	12
I008	Cheeseburger (1/4 lb)	$5.00	14
I009	Baked Potato with Sour Cream	$2.00	31
I010	French Fries	$3.00	35
I011	Garden Salad	$4.00	17
I012	Caesar Salad	$4.00	16
I013	Green Beans (1 lb)	$5.00	17
I014	Baked Beans (1 lb)	$5.00	14
I015	Kaiser Rolls (6)	$3.00	23
I016	Peanut Butter Pie (1 piece)	$2.50	12
I017	Peanut Butter Pie (8 pieces / 1 pie)	$12.00	4

CustomerOrder

OrderID	CustomerID	PickupTime
O001	C009	17:00
O002	C021	18:00
O003	C003	17:30

OrderItem

OrderID	ItemID	Quantity
O001	I004	1
O001	I009	1
O001	I012	1
O002	I001	2
O002	I009	6
O002	I011	6
O002	I013	2
O003	I008	2
O003	I010	2

FIGURE 8.23 Table data for an e-commerce restaurant scenario.

Suppose that the customer with CustId C001 now selects items and places an order. The customer selects 6 lbs. of smoked brisket (item I005), 6 packages of rolls (item I015), and 15 garden salads (item I011) for pickup at 18:30. The customer then places the order. In our scenario the created order information involves adding one row to the CustomerOrder table and adding one or more rows to the OrderItem table. The row added to CustomerOrder contains an identifier for the order (OrderID), identifier for the customer (CustomerID), and time in which the order will be picked up (PickupTime). The data added to OrderItem involves one row for each item ordered, which includes the identifier of the order (OrderID), identifier of a particular item (ItemID), and number of that item in the order (Quantity). Furthermore, in the Item table we also reduce the Available count of those ordered items, so that we maintain a current count of the number available for other orders.

With all these operations involved in an order transaction, we need to consider that one or more of them may not be successful or generate a result that is considered invalid. In that situation, we want to undo all of the operations involved with that order to appear as if the order had not yet been placed, then allow the customer to make changes to the items and attempt to place the order again. For example, the adding of a row to CustomerOrder or OrderItem may be unsuccessful because of a resource limit or referential integrity constraint violation with a foreign key. That may be a very unlikely error, but such an error may occur. More likely, we might encounter an error related to a business rule or data check constraint, such as when an item's Available value becomes negative if the transaction reduces an item's Available count to a negative value. Notice that the Item table in Figure 8.22 has a check constraint to confirm that the Available value is nonnegative.

Even though we do not involve the payment process in this example, with a more complete transaction, we may also involve the payment process as one of the transaction operations. Even though the payment process may not directly involve our database, we may wish to include the payment within the transaction so that the outcome of the payment process can affect the concluding *ROLLBACK* or *COMMIT*.[4]

If we were to carry out the processing of customer C001's order within a transaction, we would issue a series of SQL steps like those within the stored procedure PlaceOrder shown in Figure 8.24. For the purpose of this demonstration and to clearly see the data changes are involved, we show hardcoded SQL *INSERT* and *UPDATE* statements for the items in the transaction with explicit values based on the order details, and we define the stored procedure with no arguments. In an actual setting, we would use SQL statements or other language code that references the order's CustomerID, OrderID, and list of items as arguments or variables. The *INSERT* and *UPDATE* statements would then refer to those values. Let's presume the OrderID that is associated with this order is O004. After issuing the SQL statements, the procedure concludes with a *COMMIT* and sets an outgoing result session variable value to 0. The outgoing result provides the caller with a way to know whether or not the transaction ended with a *COMMIT* or *ROLLBACK*. As with many programming languages, we use a result of 0 to indicate the transaction was successful and a *COMMIT* was issued. To handle cases where the transaction is unsuccessful, we have an exception handler issue a *ROLLBACK*. The handler also sets the outgoing result to –1 to let the caller know that the transaction failed.

---

[4]An e-commerce application may involve the payment mechanism as part of the transaction involved with placing the order as described. For example, using an exception-based rollback, the transaction may add the order information and reduce the item counts. If no exception has been generated thus far to rollback the transaction, the transaction may then process the payment. If payment is successful, the transaction may simply conclude and issue a commit. If payment is unsuccessful, the payment mechanism or transaction may generate an exception, and the exception handler would issue a rollback of the order operations.

```
mysql> DELIMITER $$$
mysql> CREATE PROCEDURE PlaceOrder(OUT result INT)
    -> BEGIN
    ->
    ->     DECLARE exit handler for sqlexception
    ->     BEGIN
    ->       ROLLBACK;
    ->         SET result = -1;
    ->     END;
    ->
    ->     START TRANSACTION;
    ->     INSERT INTO CustOrder VALUES ('O004','C001','18:30');
    ->     INSERT INTO OrderItem VALUES ('O004','I005',6);
    ->     INSERT INTO OrderItem VALUES ('O004','I016',6);
    ->     INSERT INTO OrderItem VALUES ('O004','I011',15);
    ->     UPDATE Item SET Available=Available-6 WHERE ItemID='I005';
    ->     UPDATE Item SET Available=Available-6 WHERE ItemID='I016';
    ->     UPDATE Item SET Available=Available-15 WHERE ItemID='I011';
    ->     COMMIT;
    ->     SET result = 0;
    -> END;
    -> $$$
Query OK, 0 rows affected (0.09 sec)

mysql> DELIMITER ;
mysql> █
```

FIGURE 8.24 Transaction and SQL statements involved with customer C001's order.

Starting with the data shown in Figure 8.23, when customer C001's places their order, we would in practice call PlaceOrder with the necessary incoming argument values that pertain to the order, as well as an argument to receive the outgoing result value. However, because we show PlaceOrder with hard-coded values of the order for demonstrative purposes, we call PlaceOrder with only the argument that receives the outgoing result, as illustrated in Figure 8.25. We then show the returned result value of 0, which tells us that the transaction was successful and committed. Afterwards, we drop the stored procedure because of the hardcoded values for that order so that we can demonstrate another order that follows.

```
mysql> CALL PlaceOrder(@result);
Query OK, 0 rows affected (0.09 sec)

mysql> SELECT @result AS Result;
+--------+
| Result |
+--------+
|      0 |
+--------+
1 row in set (0.00 sec)

mysql> DROP PROCEDURE PlaceOrder;
Query OK, 0 rows affected (0.10 sec)

mysql> []
```

FIGURE 8.25 Placing C001's order and viewing the returned transaction result.

Presuming all the transaction operations are successful, we have the resulting data after the *COMMIT* of that transaction shown in Figure 8.26. For a complete snapshot of the data, we illustrate the data in a figure of tables rather than query each table, although if you were to query each table you would see the same data.[5]

ITEM

ItemID	Description	Price	Available
I001	Smoked Chicken (whole, 3 lbs)	$12.00	16
I002	Smoked Chicken (half, 1.5 lbs)	$8.00	23
I003	Smoked Baby Back Ribs (full rack)	$16.00	2
I004	Smoked Baby Back Ribs (half rack)	$10.00	5
I005	Smoked Brisket (1 lbs)	$6.00	2
I006	Smoked Butt (1 lb)	$5.00	9
I007	Hamburger (1/4 lb)	$4.50	12
I008	Cheeseburger (1/4 lb)	$5.00	14
I009	Baked Potato with Sour Cream	$2.00	31
I010	French Fries	$3.00	35
I011	Garden Salad	$4.00	2
I012	Caesar Salad	$4.00	16
I013	Green Beans (1 lb)	$5.00	17
I014	Baked Beans (1 lb)	$5.00	14
I015	Kaiser Rolls (6)	$3.00	17
I016	Peanut Butter Pie (1 piece)	$2.50	12
I017	Peanut Butter Pie (8 pieces / 1 pie)	$12.00	4

CustomerOrder

OrderID	CustomerID	PickupTime
O001	C009	17:00
O002	C021	18:00
O003	C003	17:30
O004	C001	18:30

OrderItem

OrderID	ItemID	Quantity
O001	I004	1
O001	I009	1
O001	I012	1
O002	I001	2
O002	I009	6
O002	I011	6
O002	I013	2
O003	I008	2
O003	I010	2
O004	I005	6
O004	I016	6
O004	I011	15

FIGURE 8.26 E-commerce database after customer C001 successfully places an order.

Now suppose customer C012 wishes to place an order of 2 smoked chickens (item I001), 3 lbs. of smoked brisket (item I005), and 10 baked potatoes (item I009) for pickup at 18:45. Let's presume the OrderID that is associated with this order is O005. Figure 8.27 shows the series of SQL statements in a hardcoded form that will be issued for that transaction.

---

[5]Depending on the e-commerce checkout implementation, the process of issuing and confirming payment may also be within the transaction that prepares the order and reduces item counts as part of the checkout process. Our example considers the ordering system processes the payment first, and if successful, only then proceeds with the transaction to prepare the order and reduce item counts.

```
mysql> DELIMITER $$$
mysql> CREATE PROCEDURE PlaceOrder(OUT result INT)
    -> BEGIN
    ->
    ->    DECLARE exit handler for sqlexception
    ->    BEGIN
    ->      ROLLBACK;
    ->      SET result = -1;
    ->    END;
    ->
    ->    START TRANSACTION;
    ->    INSERT INTO CustOrder VALUES ('O005','C012','18:45');
    ->    INSERT INTO OrderItem VALUES ('O005','I001',2);
    ->    INSERT INTO OrderItem VALUES ('O005','I005',3);
    ->    INSERT INTO OrderItem VALUES ('O005','I009',10);
    ->    UPDATE Item SET Available=Available-2 WHERE ItemID='I002';
    ->    UPDATE Item SET Available=Available-3 WHERE ItemID='I005';
    ->    UPDATE Item SET Available=Available-10 WHERE ItemID='I001';
    ->    COMMIT;
    ->    SET result = 0;
    -> END;
    -> $$$
Query OK, 0 rows affected (0.09 sec)

mysql> DELIMITER ;
mysql>
```

FIGURE 8.27 Transaction and SQL statements involved with customer C012's order.

Simulating the call to PlaceOrder in a similar manner as we did for the previous order, we have the series of statements as shown in Figure 8.28. We notice this time we have a returned result value of –1, which tells us the order's transaction failed and was rolled back.

```
mysql> CALL PlaceOrder(@result);
Query OK, 0 rows affected (0.00 sec)

mysql> SELECT @result AS Result;
+--------+
| Result |
+--------+
|     -1 |
+--------+
1 row in set (0.00 sec)

mysql> DROP Procedure PlaceOrder;
Query OK, 0 rows affected (0.07 sec)

mysql>
```

FIGURE 8.28 Placing C012's order and viewing the returned transaction result.

To review why the transaction failed and the action taken, let's review the transaction statements given in Figure 8.27. The *INSERT* statements and first *UPDATE* statement as given in this transaction add rows to CustomerOrder and OrderItem and update the Available value for item I001. However, when updating item I005's Available value, we have a negative result. Figure 8.29 shows how those tables and data appear to the transaction up to this point. We show the data that has been added and modified in the transaction so far with a gray background to indicate that those changes have not yet been finalized with a commit or rollback. Presuming the check constraint for the second item generated an exception, we never reach the point where the Available value for the third item is reduced. Consequently, Figure 8.29 does not show a reduced Available value for item I009.

ITEM

ItemID	Description	Price	Available
I001	Smoked Chicken (whole, 3 lbs)	$12.00	14
I002	Smoked Chicken (half, 1.5 lbs)	$8.00	23
I003	Smoked Baby Back Ribs (full rack)	$16.00	2
I004	Smoked Baby Back Ribs (half rack)	$10.00	5
I005	Smoked Brisket (1 lbs)	$6.00	-1
I006	Smoked Butt (1 lb)	$5.00	9
I007	Hamburger (1/4 lb)	$4.50	12
I008	Cheeseburger (1/4 lb)	$5.00	14
I009	Baked Potato with Sour Cream	$2.00	31
I010	French Fries	$3.00	35
I011	Garden Salad	$4.00	2
I012	Caesar Salad	$4.00	16
I013	Green Beans (1 lb)	$5.00	17
I014	Baked Beans (1 lb)	$5.00	14
I015	Kaiser Rolls (6)	$3.00	17
I016	Peanut Butter Pie (1 piece)	$2.50	12
I017	Peanut Butter Pie (8 pieces / 1 pie)	$12.00	4

CustomerOrder

OrderID	CustomerID	PickupTime
O001	C009	17:00
O002	C021	18:00
O003	C003	17:30
O004	C001	18:30
O005	C012	18:45

OrderItem

OrderID	ItemID	Quantity
O001	I004	1
O001	I009	1
O001	I012	1
O002	I001	2
O002	I009	6
O002	I011	6
O002	I013	2
O003	I008	2
O003	I010	2
O004	I005	6
O004	I016	6
O004	I011	15
O005	I001	2
O005	I005	3
O005	I009	10

FIGURE 8.29 E-commerce database with customer C012's order being processed. Data values in gray represent the changes within the transaction.

The exception handler is then invoked because of the negative Available value and issues a rollback. That rollback effectively undoes all of those changes in gray as shown in Figure 8.30, which is identical to the data in Figure 8.26 immediately before the transaction started.

ITEM

ItemID	Description	Price	Available
I001	Smoked Chicken (whole, 3 lbs)	$12.00	16
I002	Smoked Chicken (half, 1.5 lbs)	$8.00	23
I003	Smoked Baby Back Ribs (full rack)	$16.00	2
I004	Smoked Baby Back Ribs (half rack)	$10.00	5
I005	Smoked Brisket (1 lbs)	$6.00	2
I006	Smoked Butt (1 lb)	$5.00	9
I007	Hamburger (1/4 lb)	$4.50	12
I008	Cheeseburger (1/4 lb)	$5.00	14
I009	Baked Potato with Sour Cream	$2.00	31
I010	French Fries	$3.00	35
I011	Garden Salad	$4.00	2
I012	Caesar Salad	$4.00	16
I013	Green Beans (1 lb)	$5.00	17
I014	Baked Beans (1 lb)	$5.00	14
I015	Kaiser Rolls (6)	$3.00	17
I016	Peanut Butter Pie (1 piece)	$2.50	12
I017	Peanut Butter Pie (8 pieces / 1 pie)	$12.00	4

CustomerOrder

OrderID	CustomerID	PickupTime
O001	C009	17:00
O002	C021	18:00
O003	C003	17:30
O004	C001	18:30

OrderItem

OrderID	ItemID	Quantity
O001	I004	1
O001	I009	1
O001	I012	1
O002	I001	2
O002	I009	6
O002	I011	6
O002	I013	2
O003	I008	2
O003	I010	2
O004	I005	6
O004	I016	6
O004	I011	15

FIGURE 8.30 E-commerce database after a rollback of customer C012's order.

8.7 SUMMARY

In this chapter, we considered more complex database operations that involve multiple accesses. Now that we have familiarity with the purpose of transactions and how we may use them, we explore in the next chapter some other data integrity controls that we can employ in larger or more comprehensive environments.

CHAPTER 9

DATA INTEGRITY WITH CONCURRENT ACCESS

Chapter 8 focused on maintaining data integrity when we have multiple accesses per task. Chapter 9 focuses on another data integrity concern, this time with multiple sessions accessing the DBMS and its data. So far, we have considered rather simple data access scenarios where only one user or application session accesses the database at a given time, such that the operations by one session completes before those of another session begin. Such accesses are referred to as *serial* accesses, or those that occur one after the other. However, in larger and/or busier environments, it may be common that, at any given time, multiple user or application sessions may need to access the database and issue tasks at the same time. Such *concurrent access* introduces a risk of data integrity problems that compromise the information security objective of integrity. The following describes various data integrity problems and solutions that we can employ to solve those problems. We begin with a follow-up to the Chapter 3 topic of backups, and then expand upon the scenarios with data access from recent chapters.

9.1   CONCURRENT ACCESS AND BACKUPS

In Chapter 3, "Database Management and Administration," we described a variety of backup solutions for availability involving all databases, certain databases, or certain tables. However, we assumed a single-session DBMS environment, where at any given time, at most one user or application has a session connection to the DBMS. In larger or busier environments, such an assumption may not be practical, and at any given time we may actually have multiple users and/or applications with active sessions to the DBMS. It is the presence of these multiple active sessions that introduces the potential for data integrity problems. Such data integrity problems occur when multiple user or application sessions exist at a given time, and at least one of those concurrent sessions issue changes to DBMS components (databases, tables, stored procedures, stored functions, and so on) and/or data itself.

In the context of backups, in order to maintain data integrity, a backup that we create should have a consistent snapshot of the backed up contents. We do not want, say, part of the backup to contain database content before a session issues a change to the DBMS components or data, and another part of the backup to contain other DBMS content that does include those issued changes. Such an *inconsistency* compromises the data integrity objective with information security.

As a specific example of a data integrity compromise of DBMS components with backups, consider a session that issues data definition language (DDL) SQL statements to add a table and corresponding referential integrity constraints while a backup is in progress. This action introduces a risk of an inconsistent backup, where part of the backup may not include necessary references to the added table, but other parts of the backup do.

As another specific example of a data integrity compromise in a backup, let's look at one with the actual data itself. Consider data manipulation language (DML) statements that a session can issue to change table data. Suppose we initiate a backup that involves two tables and their data. The first table contains an inventory of items that includes the count of each item in stock. The second table contains order information, which includes with each order a list of items as well as the number of that item in that order. To maintain an item's current stock count in the first table, when an order is placed, for each item in the order, the DBMS reduces the item's stock count by the number specified in the placed order. The DBMS also inserts order details into the second table, which includes the number of each item specified in the order. If one were to place an order while a backup is concurrently in progress, we introduce the risk of an inconsistent backup, where the backup may possibly contain data in the first table with inventory and stock count before the order is placed, but also contain data in the second table after the order is placed.

Consequently, the backup would then portray an inconsistent snapshot where we have the item's stock count before the order, as well as order details which implies some of those items have been sold. Hence, the inventory stock number is larger than it should be.

In both examples, we have risks of data integrity in our backups, namely disparities or inconsistencies with DBMS components or data in the backup. Such data integrity problems can occur if operations are allowed to change DBMS components or data while a backup is in progress. To solve such data integrity problems associated with backups, we want to ensure a consistent snapshot of the database components and data during the backup task. In other words, we want to temporarily "freeze" the database components and data itself from any changes while the backup takes place. We can accomplish such a freeze by *locking* the necessary DBMS components and data. A lock is a synchronization mechanism that coordinates access to shared resources or data and can be used as a solution for a variety of data integrity problems.

We can use a lock at a variety of levels in a DBMS, depending on the scope of the resource(s) or data of which we want to coordinate access. To carry out a complete backup of all DBMS components and data, we will first consider a lock that effectively freezes all of the DBMS components and data. That way the backup task can create a copy of a single, consistent snapshot of any or all databases without introducing a data integrity risk caused by potential changes during the backup. With such a lock in place, if a session attempts to carry out a DDL or DML statement that adds, removes, or modifies a DBMS component or any data, the DBMS will make that session wait until the backup is complete and the lock is removed. Then the DBMS will allow that DDL or DML statement to be safely carried out so as to not risk data integrity of the generated backup.

To issue such a lock on all databases with MySQL, Oracle, or MariaDB, we can issue the *FLUSH TABLES* statement, as shown in Figure 9.1. Despite the mention of tables, this statement effectively freezes all database components and data so that we can achieve a consistent snapshot and resulting backup. This statement also ensures that all table data is first written to disk so that all latest changes are included in the backup. When that statement returns to the session, all table data has been written and we have a read lock in effect on all databases. For now, simply consider this read lock allows read-only access to the DBMS and data but disallows any efforts to add, remove, or modify DBMS components or data.

```
mysql> FLUSH TABLES WITH READ LOCK;
Query OK, 0 rows affected (0.02 sec)

mysql> ▌
```

FIGURE 9.1 Locking the DBMS and data for a backup.

We can then create a backup of the locked DBMS content in one of two approaches. In the first approach, with another session to the DBMS, we can then safely issue a backup statement such as with **mysqldump** as we did in Chapter 3. Notice that we mention "with another session," because if we close the session that issued the *FLUSH TABLES* lock, the DBMS will release that lock.

The second approach issues the backup within the session that established the lock. This approach leaves the session open and hence retains the lock. In Figure 9.2, within the session that established the lock on the DBMS, we issue a **system** statement to issue the **mysqldump** command. That will create a backup of the entire DBMS and data into the backup file my_consistent_backup.sql, without closing the session and releasing the lock. While the backup is in progress—namely while the lock is in effect—if any other session were to issue a DDL or DML statement to add, remove, or change a DBMS component or data, that session would wait. Later in this chapter, we discuss the use of locks in more detail and will demonstrate the effects of such waits, as well as the effects of read locks and write locks. For now, we will just consider the presence of this read lock allows the backup to proceed without a data integrity risk by causing concurrent DML or DDL modifying statements to wait for now.

```
mysql> system mysqldump -u root -p --all-databases --routines > consistent_dbms_backup.sql
Enter password:
mysql> UNLOCK TABLES;
Query OK, 0 rows affected (0.00 sec)

mysql> ▯
```

FIGURE 9.2 Issuing a backup of the locked DBMS and data and releasing that lock.

After the backup is complete, that session (the one that issued the *FLUSH TABLES* statement) can remove that lock with the *UNLOCK TABLES* statement, as shown at the end of Figure 9.2. After the *UNLOCK TABLES* statement returns, all sessions regain the ability to access and make changes to the DBMS components and data (provided they had that ability to do so before the lock was issued), and the DBMS will allow any waiting DDL or DML statements to proceed.

If we wish to backup only certain tables of a DBMS, we do not have to issue a lock on the entire DBMS as we did in Figure 9.1, but can rather lock only the tables that will be included in the backup. While we could lock the entire DBMS to maintain data integrity to a backup of only certain tables, notice that we would also disallow all but read-only access to other parts of the DBMS and data that we do not need to protect for that backup.

When issuing a backup to only certain tables, it is better to lock only those tables to freeze only the content needed in the backup. Figure 9.3 gives the general syntax for the *FLUSH TABLES* statement. If we do not specify any database(s) and/or table(s), *FLUSH TABLES* locks the entire DBMS including all data. To lock a specific table, we use a statement similar to that in Figure 9.1 for the entire DBMS, but also immediately follow the *TABLES* keyword with the table name, optionally prefixed with its database name and a period. If we specify only a table name, the statement refers to that table in the currently selected database to use. The ellipsis within square brackets indicate that to lock multiple tables, we specify the names of those tables in a comma-separated list, with each table optionally prefixed with their database name and a period.

```
FLUSH TABLES [database.]table [, ...] WITH READ LOCK
```

FIGURE 9.3 General syntax of the *FLUSH TABLES* statement to obtain a read lock.

As an example of locking a specific table for backup, suppose we wish to backup only the Patient table and its data in the MedicalCaseStudy database from Chapter 7. Figure 9.4 shows how we can issue a read lock to freeze only that table, and we also prefix the database name just in case that database is not currently selected to be used.

```
mysql> FLUSH TABLES MedicalCaseStudy.Patient WITH READ LOCK;
Query OK, 0 rows affected (0.00 sec)

mysql> []
```

FIGURE 9.4 Locking a table and its data for backup.

After locking the table, we can safely issue a backup statement and unlock that table like that in Figure 9.5. The same *UNLOCK TABLES* statement will unlock all tables specified with the previous lock, whether we locked a single table or multiple tables.

```
mysql> system mysqldump -u root -p MedicalCaseStudy Patient > patient_backup.sql
Enter password:
mysql> UNLOCK TABLES;
Query OK, 0 rows affected (0.00 sec)

mysql> █
```

FIGURE 9.5 Backup of a specific table and unlocking the table and its data.

A DBMS may have other statements to lock or freeze certain parts of the DBMS for backup, but we focused on the *FLUSH TABLES* statement because it seems more universal.

9.2 CONCURRENT ACCESS WITH DML STATEMENTS

In the previous chapters, we issued SQL statements to retrieve, add, remove, or modify data in the context of a single active session (that issues one statement after the other, or *serially*), or multiple sessions (where each session issues its own statements serially and statements are serial across sessions such that no two sessions concurrently have a statement in progress). By doing so, we ensure that only one such task is carried out on the DBMS at a given time, and therefore preserve data integrity.

However, in a larger and/or busier environment, such strict serial behavior may not be practical or desirable. Consider a larger and/or busier environment where, at a given time, we may potentially have multiple sessions that each wish to issue a task. If we require each of these tasks to be issued serially in those environments, the *turnaround time*, or elapsed time from submission of a task until that task completes, of those accesses may significantly increase as the number of tasks increases. For example, if 100 sessions each need to issue a task at the same time but are required to issue the tasks serially among each other, the tasks will be processed as if waiting in a line. The first task will be handled while the other 99 wait their turn. After that first task completes, the second task is handled while the other 98 wait. This continues until the last task is finally handled, after waiting for the other 99 tasks to complete first, one after the other. As such, the performance of serial access turnaround time does not *scale* well as the number of tasks increases.

To better scale the turnaround time in such larger and/or busier environments, we can alternatively allow simultaneous or concurrent access for those multiple users or application sessions, so that rather than wait its turn, a task can go ahead and issue its database operations while another task also does so. This concurrent approach can better utilize the database and significantly reduce task turnaround time by not imposing that requirement for tasks to wait in line. Unfortunately, such concurrency can also introduce a data integrity problem related to *data consistency*.

We described in Chapter 2, "Database Design," how a form of data integrity problems with data consistency can arise because of duplicated data and showed how we can solve that problem with database normalization. We will now describe other data integrity problems with data consistency that may occur when multiple user or application sessions concurrently access the *same* data. To illustrate this problem, consider the Financial scenario and account transfers in Chapter 8. We could involve any of the account transfer approaches from that discussion, but let's refer to the most recent implementation that we showed in Figure 8.20 for the stored procedure AccountTransferExcLog, which employs a check constraint, exception, and logging. Recall that implementation uses the AccountCC table, which we will presume still has the data as shown in Figure 8.15. If your data in that table is different, you may wish to restore that table from the backup file Financial_AccountCC.sql.

AccountTransferExcLog seems rather comprehensive to cover security concerns if only one user or application session can issue this stored procedure at any given time. However, a data integrity issue arises when multiple sessions concurrently access this stored procedure. Even though we refer to this stored procedure, rather than call it, in the following examples we take a closer look at the individual operations within that procedure.

Let's examine the data integrity concern by comparing two serial transfer cases and two concurrent transfer cases. The first serial case involves two transfers, one that sends an amount from account A00001 to account A00002, and another transfer that sends an amount from account A00003 to account A00004. When issued serially, we do not have a potential for data inconsistency among the account balances because each transfer involves different accounts. Therefore, one transfer cannot interfere with the other.

Let's now consider the second serial case that also involves two transfers, TransferA that sends an amount from account A00001 to A00002, and another transfer, TransferB, that sends an amount from account A00001 to A00003. When issued serially, TransferA will complete before TransferB begins, or vice versa. Figure 9.6 shows the sequence of data accesses to account A00001 if TransferA occurs first. These data accesses refer to the first *UPDATE* statement, which first reads the source account balance, subtracts the transfer amount from that read balance, and then writes the resulting balance back to the database. For brevity and to focus on the data integrity threat with account A00001, the account accessed by both transfers, Figure 9.6 does not include the accesses to accounts A00002 or A00003. Those accounts are not accessed by both transfers, so the accesses to read, add to, and then write their balances as the second part of each transfer occur without data integrity concerns.

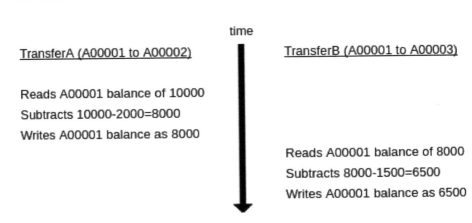

FIGURE 9.6 Steps involved in serial transfers between A00001 to A00002 and A00001 to A00003.

In this second serial case, both transfers involve account A00001 as the transfer source. If we issue the transfers in the second case serially, or one after the other, we still do not have a data integrity concern. For example, if account A00001 starts with a balance of 10000.00, and we transfer 2000.00 to account A00002, that leaves A00001 with 10000.00-2000.00 or 8000.00. Then after the first transfer completes, if we follow with the second transfer of 1500.00 from account A00001 to A00003, that leaves account A00001 with 8000.00-1500.00 or 6500.00, which is what we would expect. We even have the same resulting balance if TransferB were to occur serially before TransferA. Neither serial case presents a data integrity concern, and each account ends up with the proper balance expected.

On the other hand, suppose that we had allowed concurrent access to this stored procedure so that we can better scale as the number of transfers increases. Looking at the first case with concurrent access, again TransferA sends an amount from account A00001 to account A00002, and TransferB sends an amount from account A00003 to account A00004. As with serial access, we still do not have a potential for data inconsistency in this first case among the account balances, because each transfer accesses different accounts.

However, in the second concurrent case, we do have potential for a data integrity concern, because both transfers access a given account, namely A00001. Figure 9.7 illustrates one of the possible sequences of steps involved with these concurrent transfers. As with Figure 9.6, we focus on the steps involved with the account that is accessed by both transfers, the source account A00001.

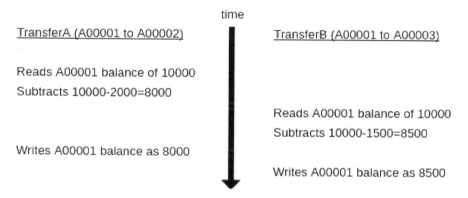

FIGURE 9.7 Possible sequence of steps involved with concurrent transfers between A00001 to A00002 and A00001 to A00003.

Again presuming account A00001 initially has a balance of 15000.00, account A00002 has 5000.00, and account A00003 has 120000.00, suppose both transfers are issued concurrently. Each transfer carries out the first *UPDATE* statement. However, an *UPDATE* statement actually consists of three data steps: a read of the data value, a modification to the read value, and a write of the resulting value back to the database. Suppose the first transfer carries out the read and modification steps, but before it issues the third step, the write, a second transfer begins to carry out its *UPDATE* statement steps. The second transfer carries out a read in the database for the data whose modified value has not yet been written back by the first transfer. So the first transfer reads a balance of 10000.00 and subtracts 2000.00 yielding 8000.00, while the second transfer reads a balance of 10000.00 (which is still the value in the database) and subtracts 1500.00 yielding 8500.00. Then each transfer proceeds to write their corresponding result back to the database.

Figure 9.8 shows a case where the first transfer carries out its write before the second transfer. So the first transfer writes back 8000.00 as the new balance, and then the second transfer then writes back 8500.00 as the new balance. That leaves the balance of account A00001 at 8500.00 after both transfers have accessed the source account, which is certainly not the outcome we want or would expect! A similar result occurs if the second transfer were to write its result of 8500.00 first, followed by the first transfer writing its result of 8000.00. The overall result is that the balance of A00001 is 8000.00, which is also not what we want nor expect! In both situations, one of the updates—or writes by one of the transfers—is lost in the end. This data integrity concern is an example of a *lost update* problem, and can occur when we have concurrent access to the same or shared data, and two or more accesses read and update that data without proper coordination.

A common solution to a lost update and similar data integrity problems for shared data involves coordinating access to the shared data with *mutual exclusion*. Mutual exclusion is a property by which only one user or application session may access shared data at a given time. A common mutual exclusion technique involves a synchronization mechanism called a *lock*, and is what we will use to solve our data integrity problem. We associate a lock with a piece or set of shared data that requires synchronized or coordinated access to prevent such data integrity problems. The lock protects the integrity of the data by requiring a session to first hold the lock associated with that data. At any given time, at most one session can hold or possess that lock. The process for a session to obtain and hold a lock begins with the session requesting the lock. If that lock is available (that is, not currently held by another session), the DBMS gives the requesting session that lock to hold. The session can then access the shared data associated with that lock. When a session finishes their access to the shared data, the session *releases* or lets go of the lock. The DBMS can then give the lock to another session that requests the lock.

On the other hand, if a session requests a lock that is currently held by another session, the requesting session must wait for the lock to be released so that the lock becomes available. Once the lock becomes available, the acquiring session finally has a chance to hold the lock and access the shared data.

By following those steps to request, hold, and release locks associated with shared data, we are assured that only one user or application session can access that shared data at a given time. As such the mutual exclusion property of a lock prevents two or more concurrent accesses to shared data, and therefore prevents lost update or data integrity problems.

In most DBMSs, we can employ a lock at various levels. Many DBMS allow us to lock the entire DBMS, which includes all of its tables, data, and other components. We demonstrated the use of DBMS locking in Chapter 3, "Database Management and Administration," in the discussion of backups. Many DBMSs allow a lock to be associated with the entire DBMS itself, an entire database table, or an individual row. Some DBMSs even provide the ability to lock a particular column. To solve our concurrent transfer problem, we can choose to either employ a lock at the table-level or row-level. We will look at both approaches, as each has its advantages and disadvantages.

Table-level locking

The first locking approach we will discuss is perhaps the simplest: a lock at the table-level, or on an entire table. If a given transfer holds a lock on the AccountCC table, that transfer can safely access the AccountCC table and issue their data accesses to the AccountCC table without risking data integrity concerns, because no other transfer can access that table in a way that changes the table data while the first transfer holds that lock. After the first transfer completes its operations, the transfer can then release the lock to allow another transfer task to have its turn with that table lock and issue their accesses to that table.

Figure 9.8 shows the general syntax for a user or application session to lock and unlock at the table-level with SQL. We begin with a *LOCK TABLE* statement and provide the name of the table to lock, followed by a *lock type* of *WRITE* or *READ*. A lock type of *WRITE* indicates that the session will write data to the locked tables, and the lock thus provides mutual exclusive access. A lock type of *READ* specifies that the session will only read the data of the locked data tables and not modify data in those tables. If a session will both read and write a locked table in its operations, we should specify a *WRITE* lock type. We will later demonstrate the use of both lock types to distinguish them and further describe their differences.

We can also lock multiple tables in a single *LOCK TABLES* statement by providing a comma-separated list of table names and their lock type. Regardless of locking one or multiple tables, if the specified table(s) are not locked when a session issues a *LOCK TABLES* statement, the statement returns, and the session is considered to now hold the lock(s) for those table(s). The session can then proceed to safely issue statements that access those locked tables. When finished accessing the tables, the session must issue an *UNLOCK*

TABLES statement, which unlocks all of the tables that were listed in the corresponding (most recent) *LOCK TABLES* statement. Finally, notice that tables accessed between the *LOCK TABLES* and *UNLOCK TABLES* statements must be listed in the *LOCK TABLES* statement, or the DBMS will report an error.[1]

```
LOCK TABLES table_name lock_type [, table_name lock_type [...] ];
statement(s)_to_access_locked_table(s)
UNLOCK TABLES;
```

FIGURE 9.8 General syntax to lock and unlock a table.

To get a better idea of this concurrent transfer example and solution, you may follow with two concurrent sql connections to the database with the AccountCC table. One connection issues the statements for TransferA, and the other connection issues the statements for TransferB. It does not matter whether both session connections are established by the same database user or by different users. To distinguish the activity of each session, the first session has a prompt of "mysql session 1>" and the second session has a prompt of "mysql session 2>".

To solve our concurrent transfer problem with table-level locking, each transfer will involve a series of statements like those shown in Figure 9.9. Here we represent the locking of the AccountCC table by TransferA for writing.

```
mysql session 1> LOCK TABLES AccountCC WRITE;
Query OK, 0 rows affected (0.00 sec)

mysql session 1> UPDATE AccountCC SET Balance=Balance-2000.00 WHERE AccountID='A00001';
Query OK, 1 row affected (0.07 sec)
Rows matched: 1  Changed: 1  Warnings: 0

mysql session 1> UPDATE AccountCC SET Balance=Balance+2000.00 WHERE AccountID='A00002';
Query OK, 1 row affected (0.13 sec)
Rows matched: 1  Changed: 1  Warnings: 0

mysql session 1> UNLOCK TABLES;
Query OK, 0 rows affected (0.00 sec)

mysql session 1> []
```

FIGURE 9.9 Table-level locking by first first session of the AccountCC table for a potentially concurrent transfer between A00001 to A00002.

---

[1]We can lock and unlock a view in the same manner as a table, by providing the name of a view rather than the name of a table. The concept is like that for a table, namely, the lock holder is able to access the data in the view according to the view lock type.

Notice the caption for Figure 9.9 mentions a "potentially concurrent transfer," because we do not know necessarily at the time the transfer is issued whether that transfer will actually be concurrent with another transfer. If there is another concurrent transfer, the other transfer must also lock the AccountCC table before similarly reading, modifying, and writing its balances involved. Locking by both transfers is necessary to maintain the data integrity we need to prevent data inconsistencies—such as lost updates—among those transfers. However, if a transfer is not concurrent with another transfer, the locking of the table just happens to be a precautionary extra step and has no effect on the resulting account balances. Thus, we take the approach of "better safe than sorry" and always lock the table to ensure we maintain data integrity and consistency.

Looking at TransferB, its statements are given in Figure 9.10. Because both TransferA and TransferB lock the AccountCC table before accessing the account data, both transfers coordinate their access to that table without risking data integrity because of inconsistencies.

```
mysql session 2> LOCK TABLES AccountCC WRITE;
Query OK, 0 rows affected (0.00 sec)

mysql session 2> UPDATE AccountCC SET Balance=Balance-1500.00 WHERE AccountID='A00001';
Query OK, 1 row affected (0.04 sec)
Rows matched: 1  Changed: 1  Warnings: 0

mysql session 2> UPDATE AccountCC SET Balance=Balance+1500.00 WHERE AccountID='A00003';
Query OK, 1 row affected (0.06 sec)
Rows matched: 1  Changed: 1  Warnings: 0

mysql session 2> UNLOCK TABLES;
Query OK, 0 rows affected (0.00 sec)

mysql session 2> []
```

FIGURE 9.10 Table-level locking by the second session of the AccountCC table for a potentially concurrent transfer between A00001 to A00003.

If we were to issue all of the statements in Figure 9.9 followed by the statements in Figure 9.10, or vice versa, we would achieve the expected outcome of both transfers successfully completing and with no data integrity problems—although such accesses are examples of serial access, and as described previously, we do not have data integrity problems with serial access, even without locking. But let's look more closely at the data integrity problems that can arise when the transfers are truly concurrent and how locks can provide the necessary mutual exclusion to prevent data integrity problems. To demonstrate this idea, we will repeat the previous transfer example.

However, for comparison we will return to that same set of data values before the transfers, and first reverse the actions of TransferA and TransferB, as shown in Figure 9.11.

```
mysql session 1> UPDATE AccountCC SET Balance=Balance+3500.00 WHERE AccountID='A00001';
Query OK, 1 row affected (0.06 sec)
Rows matched: 1  Changed: 1  Warnings: 0

mysql session 1> UPDATE AccountCC SET Balance=Balance-2000.00 WHERE AccountID='A00002';
Query OK, 1 row affected (0.04 sec)
Rows matched: 1  Changed: 1  Warnings: 0

mysql session 1> UPDATE AccountCC SET Balance=Balance-1500.00 WHERE AccountID='A00003';
Query OK, 1 row affected (0.08 sec)
Rows matched: 1  Changed: 1  Warnings: 0

mysql session 1> []
```

FIGURE 9.11 Reversing the actions of TransferA and TransferB to repeat those transfers.

We will now demonstrate the possible effects of two concurrent login sessions, where the first session issues the steps for TransferA and the second session issues the steps for TransferB. We can simulate concurrent access by first issuing only *some* of the steps for one transfer. In Figure 9.12, we have the first session issuing the *LOCK TABLES* statement, which immediately returns because there was no lock on the AccountCC table held by any session. The first session now holds the lock for the AccountCC table, and can safely access the AccountCC table as they need. However, let's not issue all of those statements for TransferA at this time, so that we can show what happens if another session concurrently issues TransferB. As such, for now we will carry out only the first few statements of TransferA for the removal of the transfer amount from account A00001.

```
mysql session 1> LOCK TABLES AccountCC WRITE;
Query OK, 0 rows affected (0.00 sec)

mysql session 1> UPDATE AccountCC SET Balance=Balance-2000.00 WHERE AccountID='A00001';
Query OK, 1 row affected (0.07 sec)
Rows matched: 1  Changed: 1  Warnings: 0

mysql session 1> []
```

FIGURE 9.12 The first session obtaining the AccountCC table lock for TransferA and starting its operations.

To simulate a concurrent issuing of TransferB, Figure 9.13 illustrates the issuing of the *LOCK TABLE* statement for the second session. You will notice that the statement does not return at this time, and this indicates that the second session is waiting for the lock that is currently held by the first session. As such, the second session cannot proceed with their statements to access the table data until the first session is finished with its access.[2]

```
mysql session 2> LOCK TABLES AccountCC WRITE;
[]
```

FIGURE 9.13 The second session requesting the AccountCC table lock and waiting on that lock.

Figure 9.14 shows the first session proceeding with their access to the table and releasing that lock. You will notice that releasing a lock will always return and does not require coordination with other sessions to do so.

```
mysql session 1> UPDATE AccountCC SET Balance=Balance+2000.00 WHERE AccountID='A00002';
Query OK, 1 row affected (0.04 sec)
Rows matched: 1  Changed: 1  Warnings: 0

mysql session 1> UNLOCK TABLES;
Query OK, 0 rows affected (0.00 sec)

mysql session 1> []
```

FIGURE 9.14 The first session continues to access the AccountCC table and releases the table lock.

It is not until the first session issues the *UNLOCK TABLE* statement that the second session has a chance to hold that lock and proceed. Figure 9.15 shows the unlocking of the table by the first session now makes that lock available for the second session. The second session's lock request returns, which means the second session now holds the table lock and can safely access that table.

```
mysql session 2> UPDATE AccountCC SET Balance=Balance-1500.00 WHERE AccountID='A00001';
Query OK, 1 row affected (0.04 sec)
Rows matched: 1  Changed: 1  Warnings: 0

mysql session 2> UPDATE AccountCC SET Balance=Balance+1500.00 WHERE AccountID='A00003';
Query OK, 1 row affected (0.06 sec)
Rows matched: 1  Changed: 1  Warnings: 0

mysql session 2> UNLOCK TABLES;
Query OK, 0 rows affected (0.00 sec)

mysql session 2> []
```

FIGURE 9.15 The second session given the AccountCC table lock and can now access the table.

---

[2]A DBMS may allow a session to only wait for a period of time (such as 60 seconds) for a lock to become available before "timing out". If such a timeout occurs, the DBMS will cancel the waiting session's lock request and transaction and allow the session to continue issuing statements to the DBMS. Notice that the session must retry the transaction and lock request if it wishes to reattempt that task.

We consider this form of table-level locking the simplest implementation of locks in a database because it involves only one lock per table accessed. As such, an advantage of table-level locking is that one or a small number of locks may be required to maintain data integrity in a given scenario. However, while such mutual exclusion does solve the data integrity problem with concurrent access, a disadvantage is that table-level locking can significantly degrade run-time performance. Specifically to the account transfer scenario, table-level locking can negatively impact the number of transfers that can be issued within a given timeframe. For example, in our first case with TransferA for accounts A00001 to A00002 and TransferB to A00003 to A00004, we do not have the potential for data integrity concerns, but each transfer still locks the entire table for mutual exclusive access anyway, because we may not necessarily know beforehand whether both transfers will access the same account. If TransferA were to lock the table first, TransferB then has to wait its turn, even though its accesses would not interfere with those of TransferA (or vice versa). Hence, table-level locking with a *WRITE* lock type on the AccountCC table always causes the accesses of each transfer to be serial, and this eliminates the performance benefit we were hoping to achieve with concurrent access.

We have two approaches to alleviate some of that performance overhead of serial access at the table-level. In one approach we can use a table-level *READ* lock type. When a session specifies a table-level *READ* lock, the session specifies that it wishes to only read data in those table(s) and not modify or delete any of that data. A *READ* lock type provides two benefits. First, it also allows other sessions to concurrently hold *READ* locks for any of those table(s) and read that data, thus allowing the performance benefits of concurrency to be achieved. Second, the *READ* lock type also specifies that no session (not even itself) can modify or delete data in those table(s) while a *READ* lock is held. This feature prevents data integrity problems where one session carries out a series of accesses and expects that certain data is not changed during that period, whether by itself or other sessions.

For example, suppose in the account transfer scenario a session issues an audit task across all accounts. During that audit task, data in the account table should remain constant and not be changed or be deleted. For example, while the audit task is carried out by one session, we do not want any other session to have the ability to carry out a transfer task that would change some of the AccountCC data. However, if a session wants to carry out a balance inquiry that simply reads an account balance and does not change it, we may want to allow such concurrent read-only access during the audit period to achieve the concurrency performance benefit.

To solve this data integrity problem where we want to read AccountCC data and not have the data change during an audit, the audit session can first request a table-level *READ* lock on the AccountCC table. If no *WRITE* lock is currently held on the AccountCC table, the DBMS will let the audit session hold a *READ* lock on the account table. The audit session may now proceed with the audit and be assured that the AccountCC table data will not change while the session holds the *READ* lock. On the other hand, if a session already holds a *WRITE* lock on the AccountCC table when the audit session requests the *READ* lock, the DBMS will cause the audit session to wait until the *WRITE* lock is released and the table becomes available for the *READ* lock.

In the second approach to alleviate the performance overhead of serial access at the table-level, we can instead turn to locking at another level, the row level.

Row-level locking

While table-level locking can effectively provide mutual-exclusive access to shared AccountCC table data, we sacrifice the possible benefits with concurrent access to that table. However, we can attempt to preserve much of the performance benefit possible with concurrent access by instead locking on the *row-level*. Row-level locking associates a lock with each row in a table, so to access a particular row, a session must first hold the lock for that row. If a session needs to access multiple rows as part of a task, the session must first obtain the locks for each of those rows. When the session finishes accessing the row(s), the session similarly releases those lock(s).

In the account transfer scenario, each transfer would involve locking two rows of the AccountCC table, namely the row that corresponds to the account that sends the transfer and the row that corresponds to the account that receives the transfer. This approach leaves the remainder of the table (that is, the unlocked rows) available for concurrent access by other sessions while a session holds the necessary locks for its two rows.

A session can lock a set of one or more rows in a table by using one of two row-level locking approaches. The first approach employs a variation of the *SELECT* statement to request the row locks, and its syntax is given in Figure 9.16. Here, the line "{begin transaction}" indicates the starting of a transaction, either explicitly with a *START TRANSACTION* statement or implicitly by setting the autocommit variable to 0 if its value is currently 1. If the autocommit variable value is already 0, we must issue a *COMMIT* or

ROLLBACK as we did before to indicate the beginning of a transaction. Even though our previous discussion and demonstration of table-level locking did not involve the use of transactions, in practice we may likely encompass a table level-locking SQL statement for a task within a transaction along with the task's other SQL data access statements.

```
{begin transaction}
SELECT * FROM table_name WHERE condition FOR lock_type;
statement(s)_to_access_locked_row_set
{end transaction}
```

FIGURE 9.16 General syntax of first approach to lock a set of rows in a table.

We then start to issue a *SELECT* statement as if we were simply retrieving data of the row(s) we wish to lock, as this is a way to identify the row set that is to be locked. The condition mentioned in the Figure 9.16 syntax defines the criteria that identifies the row set to lock, such as matching a table identifier with a certain value or range of values. In this manner, we can lock multiple rows with a single *SELECT* statement of this form. Unlike a typical *SELECT* statement, we then include at the end of this particular *SELECT* statement a *FOR* clause that defines the type of lock we wish to acquire on that row set. The two row-level lock types are *UPDATE* and *SHARE*, and we will shortly distinguish between those types and demonstrate their use. We continue with the statements to access the row set data. When we are finished accessing that data, we reach the last line with the text "{end transaction}". Here we issue a *COMMIT* or *ROLLBACK* statement, and it is then we release the locks to the rows of that row set and conclude the transaction. At that point, those rows can then be locked again by that session or by other sessions.

UPDATE locks

Back to the row-level lock types. An *UPDATE* lock type is similar to that of a table-level *WRITE* lock, in that only the lock holder may read, modify, or delete data in the locked row set. The DBMS will make other sessions that attempt to read, modify, or delete data in that row set to wait until the lock holding session releases the lock.

As before, for comparison we will again revert the actions of TransferA and TransferB as shown in Figure 9.11. Figure 9.17 shows the row-level locking and access statements issued by one session for TransferA. Like before, we distinguish the two sessions with distinctive prompts.

```
mysql session 1> START TRANSACTION;
Query OK, 0 rows affected (0.00 sec)

mysql session 1> SELECT * FROM AccountCC WHERE AccountId='A00001' OR AccountId='A00002' FOR UPDATE;
+-----------+----------+
| AccountID | Balance  |
+-----------+----------+
| A00001    | 10000.00 |
| A00002    |  5000.00 |
+-----------+----------+
2 rows in set (0.00 sec)

mysql session 1> UPDATE AccountCC SET Balance=Balance-2000.00 WHERE AccountID='A00001';
Query OK, 1 row affected (0.00 sec)
Rows matched: 1  Changed: 1  Warnings: 0

mysql session 1> UPDATE AccountCC SET Balance=Balance+2000.00 WHERE AccountID='A00002';
Query OK, 1 row affected (0.00 sec)
Rows matched: 1  Changed: 1  Warnings: 0

mysql session 1> COMMIT;
Query OK, 0 rows affected (0.05 sec)

mysql session 1> █
```

FIGURE 9.17 Row-level locking and data modifications by the first session for TransferA, which is a potentially concurrent transfer between A00001 to A00002.

Figure 9.18 shows similar statements issued by a second session for TransferB.

```
mysql session 2> START TRANSACTION;
Query OK, 0 rows affected (0.00 sec)

mysql session 2> SELECT * FROM AccountCC WHERE AccountId='A00001' OR AccountId='A00003' FOR UPDATE;
+-----------+-----------+
| AccountID | Balance   |
+-----------+-----------+
| A00001    |   8000.00 |
| A00003    | 120000.00 |
+-----------+-----------+
2 rows in set (0.00 sec)

mysql session 2> UPDATE AccountCC SET Balance=Balance-1500.00 WHERE AccountID='A00001';
Query OK, 1 row affected (0.00 sec)
Rows matched: 1  Changed: 1  Warnings: 0

mysql session 2> UPDATE AccountCC SET Balance=Balance+1500.00 WHERE AccountID='A00003';
Query OK, 1 row affected (0.00 sec)
Rows matched: 1  Changed: 1  Warnings: 0

mysql session 2> COMMIT;
Query OK, 0 rows affected (0.09 sec)

mysql session 2> []
```

FIGURE 9.18 Row-level locking and data modifications by the second session for TransferB, which is a potentially concurrent transfer between A00001 to A00003.

We can also demonstrate a concurrent execution of TransferA and TransferB by using those two sessions and issuing a few of the statements at a time for each transfer. Again, for comparison, we will revert the actions of

TransferA and TransferB as shown in Figure 9.11. Figure 9.19 and Figure 9.20 represent such a possible sequence of statements that can occur in practice. Figure 9.19 represents the first session carrying out the TransferA statements and locking its two account rows. For demonstrative purposes, we will not yet issue the data modification statements of TransferA so that we can simulate what happens when the second session concurrently attempts to carry out TransferB.

```
mysql session 1> START TRANSACTION;
Query OK, 0 rows affected (0.00 sec)

mysql session 1> SELECT * FROM AccountCC WHERE AccountId='A00001' OR AccountId='A00002' FOR UPDATE;
+-----------+----------+
| AccountID | Balance  |
+-----------+----------+
| A00001    | 10000.00 |
| A00002    |  5000.00 |
+-----------+----------+
2 rows in set (0.00 sec)

mysql session 1> []
```

FIGURE 9.19 Row-level locking by the first session for TransferA of the rows for accounts A00001 and A00002.

Turning to the second session, as before, consider TransferB issues a transfer from account A00001 to A00003. Figure 9.20 shows the locking of that row set, which does not return at this time. Although the row for A00003 is not locked, the row for A00001 is, so the lock request for that entire row set causes the second session to wait until both rows (that is, all rows in the set) are available to lock. Thus, the second session is not allowed to carry out its transfer operations because the first session has exclusive access to one of those rows that the second session is attempting to lock.

```
mysql session 2> START TRANSACTION;
Query OK, 0 rows affected (0.00 sec)

mysql session 2> SELECT * FROM AccountCC WHERE AccountId='A00001' OR AccountId='A00003' FOR UPDATE;
[]
```

FIGURE 9.20 Row-level locking and wait by the second session for a concurrent transfer between accounts A00001 to A00003.

Figure 9.21 shows the first session proceeding with its transfer operations and issuing a COMMIT to complete its transaction. That effectively unlocks the first session's hold on the rows for A00001 and A00002. Notice that if the first session were to instead issue a ROLLBACK to conclude TransferA, that would also unlock the first session's hold on those rows.

```
mysql session 1> UPDATE AccountCC SET Balance=Balance-2000.00 WHERE AccountID='A00001';
Query OK, 1 row affected (0.00 sec)
Rows matched: 1  Changed: 1  Warnings: 0

mysql session 1> UPDATE AccountCC SET Balance=Balance+2000.00 WHERE AccountID='A00002';
Query OK, 1 row affected (0.00 sec)
Rows matched: 1  Changed: 1  Warnings: 0

mysql session 1> COMMIT;
Query OK, 0 rows affected (0.05 sec)

mysql session 1> []
```

FIGURE 9.21 The first session continuing its statements for TransferA and unlocking its row set.

With the row for A00001 now unlocked, the second session will now have a chance to hold the locks for its row set. If no other sessions are competing to lock the rows for A00001 or A00003, or if the DBMS chooses the second session over other competing sessions, the second session's lock request will return, as shown in Figure 9.22. The second session now has exclusive access to the row set for accounts A00001 and A00003 and can proceed to modify data in those rows and conclude its transaction.

```
+-----------+-----------+
| AccountID | Balance   |
+-----------+-----------+
| A00001    |   8000.00 |
| A00003    | 120000.00 |
+-----------+-----------+
2 rows in set (5.83 sec)

mysql session 2> UPDATE AccountCC SET Balance=Balance-1500.00 WHERE AccountID='A00001';
Query OK, 1 row affected (0.00 sec)
Rows matched: 1  Changed: 1  Warnings: 0

mysql session 2> UPDATE AccountCC SET Balance=Balance+1500.00 WHERE AccountID='A00003';
Query OK, 1 row affected (0.00 sec)
Rows matched: 1  Changed: 1  Warnings: 0

mysql session 2> COMMIT;
Query OK, 0 rows affected (0.05 sec)

mysql session 2> []
```

FIGURE 9.22 The second session returning from its lock request for the rows of accounts A00001 and A00003 and proceeding to access that data.

SHARE locks

In contrast, with a *SHARE* row-level lock type, a session specifies that it wishes to only read data in the given row set and will not modify or delete any data in that row set. The *SHARE* lock type provides two features. First, it also allows other sessions to concurrently read data in any of those rows, thus allowing the performance benefits of concurrent access to be achieved. As a second feature, the *SHARE* lock type also ensures that no other session (or even the session holding that lock) can modify or delete data in the row set while the *SHARE* lock is held. The second feature ensures that all sessions that read data in that row set will see the same values, thus maintaining data consistency. This second feature also provides data integrity when a session carries out a task or transaction and requires certain data to remain constant and unchanged (whether by that session or other sessions) during that transaction period.

For example, suppose in the account transfer scenario a session carries out a task to audit certain accounts. During the time that session carries out the audit task, the data for those certain accounts must remain constant and not change, say by another session's transfer task that involves one of those accounts. As such, through the duration of the audit task, every read of a given piece of data in the rows of the audited accounts (the row set) always yields the same value. By following the convention that all read-only access involves a *SHARE* lock, and any access that involves modifying, creating, or deleting data involves an *UPDATE* lock, we can maintain data integrity. If one or more sessions hold a *SHARE* lock on a row set, the DBMS will cause other sessions that request an *UPDATE* lock to any part of that row set to wait until all of the *SHARE* lock holding sessions release their *SHARE* locks by ending their transaction with a *COMMIT* or *ROLLBACK* statement.

To demonstrate those features of *SHARE* locks, let's consider three concurrent sessions. The first session carries out a simple audit of summing the balances to accounts A00001 and A00002. The second session issues a balance inquiry of account A00002. The third session issues a transfer task of $1000 from account A00002 to account A00003. Because we are no longer comparing scenarios for TransferA and TransferB, we will not undo the actions of the previous case. We will also use distinctive prompts to distinguish among the three concurrent sessions.

Because the first and second sessions involve read-only access for those tasks, both sessions obtain *SHARE* locks for the accessed row(s). Figure 9.23 shows the first session carrying a *SHARE* lock request for accounts A00001 and A00002. Assuming that no locks are held at the time the first session issues the lock request, the request immediately returns.

```
mysql session 1> START TRANSACTION;
Query OK, 0 rows affected (0.00 sec)

mysql session 1> SELECT * FROM AccountCC WHERE AccountId='A00001' OR AccountId='A00002' FOR SHARE;
+-----------+---------+
| AccountID | Balance |
+-----------+---------+
| A00001    | 6500.00 |
| A00002    | 7000.00 |
+-----------+---------+
2 rows in set (0.00 sec)

mysql session 1> []
```

FIGURE 9.23 A first session issuing a *SHARE* lock request for accounts A00001 and A00002.

Now the first session can carry out its audit operations. But before that happens, let's issue a concurrent balance inquiry for the second session. As shown in Figure 9.24, the second session obtains a *SHARE* lock for account A00002. Even though another *SHARE* lock is currently held on a rowset that includes A00002, this request immediately returns to allow the concurrent read access. Thus, the second session can proceed to read the account balance and unlock that row.

```
mysql session 2> START TRANSACTION;
Query OK, 0 rows affected (0.00 sec)

mysql session 2> SELECT Balance FROM AccountCC WHERE AccountId='A00002' FOR SHARE;
+---------+
| Balance |
+---------+
| 7000.00 |
+---------+
1 row in set (0.01 sec)

mysql session 2> COMMIT;
Query OK, 0 rows affected (0.00 sec)

mysql session 2> []
```

FIGURE 9.24 A second session issuing a *SHARE* lock request for account A00002 to read that balance and given a lock to proceed with its access.

Now let's consider the third session, which requests an *UPDATE* lock for the rows to accounts A00002 and A00003, as shown in Figure 9.25. Because A00002 is part of the row set that is currently locked with a *SHARE* lock by the first session, the DBMS causes the third session to wait at this time before it can proceed with its transfer.

```
mysql session 3> START TRANSACTION;
Query OK, 0 rows affected (0.00 sec)

mysql session 3> SELECT * FROM AccountCC WHERE AccountId='A00002' OR AccountID='A00003' FOR UPDATE;
[]
```

FIGURE 9.25 A third session issuing an *UPDATE* lock request for accounts A00002 and A00003 and waiting.

Now suppose the first session continues with its audit and releases its *SHARE* locks, as shown in Figure 9.26.

```
mysql session 1> SELECT SUM(Balance) FROM AccountCC WHERE AccountId='A00001' OR AccountID='A00002' FOR SHARE;
+--------------+
| SUM(Balance) |
+--------------+
|     13500.00 |
+--------------+
1 row in set (0.00 sec)

mysql session 1> COMMIT;
Query OK, 0 rows affected (0.00 sec)

mysql session 1> []
```

FIGURE 9.26 The first session continuing with its audit operation and releasing its SHARE locks.

With no *SHARE* or *UPDATE* locks currently held on the row for accounts A00002 or A00003, the third session's *UPDATE* lock request can now be fulfilled. Figure 9.27 shows that lock request returning and the transfer task operations carried out by the third session.

```
+-----------+-----------+
| AccountID | Balance   |
+-----------+-----------+
| A00002    |    7000.00 |
| A00003    |  121500.00 |
+-----------+-----------+
2 rows in set (10.22 sec)

mysql session 3> UPDATE AccountCC SET Balance=Balance-1000.00 WHERE AccountID='A00002';
Query OK, 1 row affected (0.01 sec)
Rows matched: 1  Changed: 1  Warnings: 0

mysql session 3> UPDATE AccountCC SET Balance=Balance+1000.00 WHERE AccountID='A00003';
Query OK, 1 row affected (0.00 sec)
Rows matched: 1  Changed: 1  Warnings: 0

mysql session 3> COMMIT;
Query OK, 0 rows affected (0.05 sec)

mysql session 3> []
```

FIGURE 9.27 The third session given its *UPDATE* lock and can proceed with its transfer.

While row-level locking can greatly improve concurrency among the rows in a table, notice that a transfer now has to acquire and release two locks (one for each row), compared to just one lock for the entire table with table-level locking. With tasks that involve many accounts, that can mean even more locks involved. That additional locking and releasing increases the mutual exclusion overhead, which includes both the time taken by the DBMS to manage the lock and unlock operations as well as the wait time a session endures for a row to become available when that row is already locked by another session. In situations where a session locks many rows in the same table, that lock overhead may exceed any concurrency benefit provided by row-level locking, and actually yield worse performance compared to table-level locking. As such, in those situations, table-level locking may yield better performance because of lower lock overhead, even though there is less concurrent access.

9.3 DEADLOCK

While the use of locks can solve a variety of data integrity problems, the use of multiple locks (whether table-level or row-level) also introduces the potential for another security problem that involves the security principle of availability. This security problem with availability (or more specifically, lack of availability) is called *deadlock*. Deadlock can occur when two or more entities need concurrent access to—and attempt to acquire locks to—the same set of resources. In general, a resource refers to something (such as a single piece of data, set of data, hardware device, and so on) that is shared among the entities. For this discussion, database sessions are the entities that share the resources, and the resources are individual *tables* when locking at the table-level, or *row sets* when locking at the row-level.

Regardless of the type of resource(s), to maintain data integrity, we associate a lock with each resource like we did previously to synchronize and coordinate access to that resource. However, the data availability problem or deadlock becomes possible when two or more entities request the same set of locks, and at least two entities hold some, but not all, of the locks in that set. Because those lock-holding entities are each waiting for other lock(s) that are already held by other entities and hence unavailable, they are unable to proceed with their resource access and eventually release the locks they do hold. Consequently, none of those locks become available and those entities wait indefinitely.

We can illustrate a case of deadlock in a financial transfer scenario with two transfers: TransferA attempts to transfer from account A00001 to A00002, and TransferB attempts to transfer from account A00002 to A00001. The amount of each transfer is unimportant in such a deadlock example, because the deadlock itself is based on the locking of the data rather than the values of the data. Suppose each transfer attempts to lock the source account row first, followed by locking the destination account row. In Figure 9.28, we see a possible sequence of concurrent steps, where the TransferA session locks its source account row (for A00001) and the TransferB session locks its source account row (for A00002). Each transfer now holds the lock for the source account. Now each transfer requests the lock for the row of their destination account. The TransferA session now requests the lock for A00002, but because that lock is currently held by another session, the TransferA session must wait. Likewise, the TransferB session requests the lock for A00001, but because that lock is currently held by another session, the TransferB session must wait. Both sessions are now deadlocked and cannot proceed.

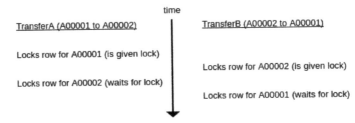

FIGURE 9.28 Example of deadlock with concurrent transfers between A00001 to A00002 and A00002 to A00001.

A common solution to avoid deadlock is to require that each session requests all of its necessary locks in a certain sequence. For example, suppose that rather than have a financial transfer session request its locks by source AccountID first and destination AccountID second, we instead require a transfer session to request its locks in order of AccountID. Revisiting our deadlock example, both TransferA and TransferB sessions would initially attempt to lock account A00001 first, and one transfer will hold the lock and proceed while the other transfer waits, and because the other transfer waits, it cannot continue and possibly create a deadlock with the first transfer. Figure 9.29 gives a possible sequence of steps where the TransferA session requests the lock for A00001 before the TransferB session does so, and the DBMS gives

TransferA the lock to hold. If the TransferB session now requests the lock for A00001, the TransferB session will wait. TransferA can then proceed to request the lock for the row to account A00002 without the TransferB session interfering and potentially causing a deadlock. If the lock to A00002 is available, the DBMS will give the TransferA session that lock to hold so that TransferA can proceed with its transfer operations and release those locks, thereby making those locks available to other transfer sessions that may be waiting for them. The TransferB session will then have a chance to hold the lock for the row to A00001, proceed with its request for the row A0003, and continue with that transfer.

FIGURE 9.29 Solution to deadlock with concurrent transfers by ordering the sequence of lock requests.

Notice that if yet another, third, transfer session were to initially hold the lock for A00002 and cause the TransferA session to wait for that lock, as long as all transfer sessions request locks in sequence of AccountID, we are assured that third session will eventually complete its transfer steps and release the lock for A00002, giving TransferA a chance to hold the lock and proceed. Looking at that third session more closely, if the third session already holds both its necessary locks—or holds one lock, requests its second lock and is given that lock to hold—the third session can freely carry out its transfer steps and release those locks. The same is true if that third session holds one lock but waits for another. For example, if the third session holds the lock for A00002 and requests another lock that a fourth transfer session already holds, we can repeat this consideration. Eventually, we will reach a transfer session that can hold all of its necessary locks and not hold one lock and wait on another, because there is not a lock for a row of a higher AccountID. This observation is due to the fact that a session which holds a lock can request only locks with a greater AccountID. In any case, locks will eventually be released so all transfers, including TransferA, can hold all of their necessary locks and continue.

9.4 SUMMARY

In this chapter, we explored risks to data integrity with concurrent access during backups and other DML statements as an expansion upon previous chapters. We described and demonstrated solutions to eliminate those risks, including DBMS locking, table locking and row locking. We elaborated on read locks and write locks, as well as also described and demonstrated the concepts of update locks and share locks. In addition, we described synchronization overhead considerations among those solutions. Finally, we explained the concept of deadlock, its risk to availability, and a solution to prevent that risk to availability.

END OF CHAPTER EXERCISES

CHAPTER 1

1. What are the three goals or principles of information security?

2. Which information security principle involves accurate data?

3. Which information security principle involves timely access to data?

4. Which information security principle may involve encryption as a solution?

5. What is a security threat?

6. What is a security control?

7. Is data security the same concept as information security? Explain why or why not.

8. In general, how does database security differ from that of data security or information security? You do not have to differentiate among the individual principles for this answer.

9. Explain the types of integrity involved with database security.

10. What are some of the controls for integrity with database security?

11. Explain the concept of high availability.

CHAPTER 2

1. Why does the data shown in Figure 2.1 have the potential for data inconsistencies?

2. In Figure 2.3, we show two examples of data inconsistencies that can occur with the Figure 2.1 data. Give two other examples of data inconsistencies that can occur with the Figure 2.1 data.

3. Why is database normalization important?

4. Explain how a functional dependency is different from a table.

5. Suppose we have a table:

    Product(ProductId, ProductName, Manufacturer, ManufacturerAddress, Price, Stock)
    with the functional dependencies

    ProductId -> (ProductName, Manufacturer, Price, Stock)
    Manufacturer -> ManufacturerAddress.

    Give an example of a data inconsistency that can occur if Product data is modified.

6. Using the normalization process to BCNF, explain the process and show the resulting table(s) for the previous question.

7. Suppose the real estate scenario described in Section 2.1 was slightly altered such that Phone is no longer unique, and therefore itself cannot be used to derive anything. In addition, a realtor may have multiple offices, each of which varies according to a given properties location. Using the normalization process to BCNF, explain the process and show the resulting table(s) if we were to start with the data in Figure 2.1 and the table structure

    Listing (RealtorName,OfficeAdr,OfficeCity,Phone,PropAdr,PropCity,NBeds, Area,Price)

    and recognize only the following functional dependencies

    (RealtorName,PropAdr,PropCity) -> (OfficeAdr,OfficeCity,Phone)
    (PropAdr,PropCity) -> (NBeds,Area,Price)

CHAPTER 3

1. Which information security principle does backups help address?

2. From a security perspective, explain why backups are an important control.

3. Explain why it may be important to keep multiple backups, each made at a different point in time, rather than just one backup that has the latest content.

4. What does a database backup that consists of SQL statements contain?

5. Even though the --**databases** option of **mysqldump** is not required for a backup of a single database, we may still want to specify that option for a single database backup. Explain why.

6. Give the **mysqldump** command that creates a backup of a database named "MyDatabase". You may assume a backup administrator account name of bkpuser with password bkppass.

7. Explain how we can restore from the backup created in question 5, using a **mysql** command that creates a client session to the DBMS and then restores from the backup file.

8. Explain how we can restore from the backup created in question 5, this time by using a client session that has already been established to the DBMS.

9. Explain how we can create a backup of one database but then restore that backup into another database, say to make a copy of the database for testing purposes.

10. In this chapter, we touched on some of the database user account controls that can be employed to support account confidentiality. Explain two other account controls not presented in this chapter that we may wish to use.

CHAPTER 4

1. Explain the risks associated with a user account that has no password.

2. Are quotes necessary around usernames and hostnames?

3. What is a host restricted account?

4. Give the SQL statement to create a user named 'guest' with no password.

5. Give the SQL statement to create a user named 'ron' with a password of '7&55ha'.

6. Give the SQL statement to create a user named 'mike' with a password of '8$mad3*'.

7. Give the SQL statement to create a user named 'carolyn' with a password of 'plmr@9' and with a host login restriction only from 192.168.2.x, where x is any number.

8. Give the SQL statement to create a user named 'mary' with a password of '3hmm4)' and with a host login restriction only from 192.168.2.9.

9. Give the SQL statement to create a user named 'mary' with a password of 'hh78u#' and with a host login restriction only from 192.168.3.1.

10. Give the SQL statement to change the password for the user account 'guest' to be 'officeguest'.

11. Explain why we may employ different passwords to a user account that has the ability to log in from multiple hosts or networks.

CHAPTER 5

1. Suppose a financial auditor needs an account to access data in the Business scenario. Give the SQL statements to create a user account named 'auditor' with password '@udit98&'.

2. Give user 'auditor' the privileges to only read the data in the Employee table.

3. Give user 'auditor' the privileges to only read the data in the Budget table.

4. Explain whether there are any security concerns with the types of access given to the financial auditor for those two tables.

5. Now we wish to allow the auditor access to only the EmpID, FName, LName, Title and Office columns in the Employee table. Explain the two approaches by which we can enforce that requirement if the auditor account already has read access to the Employee table.

6. Give the SQL statements that would be involved with your first approach.

7. Give the SQL statements that would be involved with your second approach.

8. Give the SQL statement to show the privileges for the auditor with the requirements given in (5) enacted.

9. Explain the purpose of the GRANT OPTION

10. Suppose we wanted to allow the auditor account to have the ability to modify or change the financial number data in the Budget table. Give the SQL statement(s) that would provide the ability.

CHAPTER 6

1. In the Business scenario, we created roles that had no hostname or network restriction, relying on the usernames to limit access based on the system from which a user logs in from. Can you identify scenarios where restricting a role to a particular hostname or network is necessary?

2. Suppose we were to add a financial value-based column named Projection to the Budget table with similar data access requirements to the Notes column that we added in Chapter 5. Explain how that may change our role definitions that were given for the Budget table in Chapter 6.

3. Provide the SQL statements necessary to implement your solution to (2). You may wish to back up the full DBMS first if you wish to return to the original role and/or privilege settings.

4. As part of a thorough series of testing the implementation of roles, at the end of 6.5 we give some examples of testing and the expected results. List some other tests that we could also issue and their expected results.

5. In Section 6.6.2, we handled the employee responsibility additions entirely with roles. Give the necessary statements if we were to alternatively handle the change directly with privileges. Use the BusinessCLS database for this exercise.

6. In Section 6.6.3, we handled the employee responsibility additions entirely with roles. Give the necessary statements if we were to alternatively handle the change directly with privileges. Use the BusinessCLS database for this exercise.

CHAPTER 7

1. Give the SQL statement to create a view named PatientNames of the Patient table that contains only patient FName and LName.

2. Give the SQL statement to create a view named PatientsFullyVaccinated of the Patient table that contains only data for patients who have a VaccinationStatus of 'full'.

3. Give users 'ron', 'mike', and 'carolyn' the ability to read the data in the PatientsFullyVaccinated view. Other users should not be able to see the data in that view.

4. Give the SQL statement to create a view named PatientUnder21 of the Patient table that contains only data for patients under the age of 21.

5. Give the SQL statement to create a view named Patient21OrOver of the Patient table that contains only data for patients 21 or older.

6. Explain the difference between plaintext and ciphertext.

7. Explain the differences between symmetric and asymmetric key encryption.

8. Give the SQL statement that will encrypt a message of your choosing, with a key of your choosing.

9. Give the SQL statement that will decrypt the ciphertext generated in the previous question.

10. How is hashing different from encryption and decryption?

11. How long is an SHA2 hash by default?

12. Why is storing passwords in plaintext a bad idea?

13. Explain how we can use hashing with passwords to confirm when a provided password matches the previously set password.

14. Why is salting passwords important for security purposes?

15. Give the definition of a stored function named NumUnvaccinated that returns the number of patients that have a vaccination status of 'none'.

16. Give the definition of a stored function named Num21OrOver that returns the number of patients that are 21 years of age or older.

17. Give the SQL statement(s) that would allow user 'mary' to invoke the stored function named PercentByAgeRange.

18. What are the differences between a stored function and stored procedure?

CHAPTER 8

1. Explain why database transactions may be important for data integrity.

2. Explain the difference between a COMMIT and ROLLBACK, and what individual database operations are affected by them.

3. Why must we have automatic commits disabled before we can use a COMMIT or ROLLBACK with a transaction?

4. Explain the two ways that we implement or begin a transaction.

5. Show a series of SQL statements that carry out a transfer operation on the Account table that results with valid data and a COMMIT. Show the Account table before you begin as well as at the end so that we can see a "before" and "after" set of data. Your statements should be similar to those given in Figure 8.6 and Figure 8.7 but result with valid data.

6. Show a series of SQL statements that carry out a transfer operation on the Account table that results with invalid data and a ROLLBACK. Show the Account table before you begin as well as at the end so that we can see a "before" and "after" set of data. Your statements should be similar to those given in Figure 8.6 and Figure 8.7 but result with invalid data.

7. Give an SQL CREATE TABLE statement that creates a table named ExamGrades to store grades for an exam. The columns for the table are StudentId (an integer), ExamId (also an integer), and Grade (a double floating point). Include a condition check that ensures a Grade value is between 0 and 100, inclusive.

8. Show the SQL statement and result (including the contents of the ExamGrades table) if you were to insert the values (10000, 1, 90.0);

9. Show the SQL statement and result (including the contents of the ExamGrades table) if you were to insert the values (10001, 1, 200.0);

The next three questions refer to users 'jerrysr', 'etta', 'steve', 'sindy', and 'customer'. Create user accounts for those usernames with passwords of your choosing.

10. Give users 'jerrysr' and 'steve' the ability to read, modify, add and delete data in all the tables of the Ecommerce database.

11. Give users 'etta' and 'sindy' the ability to read the data in all the tables of the Ecommerce database.

12. Give user 'customer' the ability to read only the data in the Item table.

13. Consider the implementation of the restaurant's e-commerce system chooses to store information about a user's selected items in the database itself rather than on the user's device. How would the purchase transaction differ compared to that presented in the text?

14. Give an example of calling the AccountTransferIF stored procedure that would leave a negative balance. Show the account balances before and after calling AccountTransferIF in this manner.

15. Modify AccountTransferIF to issue ROLLBACK if the transfer amount is not in a valid range of 0.00 to 999999.99, to accommodate a given requirement that transfers must be non-negative and less than 1000000.

16. We described in AccountTransferExc how a resulting negative source account balance can generate an exception that issues ROLLBACK. Can you think of other criteria or reasons why we would want an exception to issue a ROLLBACK? Hint: think of the AccountTransferExc arguments.

17. In the stored procedure AccountTransferExcLog, the exception handler issues a ROLLBACK followed by an INSERT. Must we issue those two statements in that sequence, or could we issue either one before the other? Explain why or why not.

18. In the Ecommerce scenario, we demonstrated a use of transactions for INSERT and UPDATE operations in Figure 8.24 and Figure 8.28. Come up with another use in the Ecommerce scenario where DELETE operations are involved along with INSERT or UPDATE operations. Explain what business concept the transaction handles, and provide the operations in a stored procedure like we did in Figure 8.24 and Figure 8.28.

19. In Section 8.7, we describe a data integrity concern with two account transfers involving a transfer from account A00001 to A00002 and another transfer of A00001 to A00003. Describe a data integrity concern that also involves two account transfers, but the transfers have the same account as the transfer recipient rather than the source.

20. Can you think of another data integrity example that involves two account transfers, but the source accounts of both transfers are different, and the destination accounts of both transfers are different?

CHAPTER 9

1. Explain why concurrent access to the same data presents data integrity concerns that do not exist with serial access.

2. Why may it be important to first lock database table(s) that we want to backup?

3. Give the SQL statements to lock and backup the Account table of the Financial database.

4. Figure 9.7 illustrates one possible outcome of concurrent transfers between accounts A00001 to A00002, and accounts A00001 to A00003. Show another possible outcome that leaves account A00001 with an inconsistent balance that compromises data integrity.

5. Explain the difference between a READ and WRITE lock.

6. Suppose no locks are held on a table. Session 1 issues a READ lock on that table and session 2 later issues a READ lock on the same table while session 1 still holds its READ lock. Explain whether one session waits for the other to unlock the table, or if something else happens.

7. Suppose no locks are held on a table. If session 1 issues a WRITE lock on that table and session 2 later issues a READ lock on the same table while session 1 still holds its WRITE lock. Explain whether one session waits for the other to unlock the table, or if something else happens.

8. Suppose no locks are held on a table. If session 1 issues a WRITE lock on that table and session 2 later issues a WRITE lock on the same table while session 1 still holds its WRITE lock. Explain whether one session waits for the other to unlock the table, or if something else happens.

9. Explain a scenario where table-level locking may be more efficient in terms of runtime performance than row-level locking.

10. Explain a scenario where row-level locking may be more efficient in terms of runtime performance than table-level locking.

11. Give a possible sequence of lock operations for two transfers, one from account A00001 to A00002 and the other from account A00002 to A00001, other than the one shown in Figure 9.28, that results in deadlock.